Serhy Yekelchyk

Writing the Nation
The Ukrainian Historical Profession in Independent Ukraine and the Diaspora

D1525694

Ukrainian Voices

Collected by Andreas Umland

The book series "Ukrainian Voices" publishes English- and German-language monographs, edited volumes, document collections, and anthologies of articles authored and composed by Ukrainian politicians, intellectuals, activists, officials, researchers, and diplomats. The series' aim is to introduce Western and other audiences to Ukrainian explorations, deliberations and interpretations of historic and current, domestic, and international affairs. The purpose of these books is to make non-Ukrainian readers familiar with how some prominent Ukrainians approach, view and assess their country's development and position in the world. The series was founded, and the volumes are collected by Andreas Umland, Dr. phil. (FU Berlin), Ph. D. (Cambridge), Associate Professor of Politics at the Kyiv-Mohyla Academy and an Analyst in the Stockholm Centre for Eastern European Studies at the Swedish Institute of International Affairs.

Serhy Yekelchyk

WRITING THE NATION

The Ukrainian Historical Profession in
Independent Ukraine and the Diaspora

ibidem
Verlag

Bibliographic information published by the Deutsche Nationalbibliothek
Die Deutsche Nationalbibliothek lists this publication in the Deutsche
Nationalbibliografie; detailed bibliographic data are available in the Internet at
http://dnb.d-nb.de.

Bibliografische Information der Deutschen Nationalbibliothek
Die Deutsche Nationalbibliothek verzeichnet diese Publikation in der Deutschen Nationalbibliografie;
detaillierte bibliografische Daten sind im Internet über http://dnb.d-nb.de abrufbar.

Cover illustration: Roman Bonchuk, Ukraine: A Chronicle (2006), fragment. Reproduced with the
artist's permission.

ISBN-13: 978-3-8382-1695-9
© *ibidem*-Verlag, Stuttgart 2023

Printed in the United States of America

To the memory of my history professors
Olha Lytvyn and Vitaly Sarbei

Contents

Acknowledgments

I began putting this book together in the fall of 2021. However, beginning in December 2021 media interest in Ukraine and the possibility — and, since 24 February 2022, the reality — of Russia's massive invasion, forced me to put these plans aside, because giving talks and interviews became more important for me and for Ukraine. When I finally returned to the manuscript in the summer and early fall of 2022, we were all living in a different world. In these new circumstances, the topic of Ukraine's history became more, not less, important than before the start of the Russian invasion. Completing this book became just as urgent a task as giving interviews, and this task was finally accomplished before the yellow leaves started coming down the trees on the beautiful island in the Pacific Ocean that I call home — in addition to Kyiv, which where my heart is.

I am grateful to Andreas Umland and the ibidem-Verlag team for welcoming this book project and being patient when the events of the war distracted me from working on the manuscript. I owe an apology to Kathy Bedorf for all those changing submission deadlines I kept sending her way. Publishing this monograph in ibidem's "Ukrainian Voices" series has a special meaning to me because it brought me into the company of Ukrainian intellectuals and Western scholars working on Ukraine. This is precisely the kind of transnational academic community that I describe in my book.

I would like to thank the Ukrainian muralist Roman Bonchuk, the creator of the largest painting ever made in Ukraine — *The Chronicle of Ukraine* (2007) — for allowing me to reproduce a fragment of this work on the cover of this book. Milan Zec started working as a research assistant on this project when he was my MA student, and he helped complete it in the first year of his PhD. I greatly appreciate his assistance, especially with compiling the bibliography. Marta D. Olynyk expertly copy-edited the text and translated two chapters based on articles that were originally published in Ukrainian. Many colleagues in my two departments at the Uni-

versity of Victoria supported me in myriad ways during that difficult year for Ukraine and for me personally. Olga and Lesyk did
not mind seeing my laptop on the kitchen table, and my parents in
Kyiv taught me courage by remaining in the besieged city when the
Russian army was closing in on it.

I am grateful to the journal editors, who gave me permission
to include in this book, in a significantly revised form, six articles
originally published in these journals:

- "The Location of Nation: Postcolonial Perspectives on
  Ukrainian Historical Debates," *Australian Slavonic and East
  European Studies* 11, no. 2 (1997): 161–84.
- "Writing the History of Ukrainian Culture before, under,
  and after Communism," *Australian Slavonic and East Euro-
  pean Studies* 20, nos. 1–2 (2006): 15–37.
- "Bridging the Past and the Future: Ukrainian History Writ-
  ing Since Independence," *Canadian Slavonic Papers* 53, nos.
  2–4 (2011): 45–62.
- "A Long Goodbye: The Legacy of Soviet Marxism in Post-
  Communist Ukrainian Historiography," *Ab Imperio*, no. 4
  (2012): 401–16.
- "Studying the Blueprint for a Nation: Canadian Historiography of Modern Ukraine," *East-West: Journal of Ukrainian
  Studies* 5, no. 1 (2018): 115–37.
- "Tvorchyi metod Ivana Lysiaka-Rudnytskoho: Kontseptu-
  alni ta metodolohichni vymiry," *Ukrainska biohrafistyka*, no.
  18 (2019): 54–66.
- "Prostorova istoriia: Ukrainska perspektyva," *Narodna
  tvorchist ta etnolohiia*, no. 5 (2018): 59–65.

Chapters 1, 6, and 10, as well as the Introduction and Conclusion,
are not based on any prior publications and appear here for the first
time.

This book is dedicated to the memory of two Ukrainian historians who put me on the path to joining this profession. From 1986
to 1989 Associate Professor Olha Lytvyn of the Taras Shevchenko
University of Kyiv served as the supervisor of my annual *kursovi*
papers as well as my graduate thesis. She helped me place my first

published articles and persuaded the director of the Institute of History at the Ukrainian Academy of Sciences to give me a chance at becoming a researcher. With every passing year I appreciate more and more the things she taught me about the profession, but also about life. At the Institute of History (soon to be renamed the Institute of Ukrainian History), Professor Vitaly Sarbei became my supervisor and the source of wisdom on all kinds of issues, academic and otherwise. I still do not understand how he managed to write so many texts while supervising a busy research department with numerous graduate students, but his somewhat old-fashioned manners went hand-in-hand with his personal attention to the needs of every *aspirant* (graduate student) working under him.

Introduction

Subversive Histories

In late March 2022, just a month into Russia's full-scale invasion, the Ukrainian media published the first reports about the purge of public and school libraries in the Russian-occupied territories. The Russian military police and administrators installed by the occupiers were going through the library shelves, culling textbooks of Ukrainian history and literature, as well as any academic and popular publications devoted to the history of Ukrainian resistance to the Russian Empire and the Soviet Union. For the purgers' convenience, a list of anti-Russian Ukrainian historical figures was apparently compiled, with any book mentioning them in a positive light slated for removal. It included the Cossack hetman Ivan Mazepa, who rebelled against the empire in 1708-9; Symon Petliura, the most prominent figure of the Ukrainian Revolution of 1917–20; and Stepan Bandera and Roman Shukhevych, the radical nationalist leaders of World War II and the immediate postwar period. Interestingly, the list also featured Ukrainian patriots from the late Soviet period: the great Ukrainian dissident poet Vasyl Stus, who died in the Soviet Gulag in 1985, and the former dissident Viacheslav Chornovil, who as a political figure during the late 1980s and early 1990s contributed greatly to spreading the idea of an independent Ukrainian state. The official Russian explanation for the removal of all these books was that they represented "extremist" literature.[1]

---

1   Violetta Orlova, "Rosiiany pochaly borotbu z ukrainskymy knyzhkamy na okupovanykh terytoriiakh," UNIAN, 24 March 2022, https://www.unian.ua/war/viyna-v-ukrajini-rosiyani-na-okupovanih-teritoriyah-nishchat-ukrajinski-knizhki-novini-vtorgnennya-rosiji-v-ukrajinu-11758072.html; Denys Karlovsky,"Okupanty na zakhoplenykh terytoriiakh boriutsia z pidruchnykamy istorii, Stusom i Banderoiu," *Ukrainska Pravda*, 24 March 2022, https://www.pravda.com.ua/news/2022/03/24/7334252/; Diana Krechetova, "Okupanty vyluchaiut z bibliotek ukrainski knyzhky, shchob znyshchyty ikh," *Ukrainska Pravda*, 25 May 2022, https://life.pravda.com.ua/culture/2022/05/25/248802/.

While most of the books were apparently destroyed, the occupiers also sent some of them to Moscow, where some fifty Russian historians and educators analyzed them for the presence of anti-Russian interpretations. One outcome of this process was a televised press conference on the topic "Ukrainian Textbooks as an Element in the Propaganda of Hatred." Held at the Russian Federation's Ministry of Education and co-sponsored by the ruling United Russia party, the event featured Russian officials and scholars showing some captured textbooks to the public and quoting some particularly "anti-Russian" and "extremist" passages. Among other things, the participants argued that Western historians of Ukraine had laid the foundations of a separatist, anti-Russian, Ukrainian historical narrative by justifying the existence of the "artificial" Ukrainian people. As proof of that, during the press conference, Aleksei Lubkov, president of the Moscow State Pedagogical University, showed the Russian translation of my history of Ukraine, which came out in Kyiv in 2010.[2]

Of course, it is difficult to imagine a single book, originally published in English in 2007 by Oxford University Press—even if taken together with the recent works produced by all the historians of Ukraine teaching in the West—furnishing the basis for an anti-Russian line in modern Ukrainian textbooks.[3] Clearly, the Ukrainian textbook authors were working within a much older and wider tradition going back to the great Ukrainian historian Mykhailo Hrushevsky (1866–1934), if not to his nineteenth-century predecessors. But such propagandistic aggrandizement of Western historians' role in "separating" Ukraine from Russia actually highlighted three important themes that will be developed in this book. First, the Ukrainian diaspora played a major role in the formation of a

---

2   "Press-konferentsiia Edinoi Rossii i Minprosveshcheniia Rossii ob ekspertize ukrainskikh uchebnikov," YouTube, 31 March 2022, https://www.youtube.com/watch?v=g5GnejdJiL0. See also "Materialy k press-konferentsii 'Ukrainskie uchebniki kak instrument propagandy nenavisti,'" Edinaia Rossiia, 30 March 2022, https://er.ru/pages/analiz.

3   Sergei Ekelchik [Serhy Yekelchyk], *Istoriia Ukrainy: Stanovlenie sovremennoi natsii*, trans. N. Klimchuk and E. Leenson (Kyiv: K. I. S., 2010); the original publication in English is Serhy Yekelchyk, *Ukraine: Birth of A Modern Nation* (New York: Oxford University Press, 2007).

modern Ukrainian historical narrative, both by serving as keeper of forbidden historical concepts and by introducing modern Western methodologies into Ukrainian scholarship. Second, the Ukrainian historical profession of today is increasingly global. The once-important division between Soviet Ukrainian and émigré scholars has been erased, with scholars from Ukraine actively participating in international projects, winning fellowships and positions in the West, and taking part as equals in Western academic debates. Third, and perhaps most important, this now-globalized Ukrainian historical scholarship threatens Russian imperial narratives just as much as did the works of Hrushevsky and other Ukrainian historians of the early twentieth century.[4]

The latter point needs some elaboration. The list of Ukrainian historical personalities used for purging libraries did indeed include figures whom the authorities of the Russian Empire and the Soviet Union had considered enemies or "traitors." But this only goes to show that Putin's war on Ukrainian history follows the familiar imperial models from tsarist and Soviet times. In other words, the clash of memories was not just about present-day independent Ukraine presenting a challenge to Putin's Russia, but about any version of Ukrainian history in which the Ukrainian people are endowed with agency undermining any notion of Russia as an empire.

This acknowledgement brings into the discussion of Ukrainian historiography the important concept of decolonization. It also allows historians in Ukraine to benefit from the insight into the cultural logic of imperial rule and post-imperial identity work that the discipline of Postcolonial Studies has generated over the past several decades. Ukrainian literary scholars both in Ukraine and abroad — most notably, Tamara Hundorova, Marko Pavlyshyn, and

---

4   On Hrushevsky, see Frank E. Sysyn, "Introduction to the *History of Ukraine-Rus'*," in Mykhailo Hrushevsky, *History of Ukraine-Rus'*, Volume 1: *From Prehistory to the Eleventh Century*, trans. Marta Skorupsky, ed. Andrzej Poppe and Frank E. Sysyn with the assistance of Uliana M. Pasicznyk (Edmonton: Canadian Institute of Ukrainian Studies Press, 1997), xxii–xlii; Serhii Plokhy, *Unmaking Imperial Russia: Mykhailo Hrushevsky and the Writing of Ukrainian History* (Toronto: University of Toronto Press, 2005).

Myroslav Shkandrij—have been employing the analytical instruments of Postcolonial Studies with great success since the early 1990s. However, Ukrainian historians have been more reluctant to embrace them, in large measure because they did not see Ukraine as a classic colony, an exploited and often racially different possession of a European metropole.[5]

This is bound to change as a result of the Russian Federation's massive invasion in 2022 aimed at "recovering" all of Ukraine for what can only be called a new Russian empire. The American-based historian of Russia, Ilya Gerasimov, has made a compelling case that the Revolution of Dignity as well as the unsuccessful revolt in Belarus in 2020 can be interpreted as postcolonial revolutions.[6] Moreover, Timothy Snyder has defined the 2022 invasion as Russia's "colonial war," while other social scientists have written about the war's "postcolonial" dimension.[7]

The "decommunization" policies introduced in Ukraine in 2015 had some recognizable features of decolonization. Indeed, in a 2016 interview in the Ukrainian online magazine *Korydor*, I singled out decolonization as the true nature of this process, while warning against a simplistic understanding of colonialism that could excuse the past Ukrainian elites from responsibility for what the Russian Empire and the Soviet Union did in Ukraine.[8] In 2019

5   See, e.g., Stephen Velychenko, "Post-Colonialism and Ukrainian History," *Ab Imperio*, no. 1 (2004): 391–404.

6   See Ilya Gerasimov, "Ukraine 2014: The First Postcolonial Revolution: Introduction to the Forum," *Ab Imperio*, no. 3 (2014): 22–44; Ilya Gerasimov and Marina Mogilner, "Deconstructing Integration: Ukraine's Postcolonial Subjectivity," *Slavic Review* 74, no. 4 (Winter 2015): 715–22; Ilya Gerasimov, "The Belarusian Postcolonial Revolution: Field Reports," *Ab Imperio*, no. 3 (2020): 259–72.

7   Timothy Snyder, "The War in Ukraine Is a Colonial War," *The New Yorker*, 28 April 2022, https://www.newyorker.com/news/essay/the-war-in-ukraine-is-a-colonial-war-colonial-war; Maria Mälksoo, "The Postcolonial Moment in Russia's War against Ukraine," *Journal of Genocide Research*, published online 11 May 2022, https://www.tandfonline.com/doi/full/10.1080/14623528.2022.2074947.

8   Serhii Iekelchyk [Serhy Yekelchyk], "Iakshcho kolonialnyi, znachyt my ne buly vidpovidalni za mynule," *Korydor*, 19 October 2016, http://www.kory dor.in.ua/ua/stories/sergij-yekelchyk-pamjat-reprezentacija-kultura.html.

Barbara Törnquist-Plewa and Yuliya Yurchuk argued for considering Ukrainian memory politics from a postcolonial perspective.[9]
The last step is to extend this framework's application from studies
of historical memory to wider research on Ukrainian history and
historiography. This is the approach used in this book.

Western scholars working on Ukrainian historiography have
generally focused on the challenges caused by the restoration of the
"national paradigm" as the dominant narrative of national history
at a time when history writing in the West was undermining grand
narratives by focusing on previously marginalized groups and experiences. Transnational and regional approaches have been recommended instead as being more modern and resistant to mythol-
ogizing.[10] Yet, the notion of decolonization allows re-conceptualiz-
ing the nationalizing reading of history as textual resistance to the
Russian imperial narrative. Because Ukrainian history cannot be
constructed as a continuous history of state development, it incor-
porates by definition stories that are typical of decolonizing narratives: peasants' lives and struggles, the suppression of indigenous
culture, and the ambiguous role of the national intelligentsia in re-
shaping the national culture for the empire's purposes.

Theoretical models from Postcolonial Studies allow for a better understanding of such Ukrainian phenomena as the Soviet
methods used in the creation of new historical concepts and the obsession with the exact historical positioning of Ukraine between
East and West. The more recent emphasis in historical narratives on
Ukraine's being a legitimate part of Europe is also a marker of the
postcolonial condition, but an unusual one, which propels Postcolonial Studies in a new direction. Other principal features of post-

---

9   Barbara Törnquist-Plewa and Yuliya Yurchuk, "Memory Politics in Contempo-
     rary Ukraine: Reflections from the Postcolonial Perspective," *Memory Studies* 12,
     no. 6 (December 2019): 699–720.

10   See, e.g., Georgiy [Heorhii] Kasianov and Philipp Ther, eds., *A Laboratory of
     Transnational History: Ukraine and Recent Ukrainian Historiography* (Budapest:
     SEU Press, 2009); Andrei Portnov, *Uprazhneniia s istorii po-ukrainski* (Moscow:
     OGI-Polit.ru-Memorial, 2010); Serhii Plokhy, ed., *The Future of the Past: New Per-
     spectives on Ukrainian History* (Cambridge, Mass.: Harvard Ukrainian Research
     Institute, 2017); Heorhii Kasianov, *Past Continuous: Istorychna polityka 1980-kh–
     2000-kh: Ukraina ta susidy* (Kyiv: Laurus and Antropos-Logos-Film, 2018).

Soviet Ukrainian historiography would also be recognizable to students of decolonization elsewhere. This is true of the "recovery" of national historical models preserved in the diaspora and the acquisition of modern historical methodology from the West, also with the diaspora's assistance. It is also true to say that Ukrainian history writing and memory politics are still locked in a debate with Russian ones — both in the fields preferred by the Putin administration, such as World War II, and in the ones inconvenient for the former imperial master, such as the fall of the Russian Empire in 1917 and the collapse of the Soviet Union in 1991.

Recognizing that their work is part of the decolonization process would allow the historians of Ukraine in that country and abroad to deconstruct imperial mythologies more effectively and make new Ukrainian history different from the Soviet models. The approaches based on the notions of human rights, transitional justice, and civil society would help speed up this process.

Part I

Toward a New Ukrainian History

1. The Return of Public History

On 12 July 2021, more than seven months before Russia's all-out invasion of Ukraine, President Vladimir Putin published on the web site of the Russian president's office an article entitled "On the Historical Unity of Russians and Ukrainians." Its main argument was simple: Ukrainians have always constituted a part of the Russian people, and the Ukrainian state is an artificial entity. Whenever Ukrainian and Russian histories diverged, it was always because of the West's intrigues – the actions of "those forces that have always sought to undermine our unity."[11] According to this scheme, the Bolsheviks also appeared to be Westerners – after all, they were followers of Karl Marx and wanted to dismantle the Russian monarchy. It is not surprising, then, that Putin blamed the Soviet nationality policy of the 1920s for dividing the Russian people into Russians, Ukrainians, and Belarusians. (On previous occasions, Putin ascribed the creation of Ukraine directly to Lenin, who carved out parts of Russia proper to make Ukraine.[12]) According to Putin's article, "present-day Ukraine is entirely the product of the Soviet period," and it was constituted to a large degree "at the expense of historical Russia."[13] The Ukrainian Revolution of Dignity (2013–14) was allegedly a "coup" led by "radical nationalist groups." By supporting the coup, the West "directly interfered" in Ukraine's internal affairs. In turn, the post-revolutionary Ukrainian elites surrendered their country to "direct external administration" by the West.[14]

Putin apparently believed in the persuasive power of his article, which was also posted on his site in a Ukrainian translation.

---

11 Vladimir Putin, "Ob istoricheskom edinstve russkikh i ukraintsev," Prezident Rossii, 12 July 2021, http://www.kremlin.ru/events/president/news/66181.

12 "Putin: Sovremennaia Ukraina tselikom i polnostiu byla sozdana kommunisticheskoi Rossiei," TASS, 21 February 2021, https://tass.ru/politika/13791307.

13 Putin, "Ob istoricheskom edinstve."

14 Ibid.

Such illusions reflected his long-standing belief that Ukraine's ethnic Russians and Russophone Ukrainians by default identified with
the Russian Federation and the concept of the "Russian World,"
which Putin's Russia used to mobilize ethnic and cultural Russians
living abroad and in particular in the former Union republics of the
Soviet Union.[15] That same belief led Putin to attack Ukraine in February 2022 with forces that would not be sufficient to conquer or
control that country. To put it simply, Putin believed his own propaganda. He did not realize that the Ukrainian nation as it emerged
after the Revolution of Dignity was a multiethnic community with
a vibrant civil society and a commitment to European values. The
shared values of the new Ukraine also included a reading of its history within the Russian Empire and the Soviet Union that was dras-
tically different from Putin's narrative. As a result, Putin's article
fell flat in Ukraine. The dictator's last resort was a massive military
effort but that, too, soon faltered.

This short chapter will seek to explain why Putin stood no
chance of persuading Ukrainian citizens that they are the same people as the Russians. The transformation of Ukraine's "decommunization" policies into a decolonization drive and the rebirth of
public history will serve as the principal factors explaining such an
outcome.

Toward a New Narrative

The divergence of the Russian and Ukrainian historical narratives
began in the early 1990s, when President Leonid Kravchuk saw the
national version of the past as an essential part of his state-building
efforts. However, the economic collapse that followed the dissolu-
tion of the Soviet Union allowed Kravchuk's opponents to associate
what they called "nationalism" with an economic crisis allegedly
resulting from breaking Ukraine's ties with Russia. His successor,
Leonid Kuchma (in office 1994–2004) did not halt the development

---

15   John O'Loughlin, Gerard Toal, and Vladimir Kolosov, "Who Identifies with the
    'Russian World'? Geopolitical Attitudes in Southeastern Ukraine, Crimea, Ab-
    khazia, South Ossetia, and Transnistria," *Eurasian Geography and Economics* 57,
    no. 6 (2016): 745–78.

of a new Ukrainian history – in fact, he made the first serious effort to recognize the (radical nationalist) Ukrainian Insurgent Army (hereafter UPA) as part of Ukrainian resistance to Nazism. However, Kuchma allowed both the hybridity and regionalization of historical narratives. His administration celebrated the old Soviet holidays together with the new anti-Soviet ones, and historical surveys at the time combined components of both narratives. Moreover, under Kuchma the political elites of different regions received relative freedom to interpret history in their preferred way. To enable such flexibility, the authorities even printed two different versions of the last volume of *Ukraine's Book of Memory*, the multivolume project listing the names of those who fell during World War II. One version includes a statement about the Organization of Ukrainian Nationalists and its military formations (including the UPA) having been "Nazi collaborators," while the other did not.[16]

The Orange Revolution in Ukraine (2004–5) marked the moment of the political parting of ways between the Ukrainian revolutionary leaders and Putin's increasingly insecure and anti-Western administration. Although both Kravchuk and Kuchma promoted research on the Ukrainian Famine of 1932–33 and developed commemorative ceremonies, it was President Viktor Yushchenko (2005–10) whose name became associated with the campaign to acknowledge the man-made famine, which was accompanied by attacks on Ukrainian political and cultural figures, as genocide known as the Holodomor ("murder by famine"). This campaign succeeded even though Yushchenko's approval ratings collapsed at the end of his presidency. In 2010, his last year in office, 61 percent of Ukrainian residents saw the Holodomor as genocide; by 2014, this number had risen to 72 percent.[17] The solidifying public opinion of the Holodomor as a Stalinist crime against Ukraine came to determine the attitudes to the Soviet past, which remained highly

---

16   Andrei Portnov, *Uprazhneniia s istoriei po-ukrainski* (Moscow: OGI-Polit.ru-Memorial, 2010), 49.

17   "Bilshist ukraintsiv pohodzhuiutsia, shcho Holodomor 1932–33 rokiv buv henotsydom ukrainskoho narodu," *Hromadskyi Prostir*, 17 November 2014, https://www.prostir.ua/?news=bilshist-ukrajintsiv-pohodzhuyutsya-scho-holodomor-1932-33-rokiv-buv-henotsydom-ukrajinskoho-narodu.

ambiguous in Russia, where Stalin's name continued to show up at or near the top in polling about great historical figures.

Against this background of divergent historical memories, in Ukraine, Putin's aggressive reaction to the Revolution of Dignity in 2014 led to a political mobilization in defense of national history. As is well known, in justifying his annexation of the Crimea, Putin marshaled both historical and ethnic arguments. The two Russian-sponsored separatist self-proclaimed entities in the Donbas at first relied on Soviet-style trappings of sovereignty in the form of "people's republics," then briefly reverted to the reimagined tsarist administrative-geographical concept of "New Russia," and in the end settled on the hybrid historical imagination, making use of both concepts.[18]

What followed can be described best by the widely used concept of "securitization," which has already been applied to memory politics in Europe, including Russia and Ukraine.[19] Putin's Russia was the first to treat history writing and memory politics as a state matter directly linked to foreign policy issues and political stability. In 2005 Putin famously declared that the collapse of the Soviet Union was the greatest geopolitical catastrophe of the twentieth century. That same year, the lavish celebrations of the sixtieth anniversary of victory in "the Great Patriotic War" solidified the notion that whoever opposed Putin's Russia could be denounced as a "fascist" (the Russian term traditionally used to describe the Nazis as well as

---

18   See Serhy Yekelchyk, *Ukraine: What Everyone Needs to Know*, 2nd ed. (New York: Oxford University Press, 2020), 128–30.

19   See Maria Mälksoo, *The Politics of Becoming European: A Study of Polish and Baltic Post-Cold War Security Imaginaries* (London: Routledge, 2010); idem, "'Memory Must Be Defended': Beyond the Politics of Mnemonical Security," *Security Dialogue* 46, no. 3 (2015): 221–37. For more discussion of the Russian case, see Håvard Bækken and Johannes Due Enstad, "Identity under Siege: Selective Securitization of History in Putin's Russia," *Slavonic and East European Review* 98, no. 2 (2020): 321–44 and, on the Ukrainian case, Yuliya Yurchuk, "Historians As Activists: History Writing in Times of War: The Case of Ukraine in 2014–2018," *Nationalities Papers* 49, no. 4 (2021): 691–709.

Italian fascists).[20] In 2006 President Yushchenko answered this challenge by creating the Ukrainian Institute of National Memory, modeled on the Polish one, albeit with a more limited mandate. Under his pro-Russian successor, Viktor Yanukovych, the institute lost its status as a branch of government, becoming a research institute for four years until President Poroshenko restored its role after Russia's aggression began in 2014.

From Decommunization to Decolonization

The "memory war" between Russia and Ukraine escalated during 2014–15. The 2014 Russian law "against the rehabilitation of Nazism" criminalized the "spreading of intentionally false information about the Soviet Union's actions during World War II."[21] It was aimed at both the domestic opposition, protesting the cult of Stalin, and the Ukrainian interpretation of the Soviet Union's role in the war. The latter included the depiction of the Soviet Union as a de-facto ally of Nazi Germany in 1939–41 and a belligerent party responsible for multiple war crimes. It also portrayed as national heroes the radical nationalist followers of Stepan Bandera and UPA fighters who, after a brief period early in the war when they thought that aligning with the German side would help establish a Ukrainian state, fought against both the Nazi and Soviet regimes. In the Russian interpretation, the "Banderites" were Nazi collaborators. Ukraine responded in 2015 with "decommunization" legislation, drawn up by the Institute of National Memory. The four decommunization laws banned Soviet symbols and communist propaganda, at the same time establishing Ukraine's official list of twentieth-century national heroes, including nationalists from the World War II period. The legislation criminalized the "public display of disrespectful attitudes" toward the groups that had fought for Ukrainian independence during the twentieth century, as well

---

20 Nikolai Koposov, *Memory Laws, Memory Wars: The Politics of the Past in Europe and Russia* (New York: Cambridge University Press, 2017), 249.

21 Maria Domańska, "The Myth of the Great Patriotic War As a Tool of the Kremlin's Great Power Policy," *OSW Commentary*, 31 December 2019, https://www.osw.waw.pl/en/publikacje/osw-commentary/2019-12-31/myth-great-patriotic-war-a-tool-kremlins-great-power-policy#_ftn8.

as "public denial of the legitimacy of the struggle for Ukraine's in-dependence."[22] The Institute of National Memory then coordinated a massive nationwide campaign to remove Soviet symbols and re-name streets and towns named after Soviet figures.

If this campaign could be seen as answering Russia with the same type of measures while playing on Putin's preferred field, that of World War II, subsequent years showed how the Ukrainian nar-rative was extended into periods that were more objectionable to Russia. The centennials of the revolutionary events of 1917–20 demonstrated that Ukraine saw as the foundation of its modern his-torical identity not the wartime radical nationalists, but the Ukrain-ian People's Republic, which proclaimed its independence from Russia in January 1918. Whereas the Ukrainian authorities cele-brated the string of the revolution's anniversaries as steps liberating their country from imperial rule, in Putin's Russia, which identified with the Russian Empire and viewed revolutions as illegitimate, these anniversaries were marked by a deafening silence. The thirty years since the Soviet collapse in 2021 likewise became an occasion in Ukraine for celebration and reflection on the independent na-tion's achievements, whereas in Russia they passed virtually unno-ticed.

If these developments suggested the significance of the anti-imperial struggle in Ukrainian history, it took the realization of de-communization's incomplete coverage to take the last step toward conceptualizing the recent processes in Ukrainian memory politics and historiography as decolonization. The need for a wider defini-tion became painfully obvious when the public discussion about renaming the city of Kirovohrad, which had been named after the Bolshevik functionary Sergei Kirov, revealed that the local authori-ties preferred to restore the city's previous name, Yelysavethrad, which celebrated the Russian empress Elizabeth I (r. 1741–61). Re-portedly this was also the preference of over 70 percent of the resi-dents who voted for potential new names in conjunction with the

---

22   Oxana Shevel, "The Battle for Historical Memory in Postrevolutionary Ukra-ine," *Current History* 115, no. 783 (2016): 258–63, here 261.

municipal elections of 2015.[23] Although the tsarina was not subject
to decommunization, the Ukrainian parliament overruled the municipal authorities to rename the city Kropyvnytsky after the major
Ukrainian playwright and actor Marko Kropyvnytsky (1840–1910),
who hailed from the region and lived in the city for some time.[24]

The first events at the Institute of National Memory that indicated the transition to "decolonization" as the next stage after "decommunization" took place in the spring of 2019. The Institute-pro-
duced report about the press conference, marking four years since
the decommunization legislation, was entitled "The Conclusion of
Decommunization — the Beginning of Decolonization."[25] After February 2022, the term "derussification" became routinely mentioned
together with the other two.[26]

The transition to decolonization prepared the Ukrainian state
and public well for Putin's attempt to use history as a tool for re-
cruiting supporters in Ukraine. The year 2022 saw the final parting
of ways between the Russian and Ukrainian historical narratives,
which involved the rethinking of Russian culture as an instrument
of empire building. This led to more street renamings and monument removals.

Public History Reborn

When discussing Ukraine's transition to a national historical narrative and new memory politics, it is important to highlight the

---

23 "U Kirovohradi ozvuchyly rezultaty opytuvannia pro pereimenuvannia
mista," *Ukrainska Pravda*, 26 October 2015, https://www.pravda.com.ua/
news/2015/10/26/7086321/.

24 "Verkhovna Rada pereimenuvala Kirovohrad u Kropyvnytskyi," *Den*, 14 July
2016, https://day.kyiv.ua/uk/news/140716-verhovna-rada-pereymenuvala-
kirovograd-u-kropyvnyckyy.

25 "Zavershennia dekomunizatsii — pochatok dekolonizatsii," Ukrainskyi instytut
natsionalnoi pamiati, 9 April 2019, https://uinp.gov.ua/pres-centr/novyny/
zavershennya-dekomunizaciyi-pochatok-dekolonizaciyi.

26 "UINP ta MKIP rozpochaly seriiu kruhlykh stoliv 'Derusyfikatsiia, dekomunizatsiia ta dekolonizatsiia u publichnomu prostori," Ukrainskyi instytut natsionalnoi pamiati, 13 May 2022, https://uinp.gov.ua/pres-centr/novyny/uinp-
ta-mkip-rozpochaly-seriyu-kruglyh-stoliv-derusyfikaciya
-dekomunizaciya-ta-dekolonizaciya-u-publichnomu-prostori1.

agency of historians acting as members of civil society. The year 2014 was a major watershed in this process. During the winter of 2013/14 Ukrainian civil society mobilized to secure the victory of the Revolution of Dignity; the years 2014 and 2015 witnessed continued mobilization in support of the Ukrainian army fighting the Russian and pro-Russian forces in the Donbas. Historians did not stand on the sidelines.

This was also true of the historians of Ukraine teaching in the West. In 2018 Ukraine's top award in the Arts and Humanities, the Taras Shevchenko Prize, went to the Harvard historian originally from Ukraine, Serhii Plokhy, for his popular survey of Ukrainian history published in English in 2015 and in Ukrainian in 2016.[27] This award is symptomatic of several trends of the post-2014 period. Ukrainian history as a subject became both popular and important for understanding current events. History books were now competing with popular literary works and journalism. Finally, working on the history of Ukraine was now a global project, with historians from abroad being very much part of the historiographical and political debates taking place in Ukraine.

In Ukraine, the impressive civic mobilization of 2014 and 2015 included the establishment of the *Likbez: Istorychnyi Front* (Down with Illiteracy on the Historical Front) group of volunteers, all of them professional historians employed at various Ukrainian institutions. Although sharing the state's agenda in the securitization of history and memory, the group positioned itself as a collective of volunteer social activists — much like many other groups of volunteers that appeared during the Revolution of Dignity and the early stages of the war in the Donbas.[28] The Likbez group went on to produce an enormous amount of material, which it distributed in a variety of ways: publishing the book series "History Uncensored,"

---

27   Serhii Plokhy, *The Gates of Europe: A History of Ukraine* (New York: Basic Books, 2015); Serhii Plokhii, *Brama Ievropy: Istoriia Ukrainy vid skifskykh voien do nezalezhnosti*, trans. R. Klochko (Kharkiv: KSD, 2016).

28   Iryna Vushko, "Historians at War: History, Politics, and Memory in Ukraine," *Contemporary European History* 27, no. 1 (2018): 112–24; Yurchuk, "Historians as Activists."

collaborating with the mainstream Ukrainian media, and maintaining a prominent presence on social media.

The Likbez team had a flawless understanding of the value of publicity and political engagement. When Putin published his article on the "historical unity" of Russians and Ukrainians in 2021, the Likbez collective issued its public response to Putin, demolishing his points one by one.[29]

The "History Uncensored" book series assumed a more academic tone, but the subjects of its volumes served to deconstruct the Russian narrative. This is particularly true of the volumes *In the Claws of Two-Headed Eagles: The Creation of a Modern Nation* and *Soviet Ukraine: Illusions and Catastrophes of the Communist "Paradise."*[30] Of all the volumes in the series, these two are perhaps the most innovative in terms of analysis. Authored by leading specialists on the imperial and early Soviet periods, they provide up-to-date interpretations that in some cases improve upon previously published academic history surveys. It is also worth noting that both volumes deal with Ukraine's past as part of empires — a topic of crucial importance for the process, which by 2019 would be acknowledged as the decolonization of Ukrainian history.

The writing in the other volumes of the series is more uneven, but they generally share the overall interpretive frame of deconstructing imperial mythologies. As the Ukrainian-born Swedish historian Yulia Yurchuk has noted, "the volume on the history of the Second World War is written not from the point of the subject undergoing the postcolonizing process but from the point of view of the subject that is tormented by anticolonial resentments."[31] She

---

29 "Vidpovid ukrainskykh istorykiv na stattiu V. Putina 'Pro istorychnu iednist rosiian ta ukraintsiv'," Likbez: Istorychnyi Front, 4 September 2021, https://likbez.org.ua/ua/ukrayinska-vidguk-ukrayinskih-istorikiv-na-statty u-v-putina-pro-istorichnu-yednist-rosiyan-ta-ukrayintsiv.html.

30 A. Halushka, I. Hyrych, et al., *U kihtiakh dvohlavykh orliv: Tvorennia modernoi natsii: Ukraina pid skipetramy Romanovykh i Habsburhiv* (Kharkiv: KSD, 2016); Hennadii Iefimenko, Iana Prymachenko, and Oksana Iurkova, *Ukraina radianska: Iliuzii ta katastrofy komunistychnoho "raiu": 1917–1938* (Kharkiv: KSD, 2017).

31 Yurchuk, "Historians as Activists," 703.

argues that the best volumes in the series present history as a process with multiple potential outcomes and focus on Ukraine's civic identity, while the treatment of the UPA reveals traces of an old-fashioned heroic and teleological narrative of an ethnic group fighting for its state.

The "Our Revolution" project is perhaps the most effective initiative of the Likbez group. Starting in March 2017, the participants published on two popular online news portals, *Dilova Stolytsia* and *Istorychna Pravda*, short articles familiarizing the public with events that took place a hundred years ago, beginning in March 1917. These articles, which were widely shared on social media, helped spread awareness of the Ukrainian Revolution and the Ukrainian state formations during the revolutionary period, thus refuting Putin's interpretation of Ukraine's having been created by Lenin.[32]

By the time the full-scale Russian invasion took place in 2022, a significant share of Ukrainian historians in Kyiv and the provinces were involved in a multitude of public-history projects based on the Likbez model. There could be no return to the Kuchma era with its coexistence of incompatible historical narratives and sometimes opposing regional memory policies.

* * *

When he was planning his invasion, Putin failed to account not just for the fact that after the Revolution of Dignity Ukraine had become a civic and political community rather than an ethnic one. He also overlooked the successful introduction of a Ukrainian historical narrative and the significant outreach of public-history initiatives. Above all, he missed the significance of the transition from decommunization to decolonization that began in Ukraine in 2019, although some components of this policy had been in place since the

---

32   See the first installment in the series: Kyrylo Halushko, "Na porozi novoi Ukrainy: Iak kryza staroho svitu porodyla ukrainsku natsiiu," *Dilova Stolytsia*, 10 March 2017, https://www.dsnews.ua/nasha_revolyutsiya_1917/na-poroge-novoy-ukrainy-kak-krizis-starogo-mira-rodil-ukrainskuyu-1003201722 0000.

early 1990s. The Ukraine he so brazenly attacked was a modern political community defining itself as part of European democracy rather than Russian authoritarianism. The culling of Ukrainian history books on the territories occupied by Russia will not help the Putin regime — they have already influenced the hearts and minds of Ukrainian citizens.

2. The Search for New Concepts

Ukrainian historical scholarship as it emerged after the Soviet collapse was a confusing mixture of old and new, and attempts to bridge the thematic, institutional, and methodological breaks spanning the Soviet past, the Ukrainian present, and the international future defined the next thirty years of history writing in independent Ukraine. These decades saw the rise of the "national paradigm" in historiography as well as challenges to its dominance, resulting from increased exposure to modern Western methodologies. Above all, though, the struggle between the new and the old was about liberating the historical profession from the enduring legacy of Soviet dogmatism, if often dressed up as ethnic patriotism. By the 2000s, Ukrainian historical scholarship became increasingly globalized, with the international mobility of historians and their transnational collaborations effectively turning the development of a new Ukrainian history into an international project.

From the Old Orthodoxy to the New

Beginning with the disintegration of ideological controls in the last years of the Soviet Union's existence, the study of previously forbidden topics became possible. There was little agreement in Ukrainian society of the early 1990s on the examination of such topics as Hetman Ivan Mazepa's break with Russia, the Ukrainian Revolution, the Holodomor, the Ukrainian Insurgent Army (UPA), and dissidents, but at least scholars could now write and argue about these issues. Indeed, these topics came to dominate public discourse on history and the agendas of the institutions that Ukraine inherited from the Soviet state: large research institutes and hundreds of history departments at numerous colleges — the latter's numbers increasing dramatically with the abolition of the history

33

of the Communist Party as an obligatory subject and the subsequent rebranding of all such departments as the history of political
movements or Ukrainian history.[33]

Soviet Ukrainian historiography, with its theoretical rigidity
and limited repertoire of prescribed topics (such as revolutionary
movements, cultural links to Russia, party guidance in all spheres
of life, and the construction of a socialist society), was long overdue
for a conceptual revolution. Yet, some Western observers warned
early on against the wholesale replacement of Soviet dogmatism
with a nationalist one. Writing in 1993, Orest Subtelny hoped that
the younger generation of Ukrainian historians would explore the
"great variety" of methodologies available in the West to prevent
the mechanical replacement of "one 'correct' methodology with another."[34]

The latter, however, was precisely what happened in the
1990s. The "national paradigm" of Ukrainian history — a grand narrative focusing on the Ukrainian ethnic nation's struggle for its own
state — replaced Soviet models of "socialist construction" and the
"friendship of peoples" with a similar sort of dogmatism.[35] As
Serhii Plokhy has argued, even within the history of ethnic Ukrainians and their ancestors, the emphasis on the Cossacks and the
Ukrainian national project of the nineteenth and twentieth centuries resulted in other social groups, movements, and cultural phenomena being marginalized, if not completely left out. In addition,
the "national paradigm" brought with it the danger of a retroactive
"Ukrainization" of institutions and identities that existed before the

---

33   Iaroslav Hrytsak, "Ukrainska istoriohrafiia 1991–2001: Desiatylittia zmin," *Ukraina Moderna*, no. 9 (2005): 43–68, here 46; Heorhii Kasianov, *Past Continuous:
Istorychna polityka 1980-kh–2000-kh: Ukraina ta susidy* (Kyiv: Laurus and Antropos-Logos-Film, 2018), 190–91.

34   Orest Subtelny, "The Current State of Ukrainian Historiography," *Journal of Ukrainian Studies* 18, nos. 1–2 (Summer–Winter 1993): 33–54, here 42.

35   The most comprehensive, if now somewhat outdated, study of this transforma-
tion is a book by a Polish scholar, which, ironically, has not been translated into
Ukrainian. See Tomasz Stryjek, *Jakiej przeszłości potrzebuje przyszłość?:
Interpretacje dziejów narodowych w historiografii i debacie publicznej na Ukrainie
1991–2004* (Warsaw: Instytut Studiów Politycznych PAN-Oficyna Wydawnicza
RYTM, 2007).

age of modern nationalism.[36] Even more problematic in this teleological scheme was any inclusion of Ukraine's national minorities and territories with strong regional identity. These had to be defined in relation to the titular ethnic group and its entitlement to a nation state—as friends, enemies, or fellow travellers. Indeed, in this framework even the ethnic Ukrainian population could be seen as lacking "national consciousness" and in need of being elevated to some golden standard of Ukrainian identity.

Several factors influenced the transformation of the national paradigm into a new orthodoxy. Its populist (Mykhailo Hrushevsky) and statist (Viacheslav Lypynsky and Dmytro Doroshenko) incarnations were predominant in pre-Soviet Ukrainian historical thought and thus constituted a natural fallback position for a profession that had suddenly found itself at a conceptual crossroads. The national paradigm also fit well with the young Ukrainian state's ideological stance for much of the 1990s, when attempts to create a strong Ukrainian identity translated into anti-imperialist rhetoric aimed at cultural separation from Russia. For historians trained in the Soviet era, the national school was not as difficult to accept as one might think. In much the same organicist way as the nationalists, the Soviet authorities since the late 1930s had encouraged the historical profession to think of nations as subjects of history (as in such Soviet concepts as "the great Russian people" or the "reunification of Ukraine with Russia"). The departure from the national paradigm, the direction of the nation's historical development, could easily be adjusted to lead to independence rather than to union with the Russian brethren within the socialist federation of nations. Finally, post-Soviet Ukrainian historians were not making this choice in a vacuum: Ukrainians living abroad took an active part in the reorientation of the Ukrainian historical profession. Yet, the Ukrainian diaspora's influence was more complex than is often assumed. By the 1990s, the diaspora, in addition to the majority of community activists who endorsed an unsophisticated version of the national paradigm, had also produced a number of professional

---

36   Serhii Plokhy, *Ukraine and Russia: Representations of the Past* (Toronto: University of Toronto Press, 2008), 288–89.

historians who wanted to share more sophisticated conceptual interpretations of Ukraine's history with their Ukrainian colleagues.

Ironically, in the light of his appeals to explore the diversity of Western historical methodologies, Subtelny's own survey of Ukrainian history became a symbol of the national paradigm's sweeping victory in Ukraine. What most Ukrainian historians took from it was not the author's attention to social processes or his overarching modernization paradigm, but the overall framing of Ukrainian history as the story of the ethnic nation.[37] Even though the Ukrainian translation's real print run is difficult to estimate because of widespread underreporting and outright piracy in the Ukrainian publishing world, an educated guess put it at somewhere between 900,000 and well over a million copies.[38] Subtelny's *Ukraine: A History* became a standard college textbook and a widely used text for college-entry exams, as well as a treasure trove of interpretations to be borrowed by authors of innumerable school- and college-level textbooks. In the process, this work, which at the time of its original publication in the 1980s was one of the national paradigm's best examples, incorporating, for example, Miroslav Hroch's scheme of the three-stage development of national movements in stateless nations and Bohdan Krawchenko's sophisticated sociological analysis of overcoming the "incompleteness" of the nation's social structure, was "read" at a more primitive level than it deserved.[39] Even more problematic, though, was the next stage in the restoration of the national school, wherein Ukrainian historians of the 1990s blended Hrushevsky's populist concepts with statist

37   See Orest Subtelny, *Ukraine: A History* (Toronto: University of Toronto Press, 1988) and *Istoriia Ukrainy* (Kyiv: Lybid, 1992).

38   Georgiy [Heorhii] Kasianov, "'Nationalized' History: Past Continuous, Present Perfect, Future ...," in Georgiy Kasianov and Philipp Ther, eds., *A Laboratory of Transnational History: Ukraine and Recent Ukrainian Historiography* (Budapest: Central European University Press, 2009), 7–24, here 23.

39   See Miroslav Hroch, *Die Vorkämpfer der nationalen Bewegung bei den kleinen Völkern Europas* (Prague: Universita Karlova, 1968); published in English as *A Comparative Analysis of the Social Composition of Patriotic Groups among the Smaller European Nations*, trans. Ben Fowkes (New York: Cambridge University Press, 1985), and Bohdan Krawchenko, *Social Change and National Consciousness in Twentieth-Century Ukraine* (London: Macmillan, 1985).

interpretations advanced in Galicia in the 1920s and the Soviet understanding of historical causation dating from the 1980s.[40]

Thus, post-communist Ukrainian historians by and large inherited the dogmatism and longing for a clearly-defined subject of history that was equally present in the Soviet and Ukrainian nationalist traditions. Many of them never quite managed to rid themselves of pseudo-Marxist language, even as they switched to the nationalist theories from the 1920s, as illustrated beautifully by a claim made in a collectively-written survey of the history of Ukrainian culture (authored by a group of former historians of the Communist Party) that the authors used "a psychological approach based on the principle of historical materialism."[41] More consistent, but not necessarily more sophisticated, was the introduction to the 2002 survey of twentieth-century Ukrainian history prepared at the Taras Shevchenko University of Kyiv and approved by the Ministry of Education as a textbook for students majoring in History. The book opens with the following statement: "The history of Ukraine is the Ukrainian people's path of struggle for independence." An elaboration follows in the next paragraph: "The history of the long-suffering Ukrainian people is filled with striking pages of brilliant victories for the cause of liberation and that of defeats which returned them to the previous condition."[42]

If this was the emerging, dominant scheme of Ukrainian history, it should come as no surprise that many authors of scholarly monographs published in independent Ukraine chose not to include any statements on methodology or on how their research contributes to the larger picture of Ukrainian history. In at least one case, a sense of academic integrity amid widespread frustration with the supplanting of one dogmatic ideology with another led the authors of an excellent 1994 monograph on the Soviet state and western Ukrainian intellectuals to declare that "a simple, everyday

40   Hrytsak, "Ukrainska istoriohrafiia," 52.
41   S. M. Klapchuk and V. F. Ostafiichuk, eds., *Istoriia ukrainskoi ta zarubizhnoi kultury*, 4th ed. (Kyiv: Znannia-Pres, 2002), 12.
42   A. H. Sliusarenko, V. I. Husev, and V. M. Lytvyn, eds., *Novitnia istoriia Ukrainy, 1900–2000: Pidruchnyk dlia studentiv istorychnykh spetsialnostei vyshchykh navchalnykh zakladiv* (Kyiv: Vyshcha shkola, 2002), 5.

accumulation of facts" was more important for Ukrainian historical scholarship than any "philosophy of history."[43] Ironically, this strategy of seeking refuge from ideology in a documentary approach also represented a legacy of the late Soviet period, when archaeographic research and solid empiricism were seen within the community of historians as a hallmark of true professionalism.[44]

Into the Wider World

If the diaspora's intervention helped establish the dominance of the national paradigm, it also set the Ukrainian historical profession on the road to internationalization and inclusion into the world's methodological currents. Together with the Soros network and other Western agencies and individual donors, funding from the Ukrainian diaspora helped develop new centers, journals, and translation projects that were not connected by the force of institutional inertia to the old Soviet academic world. These included the Institute for Historical Study at the Ivan Franko University of Lviv, the Kowalsky Eastern Institute of Ukrainian Studies at the Vasyl Karazin University of Kharkiv, and *Krytyka* magazine in Kyiv. The journal *Ukraina Moderna*, affiliated with the first of these and based on the Western model, soon developed into the best historical journal in Ukraine. The Krytyka Publishing House in Kyiv became a leading publisher of academic translations introducing Ukrainian audiences to the finest Western works in Ukrainian Studies and beyond. The privately-funded Center for Urban History of East Central Europe in Lviv became a leader in the field of urban studies and commemoration of Ukraine's multiethnic past. A historical school that is critical of the national paradigm and which follows recent Western epistemological trends was established in the Department of History at the National University of Kyiv Mohyla Academy. Finally, since the early 1990s an ever-increasing number of Ukrainian students has undertaken graduate training in the West. Some also

---

43   O. S. Rublov and Iu. A. Cherchenko, *Stalinshchyna i dolia zakhidnoukrainskoi intelihentsii: 20–50-ti roky XX st.* (Kyiv: Naukova dumka, 1994), 12.

44   Andrei [Andrii] Portnov, *Uprazhneniia s istoriei po-ukrainski* (Moscow: OGI-Polit.ru-Memorial, 2010), 110–12.

obtain academic positions there. Together with a small number of established Ukrainian scholars who have managed to secure positions in Western academia, they continue to publish and give public lectures in Ukraine. Today, many leading Ukrainian historians who built their reputations and schools during the post-Soviet period travel widely and read the same journals as their Western colleagues. In the emerging global and multilingual world of Ukrainian history writing, the old national history model is being increasingly challenged by new epistemological and methodological approaches. Nevertheless, it survives and even demonstrates its ability to adapt by including some of these innovations in the traditional, overall scheme of the nation's trials and victories.

Perhaps the best illustration of such adaptation and the tensions present therein may be found in the changing format of major historical surveys. The crowning achievement of Soviet Ukraine's historical scholarship was the multivolume, collectively written *History of the Ukrainian SSR*, originally published in Ukrainian in 1977–79 (eight volumes in ten books) and in a revised Russian translation in 1981–85 (ten volumes).[45] As the leading institution behind this project and, indeed, a research institute that was originally created in 1936 in order to produce a Marxist survey of Ukrainian history, the Institute of History (under the umbrella of the Ukrainian Academy of Sciences) had to redefine its very raison-d'être when Ukraine became independent. At first, a solution was sought in another multivolume history authored by a large group of scholars, this publication based on the national paradigm. In the early 1990s the Institute of History released several small-circulation brochures formulating possible conceptual approaches to this project titled *The History of the Ukrainian People*.[46] However, difficulties with

---

45   Iu. Iu. Kondufor and A. H. Shevelev, eds., *Istoriia Ukrainskoi RSR*, 8 vols. (Kyiv: Naukova dumka, 1977–79) and Iu. Iu. Kondufor, ed., *Istoriia Ukrainskoi SSR*, 10 vols. (Kyiv: Naukova dumka, 1980–85).

46   See, e.g., V. H. Sarbei, *Do vyroblennia kontseptsii bahatotomnoi "Istorii ukrainskoho narodu" (rozdumy i propozytsii)* (Kyiv: Instytut istorii Ukrainy NANU, 1994) and R. H. Symonenko, *Do kontseptsii bahatotomnoi "Istorii ukrainskoho narodu" (mizhnatsionalni i mizhnarodni aspekty)* (Kyiv: Instytut istorii Ukrainy NANU, 1993).

securing state funding for such a monumental project, as well as the realities of the post-communist publishing market, resulted in the implementation of a very different model – a book series with individual volumes single-authored or co-authored by leading specialists. Entitled *Ukraine through the Ages*, this fifteen-volume series was released in 1998–99 by the Alternatyvy Publishing House, earning its authors the State Prize for Scholarship and Technology in 2001.[47] However, the volumes varied considerably in their conceptual framing and did not provide a coherent narrative history of Ukraine.

In any case, the success of these individual authors did not quite meet the perceived need for a large, collectively-written work that would be based at the Institute and involve most of its researchers as authors. The Institute found such a project in the ten-volume *Encyclopedia of the History of Ukraine*, which appeared in ten, thick, alphabetically-arranged volumes between 2003 and 2013.[48]

---

47   K. P. Buniatian, V. Iu. Murzin, and O. V. Symonenko, *Na svitanku istorii*, Ukraina kriz viky, vol. 1 (Kyiv: Alternatyvy, 1998); S. D. Kruzhytskyi, V. M. Zubar, and A. S. Rusiaieva, *Antychni derzhavy Pivnichnoho Prychornomoria*, Ukraina kriz viky, vol. 2 (Kyiv: Alternatyvy, 1998); V. D. Baran, *Davni sloviany*, Ukraina kriz viky, vol. 3 (Kyiv: Alternatyvy, 1998); O. P. Tolochko and P. P. Tolochko, *Kyivska Rus*, Ukraina kriz viky, vol. 4 (Kyiv: Alternatyvy, 1998); M. F. Kotliar, *Halytsko-Volynska Rus*, Ukraina kriz viky, vol. 5 (Kyiv: Alternatyvy, 1998); O. V. Rusyna, *Ukraina pid tataramy i Lytvoiu*, Ukraina kriz viky, vol. 6 (Kyiv: Alternatyvy, 1998); V. A. Smolii and V. S. Stepankov, *Ukrainska natsionalna revoliutsiia (1648–1676 rr.)*, Ukraina kriz viky, vol. 7; O. I. Hurzhii and T. V. Chukhlib, *Hetmanska Ukraina*, Ukraina kriz viky, vol. 8 (Kyiv: Alternatyvy, 1999); V. H. Sarbei, *Natsionalne vidrodzhennia Ukrainy*, Ukraina kriz viky, vol. 9 (Kyiv: Alternatyvy, 1999); A. S. Rubliov and O. P. Reient, *Ukrainski vyzvolni zmahannia 1917–1921 rr.*, Ukraina kriz viky, vol. 10; S. V. Kulchytskyi, *Ukraina mizh dvoma viinamy (1921–1939 rr.)*, Ukraina kriz viky, vol. 11 (Kyiv: Alternatyvy, 1999); M. V. Koval, *Ukraina v Druhii svitovii i Velykyi Vitchyznianii viinakh (1939–1945 rr.)*, Ukraina kriz viky, vol. 12 (Kyiv: Alternatyvy, 1999); V. K. Baran and V. M. Danylenko, *Ukraina v umovakh systemnoi kryzy (1946–1980-ti rr.)*, Ukraina kriz viky, vol. 13 (Kyiv: Alternatyvy, 1999); V. M. Lytvyn, *Ukraina na mezhi tysiacholit (1991–2000 rr.)*, Ukraina kriz viky, vol. 14 (Kyiv: Alternatyvy, 2000); V. P. Troshchynskyi and A. A. Shevchenko, *Ukraintsi v sviti*, Ukraina kriz viky, vol. 15 (Kyiv: Alternatyvy, 1999). Not all the authors worked at the Institute of the History of Ukraine; some of them were from the Institute of Archeology of the National Academy of Sciences and leading universities.

48   V. A. Smolii, ed., *Entsyklopediia istorii Ukrainy*, 10 vols. (Kyiv: Naukova dumka, 2003–13).

Two additional, unnumbered volumes devoted entirely to entries on "Ukraine" and "Ukrainians" came out in 2018 and 2019. In approving this decision back in 1997, the Institute's executive apparently saw the encyclopedia as a safer and more "fact-oriented" project compared to a multivolume history. The latter, in the decades before the Revolution of Dignity and Russian military aggression, risked creating a political stir not just in relation to the appraisal of controversial topics, such as Mazepa or the UPA, but also the entire scheme of Ukrainian history.

By 2010, however, the Institute needed one more large project and grudgingly settled on another incarnation of a multivolume, collective history. Demonstrating some familiarity with Western concepts of history writing, the compilers of the prospectus missed the critical connotations of the term "grand narrative" and proclaimed their intention to develop a national grand narrative for Ukrainian history. Accordingly, the 2011 prospectus was entitled "History of Ukraine: Materials toward the Development of a Concept of a National Grand Narrative: An Invitation to a Discussion."[49] What was refreshing about this publication was its structure as a discussion piece. Together with the prospectus of the five-volume historical survey, it includes a tour-de-force paper by Heorhii Kasianov and Oleksii Tolochko, highlighting the dangers of a teleological and essentialist approach inherent in national histories, as well as an alternative prospectus by Iryna Kolesnyk and comments by a number of other leading scholars.[50] It seems that the final consensus was to produce a work modelled on *The Cambridge History of Russia* or *The Cambridge History of Scandinavia*: thematic rather than chronological within volumes and avoiding the application of modern ethnic designations to premodern societies. Moreover, the editors envisage inviting foreign specialists to contribute

---

49   V. A. Smolii, ed., *"Istoriia Ukrainy": Materialy do rozrobky kontseptsii natsionalnoho hrand-naratyvu: Zaproshennia do dyskusii* (Kyiv: Instytut istorii Ukrainy NANU, 2011).

50   A version of this paper by Kasianov and Tolochko is now available in English: Georgiy [Heorhii] Kasianov and Oleksii Tolochko, "National Histories and Contemporary Historiography: The Challenges and Risks of Writing a New History of Ukraine," *Harvard Ukrainian Studies* 34, nos. 1–4 (2015–16): 79–106.

chapters to each of the five volumes, all of which will have separate editors — unlike the old Soviet model of an "editorial board" for the entire publication.

As promising as this proposal appeared at the time, one also senses a theoretical and methodological tension between the very notion of a need for a "national grand narrative" and approaches that are designed to avoid a teleological and primordialist concept of national history. Whether or not this tension would make the new survey history innovative or conflicted, the participants' awareness of the challenges to the national paradigm places Ukrainian historical scholarship on par with other European historiographies. However, as of this writing, the project appears to be on hold because of funding challenges.

The intellectual engagement with Western historiographical debates, as demonstrated by the 2011 prospectus, developed only gradually. In 1995, when *Slavic Review*, the leading Western journal of Slavic Studies, brought together Ukrainian and Western scholars for a discussion of Mark von Hagen's provocative think-piece, "Does Ukraine Have a History?", the participants seemed to be talking at cross-purposes. Von Hagen's contribution was concerned with the early signs of "the enshrinement [in Ukraine] of a new integral nationalist dogma, a primarily diaspora narrative that charts the prehistory of the independent Ukrainian state as the teleological triumph of an essentialist, primordial Ukrainian nation."[51] In contrast, he proposed to turn the perceived "weaknesses" of Ukrainian history, such as discontinuity of state tradition and the permeable cultural frontiers of "Ukrainian" identity, into its strengths: "Precisely the fluidity of frontiers, the permeability of cultures, the historic multi-ethnic society is what could make Ukrainian history a very 'modern' field of inquiry."[52]

In his response, Yaroslav Isaievych, a leading Ukrainian historian from Ukraine, showed little appreciation for von Hagen's post-

51   Mark von Hagen, "Does Ukraine Have a History?" *Slavic Review* 54, no. 3 (Fall 1995): 658–73, here 665.
52   Ibid., 670.

modern sensibilities or even for the colonial and postcolonial approach suggested in concurrent comments by another Western commentator, George Grabowicz. Isaievych argued that Ukrainian history had been suppressed by Poles and Russians "as a means to maintain a hold on Ukrainian lands," and expressed his disenchantment that "even after the proclamation of Ukrainian independence" authoritative Western scholars, such as von Hagen, want to "discuss the very existence of Ukrainian national history."[53] Isaievych also explicitly refused to see the nation-state model of historical process as outdated, and questioned any fluidity of frontiers or permeability of cultures in the lands of what is now Ukraine, where "only the political and not the ethnic border changed comparatively often."[54] Another Ukrainian participant, Serhii Plokhy, who was by then based in Canada, offered a much more nuanced reaction to von Hagen's paper. Instead of defending or dismissing the national-history model, he saw it as essentially based on historical mythology, itself a necessary component of national identity. The only problem, then, is that this is a nationalist mythology for ethnic Ukrainians, which is facing challenges in present-day multicultural Ukraine. Plokhy noted that "contemporary Ukraine, which to a great extent is the product of one historical myth, now needs a new myth to make its way forward." In order for this to happen, Hrushevsky's historical scheme had to be reconciled with the heritage of the Ukrainian Soviet Socialist Republic.[55]

In contrast, the deconstruction of national historical myths was front and center of the follow-up discussion that was published in 2009. Originally intended as an assessment of the field ten years after von Hagen's provocative intervention, the collection of essays entitled *A Laboratory of Transnational History: Ukraine and Recent Ukrainian Historiography* came out fourteen years later. Tellingly, a Ukrainian historian and his German colleague (the latter working

---

53   Iaroslav Isaievych, "Ukrainian Studies—Exceptional or Merely Exemplary?" *Slavic Review* 54, no. 3 (Fall 1995): 702–8, here 702.

54   Ibid., 706.

55   Serhii M. Plokhy, "The History of a 'Non-Historical' Nation: Notes on the Nature and Current Problems of Ukrainian Historiography," *Slavic Review* 54, no. 3 (Fall 1995): 709–16, here 712.

in Italy at the time) conceived the project and co-edited the book.[56] Although von Hagen contributed a piece revisiting his ideas in light of recent historiographical trends, the real lead articles were written by the co-editors, Georgiy (Heorhii) Kasianov and Philipp Ther. Whereas Kasianov focuses on a critique of what he calls "national-ized history" with its teleological linear narrative, essentialism, and ethnic exclusivity, Ther proposes the "transnational paradigm" for Ukrainian history. Transnational history, of course, has been ac-tively explored by Western European and American historians as a productive way of transcending national and, indeed, even conti-nental boundaries. Understood as the study of relations between cultures and societies rather than within them, transnational his-tory focuses on episodes of cultural interaction and instances of *his-toire croisée* ("entangled history").[57] The other Western contributors to this collection also stress the need to transcend the old-style na-tional history. Andreas Kappeler provides a useful amplification of this argument by proposing that Ukrainian historiography should first move from an "ethnonational" to a multiethnic approach and from the latter to a transnational one, although his understanding of the latter differs in some respects from Ther's. Mark von Hagen fine-tunes his original thesis by proposing for Ukrainian history the interpretive frames of "borderland studies," regional history, urban studies, and the biographical approach.[58]

No less interesting is the second part of the collection, which features articles on specific problems in Ukrainian history by well-known historians from Ukraine (Natalia Yakovenko, Oleksii Tolochko, and Yaroslav Hrytsak), the West (John-Paul Himka and

---

56   Georgiy [Heorhii] Kasianov and Philipp Ther, eds., *A Laboratory of Transnational History: Ukraine and Recent Ukrainian Historiography* (Budapest: Central Euro-pean University Press, 2009).

57   Kasianov, "'Nationalized' History," 7–24; Philipp Ther, "The Transnational Pa-radigm of Historiography and Its Potential for Ukrainian History, in *Laboratory of Transnational History*, Kasianov and Ther, eds. 81–114.

58   Andreas Kappeler, "From an Ethnonational to a Multiethnic to a Transnational Ukrainian History," ibid., 51–81; Mark von Hagen, "Revisiting the Histories of Ukraine, "ibid., 25–50.

Roman Szporluk), and Russia (Aleksei Miller and Oksana Ostap-
chuk), all of whom in some form challenge the "national paradigm"
in their case studies. The editors characterize this collection of articles as "almost an alternative reader of Ukrainian history,"[59] although one wonders if they too engage in the reification of a fluid
border between the official line and revisionism. At the time, all
three Ukrainian participants were leading authorities in their fields,
a position they still hold today. Perhaps, the analytical distinction
between the "national paradigm" and revisionist challenges should
not be understood as a challenge to official historical scholarship in
either Ukraine or the diaspora. The revisionists are increasingly
well-established scholars or even leading voices in their fields, and
these days few serious scholars embrace the extreme, unmodified
version of "nationalized" history.

New Approaches in Ukraine

Thus, it would be misleading to analyze Ukrainian history writing
since independence as a clear-cut struggle between the "national
paradigm" and its opponents. Some proponents of the nation-state
framework have made important contributions to the field by documenting the development of the national movement or describing
the mechanisms of imperial repression. Even greater numbers of
solid professionals are doing excellent work on topics that occupy
a privileged place in the new canon of national history, such as the
Cossacks or the Ukrainian Revolution of 1917–20, but their sophisticated sociocultural historical approaches have little in common
with the romanticized, patriotic clichés found in older literature.
More often than not during the last thirty years, the books that
"made a splash" in Ukraine's historical community challenged the
national paradigm, but they were not rejected by some hypothetical, dominant school. These influential interventions usually stand
out because they offer new approaches that are adopted subsequently by a significant number of professional historians.

---

59   Georgiy [Heorhii] Kasianov and Philipp Ther, "Introduction," ibid., 1–4, here
      4.

The Ukrainian case demonstrates that textbooks can also make such an impact. During the late 1990s, the two companion volumes from the Heneza Publishing House, Natalia Yakovenko's *Survey of the History of Ukraine from Ancient Times to the End of the Eighteenth Century* (1997) and Yaroslav Hrytsak's *Survey of the History of Ukraine: The Formation of a Modern Ukrainian Nation during the Nineteenth and Twentieth Centuries* (1996) did much to undermine the certainties of the national paradigm. A striking feature of Yakovenko's book is the author's conscious avoidance of teleological schemes and insistence that present-day ethnic categories are not helpful tools for understanding medieval and early modern society in the lands that now constitute Ukraine.[60] Hrytsak's volume emphasizes the constructed character of the modern Ukrainian national identity, and also introduces the Ukrainian reader to the most productive Western approaches to Ukrainian history of the last two centuries.[61] Both authors are highly influential in the Ukrainian historical profession. Yakovenko was a long-serving chairperson of the History Department at Kyiv Mohyla Academy, where she has built the nation's top graduate program in History. She has also written an excellent textbook, *An Introduction to History*, which is on par with the best Western equivalents in terms of its theoretical depth and methodological sophistication.[62] Hrytsak, who was the founding director of the Institute for Historical Study in Lviv, now teaches at the prestigious Ukrainian Catholic University. A popular columnist in the national media, he takes an active part in public debates on the issues of national history and identity.

The controversies in which Yakovenko was embroiled at the turn of the century were mostly within the historical profession. The next chapter discusses in more detail her scathing critique of a volume on the seventeenth-century Cossack rebellion, co-authored by the influential director of the Institute of Ukrainian History and

---

60   N. M. Iakovenko, *Narys istorii Ukrainy z naidavnishykh chasiv do kintsia XVIII stolittia* (Kyiv: Heneza, 1997).

61   Iaroslav Hrytsak, *Narys istorii Ukrainy: Formuvannia modernoi ukrainskoi natsii XIX–XX st.* (Kyiv: Heneza, 1996).

62   Natalia Iakovenko, *Vstup do istorii* (Kyiv: Krytyka, 2007).

published in the "Ukraine through the Ages" book series. Yakovenko demonstrated that the theoretical framework and language
of this book, *The Ukrainian National Revolution of the Seventeenth Century*, are strikingly similar to that of Soviet-era books on the Bolshevik Revolution inasmuch as the concept of historical causation and
the representation of the "people" as a united force have been carried over unchanged from Marxist to neo-nationalist historiography.[63] Yakovenko's own book of highly imaginative and often revisionist essays, *Parallel World: Studies in the History of Representations and Ideas in Ukraine in the Sixteenth and Seventeenth Centuries*
(2002), took aim at a few "sacred cows" of the national paradigm,
in particular the notion of the native aristocracy's "treasonous" conversion to Catholicism beginning in the late sixteenth century and
the Cossacks' alleged unity with the people in defence of the nation
and its Orthodox faith during the wars of the mid-seventeenth century. Through a subtle textual analysis of sources Yakovenko
demonstrates that until the mid-seventeenth century the world of
Ruthenian nobles in the Polish-Lithuanian Commonwealth was
marked by religious tolerance, if not outright indifference, within
regional and family-based power networks. As for the much-lion-
ized Cossacks, they actually shared with their Polish enemies the
"knightly" ethos of condescension toward civilians and the right to
loot, including the looting of their own confession's churches and
the killing of coreligionist burghers.[64] Such interpretations have certainly acted as a healthy antidote to the traditional representations
widely encountered in the Ukrainian mass media, even if specialists
point out that Yakovenko may be going too far in her revisionism,
especially in dismissing religion almost entirely as a factor in the
Cossack wars.[65]

63   See V. A. Smolii and V. S. Stepankov, *Ukrainska natsionalna revoliutsiia XVII st.
(1648–1676 rr.)*, Ukraina kriz viky, vol. 7 (Kyiv: Alternatyvy, 1999), and Natalia
Iakovenko, "V kolorakh proletarskoi revoliutsii," *Ukrainskyi humanitarnyi
ohliad*, no. 3 (2000): 58–78.

64   Natalia Iakovenko, *Paralelnyi svit: Doslidzhennia z istorii uiavlen ta idei v Ukraini
XVI–XVII st.* (Kyiv: Krytyka, 2002), here 13–79 and 189–228.

65   Plokhy, *Ukraine and Russia*, 252–65.

Hrytsak, in contrast, is often fighting battles in the media, fending off attacks from both Ukrainian nationalists and supporters of a pro-Russian orientation. The former went into overdrive in the early 2010s after the historian's courageous refusal to endorse the cult of wartime nationalist leader Stepan Bandera, which has become a new orthodoxy in western Ukraine. In August 2011 Hrytsak wrote a newspaper column with the telling opening sentence, "They are turning me into an enemy of the people."[66]

Interestingly, Hrytsak's brilliant biography of the great Ukrainian writer and nation builder Ivan Franko (1856–1916) is no less of a threat to nationalist mythology, if only the right-wing commentators had the patience to read this bulky volume, entitled *A Prophet in His Fatherland: Franko and His Community*.[67] The phrase "his community" in the book's title could also read "his communities" because Hrytsak carefully examines the numerous micro-contexts of Franko's life and work: his native village, his school, the student circles of which he was a member, his readership, the journals he edited, the industrial city of Boryslav as the setting for his socialist propaganda and literary works, the women in his life, etc. Hrytsak shows that the image of a peasant poet, the Ukrainian national identity, and the Ukrainian-sounding stress on the last syllable of his surname are all conscious identity choices that Franko made later in life. These choices were not predetermined either. The first Ukrainian intellectual in Galicia to earn a living as a writer and editor, Franko in fact survived only because for decades he also collaborated with Polish journals, which had a much larger readership. But, historically more important was his work for the Ukrain-

---

66   Iaroslav Hrytsak, "Porady na zle i na dobre," *Gazeta.ua*, 7 August 2011, http://gazeta.ua/articles/grycak-jaroslav/poradi-na-zle-i-na-dobre/393431. The materials of contemporary discussions about Bandera in the Ukrainian media have been helpfully reprinted in Ihor Balynskyi, Iaroslav Hrytsak, and Tarik Siril [Cyril] Amar, eds. *Strasti za Banderoiu* (Kyiv: Hrani-T, 2010).

67   Iaroslav Hrytsak, *Prorok u svoii vitchyzni: Franko ta ioho spilnota (1856–1886)* (Kyiv: Krytyka, 2006). In 2018, this book also appeared in an English translation: Yaroslav Hrytsak, *Franko and His Community*, trans. Marta Daria Olynyk (Brighton, Mass: Academic Studies Press, 2018). Subsequent quotes from this book have been checked against the English edition.

ian press, where subscription numbers at the time were usually under 1,500. The print run of Franko's most popular poetry collection
in Ukrainian was only between 600 and 1,000.[68] By the early 1880s
Franko had already become a Ukrainian "Moses" for this relatively
small group of readers, a cult figure much like the poet Taras
Shevchenko had been for Ukrainians in the Russian Empire. Franko
immortalized his name early on by creating in his novels, poems,
and scholarly texts a new and very modern Ukraine—a land of industry, worker-activists, liberated women, and socialist intellectuals. In other words, in his scholarly and literary works Franko created a social and cultural space for a new generation of patriots to
inhabit. In the process, he also proved that these modern realities
could be described in the Ukrainian language, no longer just a peasant vernacular. Hrytsak argues, in contrast to much of the previous
scholarship, that it was the radical (early socialist) political culture
that Franko created rather than the cumulative result of the Ukrainian national movement which caused the final transition from pre-
national Ruthenian to a modern, national Ukrainian identity in Galicia.[69]

   The circumstance of being attacked by both the right and the
left and criticized simultaneously by nationalists, former imperial
masters, and postmodernists is nothing new to historians of modern Ukraine. This description fits the experiences of Stanislav
Kulchytsky, the leading economic historian of twentieth-century
Ukraine, who in the late 1990s took up the challenge of heading a
commission of historians evaluating the legacy of the UPA, the
Ukrainian Insurgent Army. This controversial nationalist organization is lionized in western Ukraine as a bastion of national resistance to both the Soviets and the Nazis, but seen in Russia and,
at that time, much of eastern Ukraine as a terrorist organization that
collaborated with the Germans and was complicit in the Holocaust.

---

68   Hrytsak, *Prorok u svoii vitchyzni*, 372; Hrytsak, *Franko and His Community*, 332.
69   Hrytsak, *Prorok u svoii vitchyzni*, 435; Hrytsak, *Franko and His Community*, 393.

Needless to say, the commission's reasonably balanced 2004 report failed to satisfy either side.[70]

Much the same was the outcome of Kulchytsky's other, and equally courageous, decision to engage the issue of the 1932-33 Famine, which the administration of President Viktor Yushchenko (in office 2005-2010) wanted officially recognized as the Holodomor ("murder through starvation") and a genocide of ethnic Ukrainians.[71] At that point, the notion of the Holodomor as genocide was commonly accepted in the Ukrainian diaspora but remained highly controversial in Ukraine and instrumentalized by pro-Russian and pro-Western politicians alike. Not only was Kulchytsky criticized on both sides of Ukraine's political spectrum, but a younger revisionist colleague at the Institute of the History of Ukraine, Heorhii Kasianov, made the analysis of Kulchytsky's gradual acceptance of the Holodomor concept the subject of his book on the uses of the famine in Ukrainian public discourse.[72]

One can argue, however, that the most important change in post-Soviet Ukrainian historiography took place elsewhere, not in the study of such controversial political issues as the UPA or the Holodomor. In the 2000s regional history and new social history, often informed by micro-historical and anthropological approaches, emerged as the fields where the finest Ukrainian works were on par with the best of Western historical writing in terms of

---

70   The commission's report has been published as *Problema OUN-UPA: Zvit robochoi hrupy istorykiv pry Uriadovii komisii z vyvchennia diialnosti OUN i UPA* (Kyiv: Instytut istorii Ukrainy NANU, 2004).

71   See, e.g., S. V. Kulchitskii [Kulchytskyi], *Pochemu on nas unichtozhal? Stalin i ukrainskii Golodomor* (Kyiv: Ukrainska pres-hrupa, 2007) and S. V. Kulchytskyi, *Holodomor 1932-33 rokiv iak henotsyd: Trudnoshchi usvidomlennia* (Kyiv: Nash chas, 2007). The scholar's condensed history of the Holodomor is now available in English: Stanislav Kulchytsky, *The Ukrainian Famine of 1932-1933: An Anatomy of the Holodomor*, trans. Ali Kinsella (Edmonton and Toronto: Canadian Institute of Ukrainian Studies Press, 2018).

72   Heorhii Kasianov, *Danse macabre: Holod 1932-1933 rokiv u polytytsi, masovii svidomosti ta istoriohrafii (1980- ti-pochatok 2000-kh)* (Kyiv: Nash chas, 2010), 162-89. For a lengthy book review, see Andrei Portnov, "O grazhdanskoi vovlechennosti, intellektualnoi nepredvziatosti i izuchenii pamiati," *Ab Imperio*, no. 1 (2011): 12-20.

theoretical and methodological sophistication. Such books were often authored by younger Western-educated historians. Kateryna Dysa's impressive study of witchcraft and witch-hunting in Right-Bank Ukraine during the seventeenth and eighteenth centuries, a fine example of the historical-anthropological approach, was originally a PhD thesis defended in English at the Central European University.[73] Andriy Zayarnyuk's excellent book on the "idioms of emancipation" in the life and struggles of the Galician peasantry — a new social history at its best, informed by cultural anthropology as it emerged after the "linguistic turn" — is the expanded first part of the author's doctoral dissertation defended at the University of Alberta.[74]

During the new millennium's first decade, Ukrainian-educated historians also produced excellent scholarship employing many of the same approaches. Two books on the Kharkiv region are early examples of how new Ukrainian regional history can profit from the latest social history, micro-history, cultural anthropology, borderland studies, and biographical approaches. One of them, Volodymyr Masliichuk's *A Province at the Intersection of Cultures*, was published in Ukrainian in Kharkiv, while another, Tatiana Zhurzhenko's *Borderlands into Bordered Lands*, came out in English as part of a book series issued by a German publisher.[75]

By 2010, the Institute of Ukrainian History, far from being a strict custodian of the national paradigm, published the first volumes in the series of edited collections, the very title of which speaks volumes about the growing acceptance of new social history: From the History of Everyday Life in Ukraine. Familiarity with Western scholarship is not limited to mere titles, however, as

73   Kateryna Dysa, *Istoriia z vidmamy: Sudy pro chary v ukrainskykh voievodstvakh Rechi Pospolytoi XVII–XVIII stolit* (Kyiv: Krytyka, 2008). Dysa now teaches at Kyiv Mohyla Academy.

74   Andrii Zaiarniuk [Andriy Zayarnyuk], *Idiomy emansypatsii: "Vyzvolni proiekty" i halytske selo v seredyni XIX stolittia* (Kyiv: Krytyka, 2007). Zayarnyuk is now a professor at the University of Winnipeg.

75   Volodymyr Masliichuk, *Provintsiia na perekhresti kultur: Doslidzhennia z istorii Slobidskoi Ukrainy XVII–XIX st.* (Kharkiv: Kharkivskyi pryvatnyi muzei miskoi sadyby, 2007); Tatiana Zhurzhenko, *Borderlands into Bordered Lands: Geopolitics of Identity in Post-Soviet Ukraine* (Stuttgart: Ibidem, 2010).

the works in these series feature chapters discussing French and Anglo-American new social history; in other chapters, the application of Western social-history methodology to research on everyday life in Soviet Ukraine is somewhat limited, but the intention to be up-to-date conceptually and methodologically is certainly there.[76]

More recent books by Ukrainian (and Ukraine-based) scholars confirm the further blurring of conceptual and methodological lines between the best works of Ukrainian historical scholarship within the country and abroad. The burgeoning fields of oral history and women's history both saw the advent of milestone publications that confirmed their now-prominent place in Ukrainian academia.[77] Innovative studies of the Soviet experience appeared, which use everyday material culture and food culture as the prisms through which to interpret Ukraine's Soviet past.[78] Major revisionist works appeared on the period of Kyivan Rus' and the sources of our knowledge about it, including a thick volume completely reconstructing the image of Prince Volodymyr the Great.[79] A pioneering study of the everyday life, code of honor, and identities of the Ukrainian nobility in the Polish-Lithuanian Commonwealth shows that Cossacks and peasants need not be seen as the only ancestors of modern Ukrainians.[80]

---

76   S. V. Kulchytskyi, ed., *Narysy povsiakdennoho zhyttia Radianskoi Ukrainy v dobu NEPu (1921–1928 rr.)*, 2 vols. (Kyiv: Instytut istorii Ukrainy NANU, 2010); V. M. Danylenko, ed., *Povoienna Ukraina: Narysy sotsialnoi istorii (druha polovyna 40-kh–seredyna 50-kh rr.)*, 2 vols. (Kyiv: Instytut istorii Ukrainy NANU, 2010).

77   Helinada Hrinchenko, ed., *Slukhaty, chuty, rozumity: Usna istoriia Ukrainy XX–XXI stolit* (Kyiv: Ukrainska asotsiatsiia usnoi istorii, 2021); Oksana Kis, ed., *Ukrainski zhinky u hornyli modernizatsii* (Kharkiv: KSD, 2017).

78   See Oksana Ovsiiuk, *Zhyttia pislia okupatsii: Pobut kyian, 1943–1945 rr.* (Kyiv: Duliby, 2017); Olena Stiazhkina, *Smak radianskoho: Izha i idtsi v mystetstvi zhyttia i mystetstvi kino (seredyna 1960-kh–seredyna 1980-kh)* (Kyiv: Dukh i litera, 2021).

79   Aleksei [Oleksii] Tolochko, *Ocherki nachalnoi Rusi* (Kyiv: Laurus, 2015); Vadim [Vadym] Aristov, *Aleksei Shakhmatov i rannee letopisanie* (Kyiv: Laurus, 2018); Oleksandr Filipchuk, *Zabutyi sviatyi: Kniaz Volodymyr Velykyi mizh Skhodom i Zakhodom* (Kyiv: Laurus, 2020).

80   Natalia Starchenko, *Ukrainski svity Rechi Pospolytoi: Istorii pro istoriiu* (Kyiv: Laurus, 2021).

All of these books (and many more not referenced here) could have easily been originally published in English and other main Western languages. Indeed, it is telling that in recent years the Harvard Ukrainian Research Institute and the Canadian Institute of Ukrainian Studies, which had sponsored translations of Western literature into Ukrainian in the 1990s and early 2000s, have developed strong programs of translation from the Ukrainian. Historical concepts and innovative findings now flow in both directions.

* * *

As Ukraine enters the fourth decade of its independent state existence, historical scholarship is coming of age as a worthy partner in the family of the world's "national" yet increasingly international historiographies. Internationalization in this sense is not limited to similar theoretical and methodological apparatus; acceptance of women's history, regional history, micro-history, and historical anthropology are some other approaches to the once-sacred "wholeness" (*sobornist*) of the Ukrainian nation and its past. Just as the Revolution of Dignity affirmed the notion of a modern political rather than ethnic Ukrainian nation, the now-global Ukrainian historical profession is drawing closer and closer to a more open and inclusive national history, and becoming more of a mosaic than a monolith.

3. Soviet Ghosts in Post-Communist Ukrainian Historiography

One of the common assumptions about history writing in the post-Soviet political space is that it is undergoing a long process of liberating itself from the legacy of Soviet dogmatism. In fact, as is also the case with other aspects of post-communist transition, old traditions die hard and, with the heritage of Soviet historical concepts not having been systematically examined, their traces can still be found in works positioning themselves as anti-Soviet. One can also argue that the majority of Ukrainian historians never fully caught up with the Western school of social history that was so prominent worldwide from the 1960s to the 1980s, perhaps because its terminology and methods sounded so "Soviet." The transition to the most recent Western historical methodology "after the linguistic turn" is thus encumbered in today's Ukraine by missing the social-history link and proceeding instead from a nation-centric starting point with concepts and methodology that are still unwittingly Marxist-Leninist in methodology but in denial of their Soviet lineage.

This chapter argues that Soviet-style historical methodology persists in contemporary Ukrainian historiography both at the level of terminology (itself reflecting historians' understanding of causation) and of the conceptual framework in which the dominant grand narrative of the ethnic nation for much of the 1990s and 2000s hindered the transition to modern microhistorical, regional-history, and cultural-history approaches. During the 2010s, the reign of traditional national history was challenged decisively from within the Ukrainian historical profession, but a serious debate about the Soviet legacy in historical methodology has yet to unfold.[81]

---

[81] There have been some interesting attempts to approach this issue: Leonid Zashkilniak, "Radianski istorychni mify v suchasnii ukrainskii istoriohrafii: 'Stare vyno v novykh mikhakh'," in *Svitlo i tini ukrainskoi radianskoi istoriohrafii: Materialy mizhnarodnoi naukovoi konferentsii*, ed. V. A. Smolii (Kyiv: Instytut istorii Ukrainy NANU, 2015), 17–30; H. V. Kasianov and O. P. Tolochko, "Natsionalni

Bringing Back the Nation

There are few signs of methodological self-awareness in the body of literature that was generated during the period of "revelations" in the late 1980s and early 1990s. Of course, Soviet Ukrainian historians realized the inadequacy of their general theoretical and methodological premises, but it was easier to speak of overcoming Soviet dogmatism than to analyze its structures or offer a recipe for the future. In the July 1991 issue of *Ukrainskyi istorychnyi zhurnal* (The Ukrainian Historical Journal), which was published literally on the eve of the Soviet collapse, the director of the premier historical research institute in Ukraine, Yuri Kondufor, announced that "the majority of the institute's researchers had managed to overcome (or was overcoming) vulgar sociologism, politicization, dogmatism, descriptiveness, simplification, and other shortcomings."[82] However, this short and rather superficial reference to methodology came in the middle of a long interview devoted primarily to previously proscribed topics and the legacy of prerevolutionary Ukrainian historians. Likewise, the leading authority on the Soviet period, Stanislav Kulchytsky, focused, in his 1991 introduction to a new collection of essays supposedly representing a break with Soviet models, on such issues as the famine of 1932–33, the Terror, and the abolition of special-access library collections containing the works of prerevolutionary and diaspora historians. He did offer some excellent observations on the Stalin-approved 1938 *Short Course* on party history and later party documents from which derived the theoretical frameworks of Soviet historical scholarship. The "vulgarized concepts" from the *Short Course* became "an obligatory matrix of all historical works." Later, the "stillborn but obligatory concepts of the 'complete and final victory of socialism,' 'developed socialism,'

---

istorii ta suchasna istoriohrafiia: Vyklyky i nebezpeky pry napysanni novoi istorii Ukrainy," *Ukrainskyi istorychnyi zhurnal*, no. 6 (2012): 5–24.

82   Iu. Iu. Kondufor, "Sohodennia Instytutu istorii Ukrainy AN URSR," *Ukrainskyi istorychnyi zhurnal*, no. 7 (1991): 57–60, here 58.

'socialist way of life,' [and] the 'Soviet people as a new historical entity' led to primitivism in historical works."[83]

However, like other historical writings of the time, even Kulchytsky's subtle analysis reflected the ethos of "liberating" historical scholarship from external constraints that should have resulted, almost by default, in "a new picture of a historical process" "stripped of the elements of totalitarian thinking heretofore imposed on historians 'from above.'"[84] Yet, in the very next sentence, listed first among the new features of the projected survey, was the phrase "the great attention devoted to the problems of the formation of Ukrainian statehood" — the very crux of the traditional national-history canon and a regression from the contemporary orientations of Western historical scholarship.

As Ukrainian historians celebrated their liberation from totalitarian thinking, their colleague on the other side of the Atlantic, Orest Subtelny, cautioned them against the wholesale abandonment of their Soviet training. In his 1993 article on "The Current State of Ukrainian Historiography," Subtelny suggested that it could be more productive for his Ukrainian colleagues to transition directly to such a mainstream Western field as social history:

> Rather than precipitately abandoning the Marxist methodology, which they know well, for unfamiliar Western approaches, it may be more fruitful for Ukraine's historians to concentrate instead on applying the Marxist approach more creatively. For example, those historians who dealt with classes, class struggles, and class consciousness throughout their careers could now apply their expertise to the study of labour history, urban and rural studies, or the history of women and the family. In other words, they might move into the currently popular new social history.[85]

Of course, Subtelny's proposal rested on the assumption that Soviet Ukrainian historians received rigorous theoretical training in what he imagined to be similar to the West's more open-minded and cre-

---

83 S. V. Kulchytskyi, "Istoriia Ukrainy: Sproby novoho bachennia," *Ukrainskyi istorychnyi zhurnal*, no. 4 (1991): 3–5, here 3–4.

84 Ibid., 5.

85 Orest Subtelny, "The Current State of Ukrainian Historiography," *Journal of Ukrainian Studies* 18, nos. 1–2 (Summer–Winter 1993): 33–54, here 42.

ative Marxist social history. In reality, the Soviets practiced a dogmatic variety of Stalinist historical materialism, which could not be
easily transformed into modern Western approaches.[86] As Nikolai
Koposov has shown, beginning in the 1960s, some leading Soviet
historians in Moscow and Leningrad could push beyond the conventional framework by emphasizing the role of culture in historical processes, but this freedom certainly did not extend to their colleagues in the non-Russian republics.[87] In their case, any such attempt could lead to the ominous accusation of, say, Ukrainian nationalism.[88]

It was thus not surprising that the established historians in
Ukraine began constructing a new master narrative of the ethnic
nation cobbled together from the same pseudo-Marxist clichés that
they knew so well. The same issue of *Ukrainskyi istorychnyi zhurnal*
that published a translated excerpt from Subtelny's history of
Ukraine also included, for example, Vitalii Sarbei's article, "The Development and Consolidation of the Nation and the Growth of the
National Movement in Ukraine in the Second Half of the Nineteenth Century." The historian argued that the consolidation of the
Ukrainian nation was "closely connected with the gradual development of capitalist relations," which strengthened "an objective
trend toward the reunification of all the Ukrainian lands."[89] However, Sarbei still emphasized that the development of capitalism underlined the nation-building process "even before the consolidation

86   See Andrei [Andrii] Portnov, *Uprazhneniia s istoriei po-ukrainski* (Moscow: OGI-
Polit.ru-Memorial, 2010), 113.
87   N. E. Koposov, *Khvatit ubivat koshek! Kritika sotsialnykh nauk* (Moscow: Novoe
literaturnoe obozrenie, 2005), 169–71.
88   For an excellent survey of recent research on Soviet Ukrainian historical scholarship, see Vitalii Iaremchuk, "Ukrainska radianska istoriohrafiia: Suchasnyi
stan doslidzhen," *Naukovi zapysky Natsionalnoho universytetu "Ostrozka akademiia": Seriia Istorychni nauky*, no. 27 (2018): 242–49.
89   V. H. Sarbei, "Stanovlennia i konsolidatsiia natsii ta pidnesennia natsionalnoho
rukhu na Ukraini v druhii polovyni XIX st.," *Ukrainskyi istorychnyi zhurnal*, no.
5 (1991): 3–16, here 3.

of capitalist socio-economic order," because for him, like for all Soviet historians, capitalism in the Russian Empire formally began
only in 1861.[90]

Such periodization was reversed in the space of only a few
years, with the nation triumphing over Marxist economic formations, at least on the surface. This process is well illustrated by
Oleksandr Reient's 1994 article on "Ukraine's Proletariat and the
Central Rada." In making the point that the late nineteenth and
early twentieth centuries ushered in a new period of Ukrainian history, the author seeks to distance himself from Soviet historical
scholarship's definition of this period as "imperialism." Instead, he
employs the name proposed by the diaspora historian Ivan Lysiak-
Rudnytsky, "the modernist age," and also claims that the influence
of economic and social factors actually decreased during this period, which was marked first and foremost by the advances in nation building. However, Reient's topic was the working class, and
therefore he needed somehow to bring it back into the picture now
dominated by the nation. This was achieved by his stating that the
time in question "marked the beginning of a qualitatively new period in the history of the Ukrainian people and, therefore, also their
working class."[91] At the same time, the term "proletariat" is used in
the article's title, and the text discusses such things as the "development of market relations and industrial production."[92]

One can argue that at the time Ukrainian historians were misreading the message from their Western colleagues, none of whom
would have recommended a simple change in the subject of history
without the rejection of Soviet clichés. Today it is curious to read
the report that I published as a graduate student in 1991 about a
meeting that took place at the Institute of History between Ukrainian scholars and the Canadian historian John-Paul Himka. Even
though the visitor was best known for his work on the history of
socialism in Galicia, the report is framed as a summary of the advice

---

90   Ibid.
91   O. P. Reient, "Stavlennia proletariatu Ukrainy do Tsentralnoi Rady," *Ukrainskyi
      istorychnyi zhurnal*, no. 4 (1994): 3–18, here 3.
92   Ibid., 5.

received from the "well-known researcher of the history of the Ukrainian national movement." Himka's comments on the diaspora's potential role in helping Ukrainian historians to master modern methodology, which were probably intended as cautionary words against borrowing from outdated nation-centric narratives, are also presented as a further appeal to learn from the West how to study nation building.[93]

Tellingly, Himka's first book, on the development of Polish and Ukrainian socialism in Galicia (1983), was not published in a Ukrainian translation until 2002, and even then it was issued by a publishing house associated with the Social Democratic United Party of Ukraine—at that point, a misleadingly-called political project by Viktor Medvedchuk having little in common with the early Galician Radicals about whom Himka wrote—rather than a mainstream publisher specializing in the Humanities and Social Sciences.[94] Likewise, the more influential Ukrainian translation of Bohdan Krawchenko's book on the social composition of Ukraine during the twentieth century was generally perceived in Ukraine as the story of a nation overcoming the "incompleteness" of its social structure (meaning, the underdevelopment of the native working class and educated strata), with the Marxist framework and political implications of Krawchenko's analysis not registering fully with his Ukrainian readers.[95] In the early 2000s, Hrytsak characterized Krawchenko's book as simply the best example of applying to

---

93 S. Yekelchyk, "Zustrich z kanadskym istorykom Dzh.-P. Hymkoiu," *Ukrainskyi istorychnyi zhurnal*, no. 12 (1991): 152.

94 Dzhon-Pol Khymka [John-Paul Himka], *Zarodzhennia polskoi sotsial-demokratii ta ukrainskoho radykalizmu v Halychyni (1860–1890)*, trans. S. Levchenko (Kyiv: Osnovni tsinnosti, 2002). For the original publication in English, see John-Paul Himka, *Socialism in Galicia: The Emergence of Polish Social Democracy and Ukrainian Radicalism* (Cambridge, Mass.: Harvard Ukrainian Research Institute, 1983).

95 Bohdan Kravchenko [Krawchenko], *Sotsialni zminy i natsionalna svidomist v Ukraini XX st.*, trans V. Ivashko and V. Korniienko (Kyiv: Osnovy, 1997). For the original publication in English, see Bohdan Krawchenko, *Social Change and National Consciousness in Twentieth-Century Ukraine* (London: Macmillan, 1985).

Ukrainian history the modernization approach, which from the distance of time appeared increasingly outdated.[96]

It is also possible that in the wake of the Soviet collapse Western colleagues in turn were misreading their Ukrainian interlocu-
tors. In his book on Ukrainian history writing and memory politics,
Andrii Portnov calls Subtelny's 1993 appeal "both tragic and
comic" because Soviet Ukrainian historical scholarship was not really Marxist, but used quasi-Marxist clichés to justify whatever version of the past was most convenient for the Soviet authorities at
any given time.[97] Just as historians in Ukraine assumed that their
diaspora counterparts must all be studying nation building, visitors
from the West may have taken for granted the Marxism of their
Ukrainian colleagues, based on what they knew about Marxist categories of contemporary Western social history. An authority on
Soviet Ukrainian historiography, Vitaliy Yaremchuk, shares
Portnov's overall scepticism about its connection to classical Marxism. He writes that obligatory references to Marx, Engels, and Lenin
served to justify changing historical interpretations that were themselves merely part of the Soviet "ideological discourse."[98] At the
same time, Yaremchuk does not see the Soviet Ukrainian historical
grand narrative as a totally flexible political tool devoid of established theoretical concepts. For the postwar period, he singles out
at least three theoretical notions commonly found in historical
works: periodization by economic formations, emphasis on class
analysis, and discussion of the beneficial role of the "fraternal" Russian people.[99]

In any case, it is significant that no serious discussion of the
inadequacy of Soviet "Marxist" methodology or the need for methodological change took place in Ukraine during the first post-com-

---

96   Iaroslav Hrytsak, "Paradoksy ukrainskoi modernizatsii," in Iaroslav Hrytsak,
      Strasti za natsionalizmom: istorychni ese (Kyiv: Krytyka, 2004), 37–45.
97   Portnov, *Uprazhneniia*, 113.
98   Vitalii Iaremchuk, *Mynule Ukrainy v istorychnii nautsi URSR pisliastalinskoi doby*
      (Ostroh: Vydavnytstvo Natsionalnoho universytetu "Ostrozka akademiia,"
      2009), 464 and 471.
99   Ibid., 471.

munist decade. The only book-length study of post-Soviet Ukrainian historiography, the work of Polish historian Tomasz Stryjek,
documents the 1990s debates about the "blank spots" of Ukrainian
history and the origins of the nation, but not methodological issues.
Whatever opposition there was to the now-dominant conception of
national history, it was largely limited to questioning the primordialist understanding of the nation.[100] Perhaps even more tellingly,
Stryjek's book still has not been translated into Ukrainian, thus in-
dicating how little interest there is in conceptualizing the transition
to the nation as a new — and, for all that, traditional — subject of history.

A New History in the Old Style

Yet, it was probably the level of conceptualization, called "mode of
emplotment" by Hayden White — rather than mode of argument or
of an ideological implication — which truly defined the nature of Soviet historical writing.[101] "Mode of emplotment" may also be its
longest-lasting legacy. As the leading authority on the early modern period, Natalia Yakovenko showed in her scathing review article (2000) of a book about the central event of the new nation-building narrative, the Khmelnytsky Rebellion (1648–54), decades of
writing about the revolutionary movement left even good historians mired in the Soviet linguistic and conceptual apparatus. Although Valerii Smolii and Valerii Stepankov wrote a book about
what they termed "the Ukrainian national revolution" and not the
Great October Socialist Revolution, one encounters familiar Soviet
terminology at key junctures in the text. Such notions as "exacer-
bating socioeconomic contradictions," "the powerful revolt of the
masses," and the political avant-garde "formulating a program"

---

100 Tomasz Stryjek, *Jakiej przeszłości potrzebuje przyszłość?: Interpretacje dziejów
narodowych w historiografii i debacie publicznej na Ukrainie 1991–2004* (Warsaw:
Instytut Studiów Politycznych PAN-Oficyna Wydawnicza "Rytm," 2007).

101 These notions, although not in application to the Soviet historical profession,
are elaborated in Hayden White, *Metahistory: The Historical Imagination in Nineteenth-Century Europe* (Baltimore: Johns Hopkins University Press, 1973), 5
passim.

make sense to the two historians and their readers precisely because this is how history was written during the Soviet period.[102] Andrii Portnov, too, noted the tenacity of the Soviet professional vocabulary in post-Soviet Ukrainian historical works, for example, the persistence of such expressions as "selfless struggle," "showing their people the way," "autocratic oppression," and "the domination of foreign capital."[103]

Far from being examples of playful postmodern intertextuality, these are actually indications of the nation-state, as the teleological aim of the historical process, being mechanically inserted into a familiar narrative that previously pointed toward the union with Russia and the victory of socialism. Or perhaps one could speak of the narrative being simply recentered from socialism to the nation because, after all, Soviet historical accounts did not ignore the existence of the Ukrainian nation, but presented incorporation into Russia and the Bolshevik Revolution as best reflecting the interests of the Ukrainian toiling masses.[104]

It is instructive to compare the introduction to the last edition of Ukrainian historical scholarship's crowning achievement, the multivolume *History of the Ukrainian SSR*, with the introduction to the most authoritative, one-volume history of Ukraine that went through three editions between the late 1990s and early 2000s. The Soviet-era introduction reveals a certain hierarchy of conceptual and methodological statements. It begins by asserting that the history of the Ukrainian people is inseparable from that of the "great" Russian people and other peoples of the USSR and that the struggle of the Ukrainian people for their social and national liberation cannot be separated from the role of the Communist Party. Following some token references to Marx, Engels, and Lenin, the methodological principles are introduced, such as Marxist-Leninist teachings about socioeconomic formations, the class struggle, the masses as

102 Nataliia Iakovenko, "U kolorakh proletarskoi revoliutsii," *Ukrainskyi humanitarnyi ohliad*, no. 3 (2000): 58–78, here 61–64.

103 Portnov, *Uprazhneniia*, 119.

104 Serhy Yekelchyk, *Stalin's Empire of Memory: Russian-Ukrainian Relations in the Soviet Historical Imagination* (Toronto: University of Toronto Press, 2004).

the true creators of history, and the party's leading role. Then, however, the text mentions the concept of "Ukrainian statehood," which began forming during the Khmelnytsky Rebellion, called "a people's liberation war."[105] The development of capitalism forms the basis of subsequent history, yet the nation-state theme reappears in the section on the Bolshevik Revolution and the Ukrainian Soviet Republic: "With the victory of October, the Ukrainian people created a sovereign nation-state (*natsionalnoe gosudarstvo*) for the first time in their history."[106] In a sense, the legacy of Soviet Ukrainian scholarship has made it easy for historians to refocus their narratives on the nation-state by doing away with Marxist rhetoric but not necessarily Soviet methodology.

It is telling, then, that clear methodological statements or long introductions have become a rarity in post-Soviet Ukrainian historical scholarship. No new multivolume, collectively-written history of Ukraine having been produced to this day, the most representative and coherent expression of mainstream scholarship's position remains the one-volume history of Ukraine authored by the leading historians of the Institute of Ukrainian History. In the brief introduction to the book's third edition (2002), the institute's director, Valerii Smolii, writes: "Missing from this text is the Soviet historical concept that originated from Stalin's [*Short*] *Course on the History of the VKP(B)* and successfully survived both de-Stalinization attempts, the first under Khrushchev and the second under Gorbachev. The authors have developed their own approaches to the periodization of historical processes, to the clarification of true causal connections between events, and to the evaluation of historical actors. These approaches are based on the firm foundation of Ukrainian historiography from the late nineteenth century and the first third of the twentieth, and above all on the works of M. Hrushevsky."[107]

---

105   Editorial Board, "Predislovie," in *Istoriia Ukrainskoi SSR*, ed. Iu. Iu. Kondufor (Kyiv: Naukova dumka, 1981), vol. 1, 5–16, here 5–7.

106   Ibid., 10.

107   V. Smolii, "Peredmova," in *Istoriia Ukrainy: Navchalnyi posibnyk*, ed. Valerii Smolii, 3rd ed. (Kyiv: Alternatyvy, 2002), 3–8, here 6.

As in so many other works written by contemporary Ukrainian historians, the reference to the legacy of Mykhailo Hrushevsky is misleading and very much serves the same purpose as obligatory mentions of Marx and Lenin in Soviet-era histories. In fact, it can be argued that the Hrushevsky cult in post-Soviet Ukraine was created with the aim of legitimizing the political regimes of the 1990s and, perhaps, to recycle the familiar Soviet model of paying homage to great visionaries.[108] In reality, the 2002 *History* has very little in common, in terms of its theoretical and methodological approaches, with the writings of the populist and positivist Hrushevsky, who wrote a history of the people rather than the state. In its periodization, the post-Soviet *History* is based explicitly on the development of Ukrainian statehood, sometimes in an unashamedly teleological fashion, as, for example, when the chapter on Gorbachev's reforms is entitled "On the Road to Independence." However, a closer look at the text reveals some instantly recognizable language about the pre-feudal and feudal periods and the role of the development of capitalist relations of production in the "objective process of nation building."[109] The book's longest chapter, "The National Revolution: The Creation of the Cossack State," features all the terminological and epistemological holdovers from Soviet historical thinking that Natalia Yakovenko spotted in the book by the same two authors. Moreover, the "revolutionary movement" makes an appearance in the title of a chapter devoted to the attempts to establish a Ukrainian republic in Galicia and the subsequent Ukrainian-Polish war there—essentially the story of nationalist mobilization leading to an ethnic conflict that had little revolutionariness. As if to emphasize that Ukrainian statehood, on which the authors focus, refers primarily to a nation-state for ethnic Ukrainians, there is little mention of minorities, yet the entire concluding chapter is devoted to the Ukrainian diaspora. Naturally, it begins with the more influential Ukrainian diaspora in North America and ends with much larger "eastern diaspora" in Russia and other post-Soviet countries. It is

---

108 See Iaroslav Hrytsak, "Ukrainska istoriohrafiia 1991–2001: Desiatylittia zmin," *Ukraina Moderna*, no. 9 (2005): 43–68, here 52 and chap. 9 of this book.

109 Smolii, *Istoriia Ukrainy*, 40 and 152.

the former that "supported nation-building processes" in the hope that "this time the building of an independent and democratic Ukrainian state will be completed."[110]

Toward a New Approach to "Soviet" Topics

The more post-communist Ukrainian historical narratives had in common with their Soviet predecessors in terms of narrative structure and rhetoric, the less willing they were to address their Soviet pedigree. Abandoning the concept of class for that of nation provided an easy solution and a convenient excuse for the slow transition to the contemporary mode of historical writing. This is particularly obvious in situations where historians were writing about a topic that was traditionally prioritized in Soviet-era scholarship and where the evaluation of Marxist (or pseudo-Marxist Soviet) methodological legacy would have seemed inescapable.

One noteworthy example is the two-volume *Economic History of Ukraine* (2011), also prepared by a group of authors under the aegis of the Institute of Ukrainian History. The two-page introduction, signed by the head of the Editorial Board and the then-speaker of the Ukrainian parliament, Volodymyr Lytvyn, a trained historian, does not mention any common theories or methodological principles of the work. The chapters are very uneven, the authors of some clearly aiming for a positivist description of the "facts," but more often than not still relying on Soviet terminology, while others simply stick to the old Soviet narrative, if not one that is slightly tilted toward the nation. The chapter on the economic development of Eastern Ukraine in 1861–1900 demonstrates with particular clarity that present-day Ukrainian historical scholarship has not developed a new conceptual or terminological apparatus to describe what the authors still call "the development of capitalist relations" and the emergence of "two new social strata — the bourgeoisie (industrialists) and the proletariat."[111] Of course, substituting "social

---

110 Ibid., 454.

111 V. M. Lytvyn, ed., *Ekonomichna istoriia Ukrainy* (Kyiv: Nika-Tsentr, 2011), vol. 1, 604.

strata" for "classes" does not change the essence of the analysis offered in the text; neither does special attention to just how "Ukrainian" these two groups were in the Ukrainian lands.

In general, the introduction of nation as the central category of
historical analysis has made it difficult for Ukrainian historians to
recover the inner dynamics of social and economic history that did
not always coincide with major advances in nation building. For
example, the chapter on the Gorbachev period in *Economic History*
is entitled "On the Road to Independence," an exact copy of the
chapter title from the 2002 *History*, yet the text does not establish
any logical progression toward the nation-state. In fact, it speaks of
half-hearted attempts at reform and the descent into economic
chaos, neither process logically connected with the supposed historical progression toward a Ukrainian nation-state.[112]

National history's difficulty with workers is nothing new, of
course, even in the case of Ukraine. When the advent of Solidarity
in Poland sparked Western scholars' interest in the condition of industrial workers in the Eastern Bloc, the leading journal of the
Ukrainian diaspora, *Suchasnist*, managed only with great difficulty
to put together a special issue on Ukrainian workers (1980). The editor, Yuri Shevelov, felt it necessary to add a personal postscript to
the issue explaining that it was a year late primarily because he
could not find contributing authors. Scholars were willing to write
about urbanization in general, about Ukrainian literature in the
Donbas, or the representation of workers in Ukrainian literature –
just not about workers. Shevelov concluded that the diaspora
wanted to perpetuate the traditional myth of Ukraine as a peasant
nation with a small but committed stratum of the intelligentsia. The
potential authors whom he had approached did not know – and
preferred not to know – that one of every two Ukrainian residents
at the time was either a worker or a dependent of one.[113] Shevelov
was able to secure a solid historical and statistical overview of the

---

112   Ibid., 499–520.
113   [Iurii Shevelov], "Postskryptum redaktora," *Suchasnist*, no. 2 (1980): 157–59,
      here 158.

Ukrainian working class from Bohdan Krawchenko, a Canadian sociologist in the Marxist (perhaps, even the Ukrainian national-communist) tradition, and two elegant essays from the historians Roman Szporluk and Alexander Motyl, both of whom, however, looked at workers as a problem for the nation or the national movement. Szporluk even titled his short essay "In Lieu of the Promised Article."[114] Other contributions to the forum did not rise above assorted personal thoughts on the issue. In order to have a forum of respectable size, Shevelov had to add several samples of Soviet Ukrainian poetry and prose of the 1920s describing the lives of workers.

Ironically, history repeated itself in 2009, when the most interesting historical journal in post-Soviet Ukraine, *Ukraina Moderna*, decided to publish a special issue devoted to "Marxism in Europe's East." The editor, Andrii Portnov, was having difficulties securing contributions from Ukrainian historians, who apparently simply did not find stimulating his intellectual project of re-examining Marxism either as their own past methodology or their Soviet past. The only article in the issue penned by a contemporary Ukrainian historian, an excellent piece by Volodymyr Masliichuk, who wrote about the Ukrainian Marxist historians of the 1920s, dealt with Marxist methodology as history and as part of the suppressed heritage of the Ukrainization period, a topic that could still be seen as a legitimate part of a nation-centric narrative. The only article in the issue that even briefly touched on the relevance in today's Ukraine of "working class" as a category of social analysis was written by the sociologist Anastasiia Riabchuk, further confirmation that in post-communist Ukraine sociologists and art critics are far more likely than historians to pay special attention to workers.[115]

---

114   Bohdan Kravchenko [Krawchenko], "Zminy v strukturi robitnychoi kliasy na Ukraini (1897–1970 rr.)," *Suchasnist*, no. 2 (1980): 7–25; Roman Shporliuk [Szporluk], "Zamist obitsianoi statti," ibid., 26–33; Oleksandr [Alexander] Motyl, "Orhanizatsiia ukrainskikh natsionalistiv i robitnytstvo (kilka zavvah), ibid., 51–63.

115   Volodymyr Masliichuk, "Marksystski skhemy ukrainskoi istorii: Matvii Iavorskyi, Volodymyr Sukhyno-Khomenko, Mykola Horban," *Ukraina Moderna*, no. 3 (2009): 63–77; Anastasiia Riabchuk, 'Formuvannia' i 'zanepad' robitnychoho klasu (Sproba ohliadu)," ibid., 126–42.

Unlike in present-day sociology and art criticism, neo-Marxist theories arriving from the West have not provided current Ukrainian historiography with a methodological base from which to deconstruct the dogmatic legacy of the Soviet period. Inasmuch as neo-Marxist theories hold such a promise at all, it seems to be mediated through mainstream Western historical scholarship as it is emerging after the "linguistic turn." When two prominent Western practitioners of "new social history," Geoff Eley and Keith Nield, attempted to resurrect the notion of "class" as a category of historical analysis, they could do so only from the position of considering "class" as a discursive construct.[116] Ironically, the specialist in Soviet history whom they invited to contribute to a special issue on this topic, Stephen Kotkin, immediately pointed out that this was precisely the Bolshevik understanding of turning theory into practice, that is, institutionalizing the discursive construct of "class" as a category of governance and violence, of forming classes according to the (Soviet) ideological blueprint.[117] Untangling the layers of political practice under each discursive construct proposed for revitalization could indeed be a fruitful exercise.

Yet, for the Ukrainian historical profession overall, a productive way of moving beyond the dogmatic Soviet model of Marxism or its often unacknowledged legacy would probably consist of engaging some of the most popular clichés of Soviet and nation-centric historical scholarship with the new instruments that modern Western methodology has provided, such as cultural history, micro-history, or gender studies. Take, for example, a chapter from Yaroslav Hrytsak's ground-breaking biography of the literary figure Ivan Franko (1856–1916), a great figure revered by Soviet and post-Soviet Ukrainians alike because he could be presented as both a socialist and an ideologist of the national movement. Hrytsak demonstrates that Franko's own identity as a "son of a peasant" and an ethnic Ukrainian was the writer's own ideological construct.

---

116 Geoff Eley and Keith Nield, "Farewell to the Working Class?" *International Labor and Working-Class History*, no. 57 (Spring 2000): 1–30.

117 Stephen Kotkin, "Class, the Working Class, and the Politburo," *International Labor and Working-Class History*, no. 57 (Spring 2000): 48–52.

Franko also imagined the "peasantry" in a certain way, which explains the misunderstandings that arose between his radical friends and peasants when they encountered each other in village reading rooms. In the end, abstract socialist concepts were translated into a "national" language that the peasants found more accessible — "Polish land for the Poles and Ruthenian land for the Ruthenians." This reverse influence of the peasantry's worldview on political discourse can be seen in the program of the Radical Party that Franko helped establish.[118] Hrytsak then examines Franko's prose works, which in Soviet times served as the best example of narrative realism, as well as his socialist convictions, famously reflected in his "Boryslav cycle" of short novels. Through micro-historical analysis of actual industrial settlement patterns, Hrytsak shows that Franko did not so much describe as invent new character types in Ukrainian literature, including that of a worker activist. Like other socialists of his time, Franko was looking in his imaginary Boryslav for an industrial proletariat at the very same time as he was translating parts of *Das Kapital* into Ukrainian. As Hrytsak shows, the writer's imagination was ahead of the times: the workers' strike at the Boryslav oil fields depicted in *Boryslav Is Laughing* actually happened twenty years after the novel's publication.[119]

Andriy Zayarnyuk's book on the Galician peasantry before and after the abolition of serfdom in Austria-Hungary in 1848 pursues somewhat similar strategies, but with a more explicit methodological positioning more appropriate for an academic monograph than a biography. The author registers his uneasiness with the smooth transition from the Marxist category of "consciousness" to a more nation-friendly "identity," as well as with the general rewriting of the same events as part of the national movement. He does not shy away from quoting Marx on the significance of the

---

118 Iaroslav Hrytsak, *Prorok u svoii vitchyzni: Franko ta ioho spilnota, 1856–1886* (Kyiv: Krytyka, 2006), 272. All quotations are from the English-language edition: Yaroslav Hrytsak, *Franko and His Community*, trans. Marta Daria Olynyk (Brighton, Mass.: Academic Studies Press, 2018), 242.

119 Hrytsak, *Prorok u svoii vitchyzni*, 285 and 301; Hrytsak, *Franko and His Community*, 252–53 and 269.

property question for the Galician peasantry, which, for the German thinker, meant the transformation of feudal land tenure into petit-bourgeois ownership.[120] More important, however, is Zayarnyuk's microhistorical approach, informed by the fusion of social and cultural history. He studies the language of peasant emancipation, which shaped the social practice of emancipation, in an effort to go beyond the grand narratives of social and national liberation—both problematic frameworks for understanding events because both, like Kotkin's "class," were developed by members of the emancipation generation, who used them as political mobilization tools.[121] Zayarnyuk thus uses his close reading of a series of events in the rural Sambir district between 1846 and the 1860s, set against the background of emancipatory discourse of all varieties, to uncover the social expectations that the codes of emancipation developed among villagers, a stratum that we would now categorize as "peasants." A social history with discourse left in and grand narratives left out, this book is also an example of Ukrainian historiography's new international horizons.

More recently, there have been some interesting examples of how a historian of Ukraine can analyze in an innovative way such a paradigmatic Marxist topic as the development of capitalism in Ukraine. It is fitting that one of them comes from the work of a Ukrainian historian based in Ukraine and another, from the work of a Ukrainian-born historian working in Germany. In her book entitled *The Space of Possibilities: Ukraine in the Age of Iron and Steam* (2018), Tetiana Vodotyka takes an interdisciplinary approach to her subject. She puts the development of industrial capitalism and the new entrepreneurial class in a global context (the inclusion of Ukrainian lands into international markets and chains of production), connects these processes to social and cultural changes (in particular, the rise of new urban elites and new educational institutions), and links them to the present (through the traditions and

---

120 Andrii Zaiarniuk [Andriy Zayarnyuk], *Idiomy emansypatsii: "Vyzvolni" proekty i halytske selo v seredyni XIX stolittia* (Kyiv: Krytyka, 2007), 17.

121 Ibid., 18–19.

practices that survive to our day).[122] Olena Petrenko focuses specifically on how technological revolution in one industry – the production of sugar from sugar beets, in which Ukraine became a world leader in the late nineteenth century – created powerful social lifts that made the new industrialists a very diverse group. The new "sugar barons" of central Ukraine included Jews (the Brodskys) and Ukrainians (the Tereshchenkos, Yakhnenkos, and Symyrenkos), whose patronage practices changed the region's cultural landscape.[123]

Among the new wave of Ukrainian historical periodicals, the almanac *Socium: Almanac of Social History*, which began publication in 2002 and is based at the Institute of Ukrainian History in Kyiv, stands out as the main forum for innovative research and theoretical discussions about the new ways of analyzing social processes in Ukraine's past. The 2005 article by deputy editor Viktor Horobets, a specialist in the early modern period, provides a counterpoint to Orest Subtelny's 1993 suggestion that Ukrainian historians use their "Marxist" training in order to transition to a Western-style social history. In this short programmatic essay entitled "How New Is the 'New Social History' in the Ukrainian Reception? (From the Editorial Board)" Horobets noted that the most active group of authors comes from the fields of medieval and early modern history of Ukraine, that is, the ones where field-specific training was always more important than pseudo-Marxist terminology. The research published in *Socium* has featured innovative studies of Ukrainian social or confessional groups (such as Cossacks of various categories, lawyers, students, and Old Believers) and new methodological approaches ranging from micro-history to conflict studies and representations of masculinity.[124] It is difficult to overlook the fact that

---

122 Tetiana Vodotyka, *Prostir mozhlyvostei: Ukraina v dobu zaliza ta pary* (Kyiv: Klio, 2018).

123 Olena Petrenko, "Die Rübenzuckerindustrie im Süd-Westen des Zarenreiches und die neuen Agrareliten," *Jahrbuch für Wirtschaftsgeschichte / Economic History Yearbook* 60, no. 2 (2019): 433–47.

124 Viktor Horobets, "Naskilky novoiu ie 'nova sotsialna istoriia' v ukrainskomu prochytanni? (Vid redaktsiinoi kolehii)," *Sotsium: Almanakh sotsialnoi istorii* 5 (2005): 7–9, here 8.

such up-to-date Western approaches are being adopted by historians in the field who have been least exposed to Soviet class-based
history, whereas their colleagues who are working on the nineteenth and twentieth centuries are lagging behind. If this interpretation is correct, Subtelny has been proven wrong, but there are different reasons for optimism about the future of the Ukrainian historical profession. They have a lot to do with the transfer of Western
methodology, but also with the ideas of professionalism and specialist training embedded in certain "historical schools" and institutional niches, even during the late Soviet period.

* * *

The overcoming of Soviet historical methodology has not been addressed in Ukrainian historiography for a very good reason,
namely, that it has not happened yet. The wholesale restoration of
the traditional canon of national history was accomplished in
Ukraine without abandoning Soviet narrative models or conceptualization tools. As a result, the "national" version of the Ukrainian
past looks surprisingly "Soviet," and belated resistance to this Soviet legacy is taking the form of questioning the national-history
paradigm, in which both the teleological vision and the template of
multivolume, collectively written histories point to the historiographical practices of the Soviet past. At the same time, the new
social history, which is cognizant of social categories as discursive
constructs, is making inroads into the traditional territory of grand
narratives. It promises to construct a multidimensional Ukrainian
history not beholden to Soviet models.

Part II

Diaspora Historians Conceptualizing the Modern Nation

4. Canadian Historians of Ukrainian Modernity

When the Ukrainian-Canadian historian Orest Subtelny died in 2016, the prominent Ukrainian journalist Vitaly Portnikov wrote that Subtelny's *Ukraine: A History* "gave us Ukraine, not the one that had been, but the one that shall be."[125] Portnikov goes on to explain the meaning of his striking statement, although he lacks the academic vocabulary to express his impressions as a reader. Subtelny's survey history came out in 1991, just as the new Ukraine and a new narrative of Ukrainian history were being constructed, and he wrote "not just the history of the people, not just the history of the regions – he wrote the history of the country."[126] In other words, the Canadian historian presented Ukraine as a nation struggling continuously for its independence – a nation-state in the making.

One can argue that such a teleological reading simplified the complex arguments of Subtelny and other Western historians, but it is telling that Ukrainian audiences saw such a scheme as an exciting discovery of their nation's past and future. Yet the relationship between the Canadian historiography of Ukraine and Ukrainian readers in independent Ukraine can also be seen as a more complex case of mutual cross-pollination. The idealistic enthusiasm in Ukraine of the early 1990s did not last long. The persistence of ambiguous national identities within the country and unabating Russian cultural domination called for a more detailed inquiry into the construction and deconstruction of nations in the imperial and post-imperial contexts. The two popular Ukrainian revolutions of the twenty-first century and the subsequent war in the Donbas since 2014 have emphasized the political nature of identity-building processes. They have also marked the development of a civic, multicultural Ukrainian identity that defines itself in opposition to

---

125 Vitalii Portnikov, "Nash Hrushevsky: Pamiati Oresta Subtelnoho," Espreso TV, 26 July 2016, http://espreso.tv/article/2016/07/26/nash_grushevskyy_pamyati_oresta_subtelnogo.
126 Ibid.

the corrupt authoritarian regimes past and present, both at home and abroad.[127]

Precisely because of their interest in nation building, Canadian historians of modern Ukraine were in a position to help their Ukrainian colleagues and the general public make sense of the complex processes underway in their country. The concepts and methodological approaches they could offer were neither teleological nor partisan, but based on a comparative study of European national movements and the importance of the state and the national intelligentsia – acting either in unison or at cross-purposes – in the cultural and political processes producing modern nations. The original impetus for the development in Canadian historiography of such a focus on Ukrainian nation building may well have been patriotic, reflecting the interests of the influential Ukrainian-Canadian community, but already in the 1970s Ukrainian-Canadian scholars began advancing innovative interpretations of Ukraine's historical development. In so doing, they often found themselves revising the national paradigm that had been established in the early twentieth century. Social history soon emerged as a methodological tool indispensable to the study of the Ukrainian national movement. In the next generation of Canadian historians of modern Ukraine, cultural history, post-colonial studies, and the linguistic turn provided new ways of examining the discourse of the nation. The concept of total war and a more complex understanding of imperial projects came to supplement the earlier emphasis on the national intelligentsia's organic work. Finally, in the twenty-first century, joint projects, translations, and academic mobility weakened the borders between the Canadian and Ukrainian academic worlds, making the study of modern Ukraine an increasingly global and collaborative enterprise.

The Beginnings

The mass immigration of Ukrainian peasants to Canada's Prairie Provinces, which began in the 1890s, was bound to generate, at least

---

127   For a more detailed analysis, see Serhy Yekelchyk, *The Conflict in Ukraine* (New York: Oxford University Press, 2015).

in the long run, academic interest in Ukrainian Studies in this country. By the time the second generation of Ukrainian Canadians,
more assured of its social standing and more confident in English,
came of age in the 1930s, Ukraine had become the subject of international attention owing to the repressive Polish policies in Eastern
Galicia and the state-engineered Holodomor (the Famine of 1932–
33) in Soviet Ukraine. The combination of these two factors generated interest in Ukraine among some influential Canadian academics, such as the historian George W. Simpson and the poet and
translator Watson Kirkconnell. Both of them worked indefatigably
to include Ukrainian language and literature as regular subjects at
Canadian universities, which effort began to bear fruit in the 1940s.
However, Simpson in particular also sought to establish Ukrainian
history as an academic subject; already in 1935, instead of a survey
of Russian history, he created an introductory course at the University of Saskatchewan on the history of the Slavic peoples.[128]

Simpson also supported Ukrainian community activists on
two projects in the late 1930s that tested the waters for the establishment of a Ukrainian history course. He welcomed a proposal by
the Ukrainian Self-Reliance League of Canada to invite a leading
Ukrainian historian, Dmytro Doroshenko, to tour Canada with lectures on Ukrainian history and culture. The tour included a sixty-
hour lecture course for schoolteachers (but open to students and the
general public), which was originally planned at the Petro Mohyla
Institute in Saskatoon but later moved to the Hrushevsky Institute
in Edmonton. By all accounts, the tour was a success. Doroshenko
went on a similar tour of Canada again in 1938, and only the start
of World War II prevented him from repeating it in 1939.[129] Simpson also got involved in a second project, arising from the success
of Doroshenko's first visit: the preparation of an abridged translation of Doroshenko's *Narys istorii Ukrainy* (2 vols., 1932–33), the
most up-to-date history of Ukraine at the time. Simpson edited

---

128 Thomas M. Prymak, *Gathering a Heritage: Ukrainian, Slavonic, and Ethnic Canada
and the USA* (Toronto: University of Toronto Press, 2014), 121.
129 Thomas M. Prymak, "Dmytro Doroshenko and Canada," *Journal of Ukrainian
Studies* 30, no. 2 (Winter 2005): 1–25, here 6–10.

Hanna Chykalenko-Keller's English translation and also wrote the introduction and the explanatory note on terminology. Funded by the Ukrainian Self-Reliance League, the abridged translation came out in 1939 and was reprinted in 1940 — the very period when Canadian interest in the Ukrainian question in Europe, as well as the political allegiances of the Ukrainian-Canadian community, was at its peak.[130] The following chapter will discuss this historical survey in greater detail.

Doroshenko resumed his contacts with Canada after the war, and in 1947 he moved to Winnipeg to lecture at St. Andrew's College, an educational institution run by the Ukrainian Greek Orthodox Church of Canada. During his eighteen-month sojourn in Winnipeg the pre-eminent Ukrainian historian in the West accomplished much. He taught courses on Ukrainian and church history, as well as the history of Ukrainian literature, but also wrote at an impressive pace. While in Winnipeg, Doroshenko also produced several new chapters for the second edition of *Velyka istoriia Ukrainy* (An Expanded History of Ukraine), a collectively written popular survey whose first edition (Lviv, 1935) had been a bestseller, and wrote his immensely valuable memoirs about the Ukrainian national movement before World War I.[131] In addition, he produced two short books on church history, likely based on his lectures, and prepared a brief survey of the history of Ukrainian literature, which remains unpublished. He also discovered a new research opportunity: the history of Ukrainian immigration to Canada. Doroshenko edited a volume of materials on Ukrainian Canadians for the Ukrainian National Home in Winnipeg and prepared, with the

---

130 Dmytro Doroshenko, *History of the Ukraine*, trans. Hanna Chykalenko-Keller, ed. and with an introduction by G. W. Simpson (Edmonton: Institute Press, 1939). On the Canadian context, see Bohdan S. Kordan, *Canada and the Ukrainian Question, 1939 –1945* (Montreal: McGill-Queen's University Press, 2001); and Thomas M. Prymak, *Maple Leaf and Trident: The Ukrainian Canadians during the Second World War* (Toronto: Multicultural History Society of Ontario, 1988).

131 Ivan Krypiakevych and Mykola Holubets, eds., *Velyka istoriia Ukrainy*, supplemented by Dmytro Doroshenko and Iaroslav Pasternak (Winnipeg: Ivan Tyktor, 1948); D. Doroshenko, *Moi spomyny pro davnie-mynule (1901–1914)* (Winnipeg: Tryzub, 1949).

assistance of the graduate student Paul Yuzyk, a card bibliography on this subject.[132]

If Doroshenko had continued his work in Winnipeg, he could have become the mentor of a new generation of historians. His concept of Ukrainian history, as expressed in his *History of the Ukraine*, represented a remarkable symbiosis of Mykhailo Hrushevsky's history of the Ukrainian people as an ethno-linguistic community and the Ukrainian "statist" school's emphasis on the continuity of state formations and elites, including the non-Ukrainian nobility, as in Viacheslav Lypynsky's territorial concept of Ukraine. Instead of Hrushevsky's emphasis on popular revolts, Doroshenko focused on the autonomist and separatist strivings of the Ukrainian elites as the moving force of the national history, but his notion of Ukraine was ethnographic.[133] Striking parallels between Doroshenko's vision of Ukrainian history and the one found two generations later in Subtelny's survey suggest that the elder historian may have created his school in Canada. The paradigm shift in historiography, which occurred in the United States thanks to Oleksander Ohloblyn's mentorship of young Ukrainian-American, Anglophone historians in the 1960s, could have happened in Canada even earlier. However, after living for many decades in major European cities, Doroshenko never quite adjusted to the harsh climate and relative isolation of the Canadian Prairies. Furthermore, St. Andrew's College's financial difficulties, combined with a conflict— or, in another interpretation, a misunderstanding arising from indifference and circumstances—between Doroshenko and the college administration resulted in his appointment first being reduced then not renewed.[134] Depressed and in increasingly ill health, Doroshenko left for Europe in 1950 and died in Munich the following spring.

---

132 Prymak, "Dmytro Doroshenko and Canada," 18–20.
133 See Thomas M. Prymak, "Dmytro Doroshenko: A Ukrainian Émigré Historian of the Interwar Period," *Harvard Ukrainian Studies* 25, nos. 1–2 (Spring 2001): 31–56, here 39.
134 For the two interpretations, see Oleh W. Gerus, "The Reverend Semen Sawchuk and the Ukrainian Orthodox Church in Canada," *Journal of Ukrainian Studies* 16,

Paradoxically, as he was crossing the Atlantic in one direction, hundreds of thousands of Ukrainians and other postwar displaced persons were travelling in the opposite direction — to North America. The arrival of this new wave of immigrants, better educated and politically more assertive than the earlier émigrés, transformed the Ukrainian-Canadian community. The early period of the Cold War also contributed to renewed interest in Ukraine as a major component of the Soviet nationality problem. In these new circumstances, Canadian universities started opening up positions in Ukrainian Studies, although primarily in language and literature rather than history. Yet some Canadian Slavists hired to teach Ukrainian did research that would be called interdisciplinary today. Professor George S. N. Luckyj (also known as Iurii Lutskyi, University of Saskatchewan, 1947–49, and University of Toronto, 1952–84) was, perhaps, the best example of a scholar working on the porous border between literary studies and cultural history. His influential books were read by historians and literary scholars alike; together with his wife, Moira, he also translated into English a number of important Ukrainian works, both literary and historical.[135]

Other disciplines related to modern Ukrainian history also developed in Canada in the 1950s and 1960s. Doroshenko's close friend and colleague Metropolitan Ilarion (Ivan Ohiienko) continued publishing on church history and Ukrainian culture in both the early modern and modern periods after becoming the head of the Ukrainian Greek Orthodox Church of Canada in 1951. He also reformed St. Andrew's College, which became an affiliated college of

---

no. 1 (Summer 1991): 61–88; and Prymak, "Dmytro Doroshenko and Canada," 21–22.

135 George S. N. Luckyj, *Literary Politics in the Soviet Ukraine, 1917–1934* (New York: Columbia University Press, 1956; rev. and updated ed., Durham, N.C.: Duke University Press, 1990); idem, *Between Gogol' and Ševčenko: Polarity in the Literary Ukraine, 1798–1847* (Munich: W. Fink, 1971); idem, *Young Ukraine: The Brotherhood of Saints Cyril and Methodius, 1845–1847* (Ottawa: University of Ottawa Press, 1991); *Towards an Intellectual History of Ukraine: An Anthology of Ukrainian Thought from 1710 to 1995*, ed. Ralph Lindheim and George S. N. Luckyj (Toronto: University of Toronto Press, 1996). The translations of the above-cited Ukrainian historical works include some by Dmytro Doroshenko, Hryhorii Kostiuk, and Ivan Maistrenko (also known as Iwan Majstrenko).

the University of Manitoba in 1962.[136] Paul Yuzyk, a historian and community leader, who as an MA student had helped Doroshenko to compile a bibliography on Ukrainian Canadians, obtained a teaching position at the University of Manitoba in 1951 and went on to publish influential works about Manitoba's Ukrainian community, the two main Ukrainian churches in Canada, and other aspects of Ukrainian-Canadian history. After being appointed to the Senate in 1963 as a Progressive Conservative from Manitoba, he moved from the University of Manitoba to the University of Ottawa and became an important spokesperson for what subsequently became known as the policy of multiculturalism.[137] In 1958, in another Prairie Province with a significant Ukrainian population, the University of Alberta hired Manoly R. Lupul, a historian of the Canadian educational system who went on to lead the Ukrainian community's efforts to create a bilingual English-Ukrainian school system, and transformed his university into a major centre of Ukrainian Studies. He was also a prominent advocate of multiculturalism.[138]

All these trends — the continued importance of church history, the lasting legacy of Doroshenko and Metropolitan Ilarion, and the focus on the history of Ukrainian Canadians — can be seen in the long career of Oleh W. Gerus. Trained as a historian of imperial Russia and hired to teach at the University of Manitoba in 1969, he wrote primarily on Ukrainian Canadians and the Ukrainian Greek Orthodox Church in Canada (after 1990: the Ukrainian Orthodox Church of Canada). Significantly, however, Gerus also undertook the updating of Doroshenko's history in English. Published in 1975 as *A Survey of Ukrainian History*, a title that was more faithful to

---

136 See M. S. Tymoshyk, *Holhofa Ivana Ohiienka: Ukrainoznavchi problemy v derzhavot-vorchii, naukovii, redaktorskii ta vydavnychii diialnosti* (Kyiv: Zapovit, 1997).

137 Vera   Yuzyk,   "Biography,"   Honourable   Senator   Paul   Yuzyk, https://yuzyk.com/biography/#Moving-Multiculturalism-from-Idea-to-Offi cial-Recognition.

138 See Manoly R. Lupul, *The Politics of Multiculturalism: A Ukrainian-Canadian Memoir* (Edmonton and Toronto: Canadian Institute of Ukrainian Studies Press, 2007).

Doroshenko's original two-volume set, it included the text of Doroshenko's 1939 abridged edition, Gerus's introduction, a select bibliography of English-language works, and six new chapters by Gerus covering the period from 1914 to the mid-1970s. Gerus's fast-paced narrative is generally in keeping with Doroshenko's overall framework. Thus, he endorses Pavlo Skoropadsky's promotion of "territorial patriotism with the emphasis on Ukrainian citizenship rather than on Ukrainian nationality."[139] At the same time, one can see in Gerus's chapters the influence of social history and other modern concepts. For example, in explaining the Ukrainian Revolution's outcome, Gerus focuses first and foremost on the leadership's failure to address the peasantry's concerns. The chapter on the 1920s stresses the process of urbanization that unfolded in tandem with the policy of Ukrainization. When discussing the political dissent of the 1960s and 1970s in Soviet Ukraine, Gerus offers a subtle explanation of how Marxism could provide an ideological foundation for the majority of dissidents, the ideological descendants of the "national communists." Gerus already deemed the Famine of 1932–33, which was not known as the Holodomor yet, "a form of genocide."[140] The book sold well, thus proving the demand for a college-level textbook on Ukrainian history. A new printing of the *Survey* was released in 1980.

Focus on the Nation

The postwar wave of Ukrainian immigrants brought to Canada many participants of momentous historical events in Ukraine who were eager to tell their stories. Most of them published their works in Ukrainian and never held academic appointments at Canadian institutions. However, the Shevchenko Scientific Society of Canada (est. 1949) and other community organizations provided a useful platform for amateur and trained historians alike. This diverse group of authors included Semen Pidhainy, Zynovii Knysh, Roman

---

139 Ibid., 638.
140 Ibid., 698.

Kolisnyk, and Wasyl Veryha, among others. Most of them published memoirs in addition to historical works, as well as books fitting somewhere between these two categories; they also usually focussed on the Ukrainian Revolution and World War II. There was now a readership in Canada for such works and there were publishers, too, most notably Ivan Tyktor, who had published important historical surveys in interwar Lviv and reissued their updated versions in postwar Winnipeg.

By the early 1970s, however, the changing Canadian context set the stage for the establishment of Ukrainian history as a legitimate academic discipline at Canadian universities. In 1971 the Liberal government of Pierre Elliott Trudeau declared its official commitment to the policy of multiculturalism, an inclusive vision of Canada as a land of many equally valuable cultures. The Ukrainian-Canadian community, which had lobbied for this change, saw the new policy as paving the way to recognition of Ukrainian immigrants' contributions to Canada, as well as to a host of cultural and educational initiatives aimed at supporting Ukrainian culture. The early- to mid-1970s saw important advances in Ukrainian-Canadian schooling, cultural life, and the academic sphere. New developments at the University of Alberta made the greatest impact on the academic study of modern Ukrainian history.

In 1970 the Department of History at the University of Alberta invited Ivan Lysiak-Rudnytsky (also known as Ivan L. Rudnytsky) as a guest professor to teach a course on "The Beginnings of Modern Ukraine." This invitation came about as a result of several fortuitous factors. The Royal Commission on Bilingualism and Biculturalism had just released the last volume of its report, which endorsed what would become known as multiculturalism. Among other practical recommendations, the report proposed the creation of university positions in the history and culture of Canada's immigrant groups. At the same time Rudnytsky, who had been teaching at the American University in Washington, D.C., was looking for a way to move to Edmonton to reunite with his spouse. Professor Lupul and the Edmonton lawyer Peter Savaryn, who was an influential figure in the Progressive Conservative Party, mounted a campaign to have him hired. The 1970 guest course proved a success, and Rudnytsky confirmed his reputation as an original thinker and engaging speaker, who was popular with students. Lupul and Savaryn then pushed for a permanent appointment, which materialized in 1971, after Alberta's Ministry of Education and the Ukrainian Canadian Foundation of Taras Shevchenko provided additional funds.[141]

The establishment of a position in Ukrainian history paved the way for other Ukrainian initiatives at the University of Alberta and throughout the province. Following the introduction of the bilingual English-Ukrainian school network in 1974, community leaders focused their attention on obtaining government funding for a Ukrainian research institute on the University of Alberta campus. Lupul, Savaryn, and the Edmonton lawyer and politician Laurence Decore spearheaded the effort, which the then provincial minister of education, Albert Hohol, endorsed. In 1976 the Alberta provincial government established the Canadian Institute of Ukrainian Studies (CIUS) as a regular part of the University of Alberta. Professor Lupul was appointed its first director, with Professors Rudnytsky and Luckyj (based in Toronto) as its two associate directors.[142] The CIUS provided a crucial platform for research and community outreach. It also facilitated collaboration among Ukrainian specialists in various disciplines and countries by awarding scholarships and organizing conferences. Within Canada, the CIUS fostered inter-regional research collaboration by appointing as associate directors the literary scholar Luckyj and, after Rudnytsky's departure from the CIUS in 1978, the political scientist Bohdan Bociurkiw (also known as Botsiurkiv) of Carleton University in Ottawa.

---

141 Ivan Khymka [John-Paul Himka], "Istoriia Ukrainy ta ukraintsiv u Kanadi u Viddili istorii ta klasyky Albertskoho universytetu," in *Zakhidnokanadskyi zbirnyk*, ed. Yar Slavutych, (Edmonton: Kanadske naukove tovarystvo im. Shevchenka, Oseredok na Zakhidniu Kanadu, 1998), vol. 3, 99–119, here 100–105.

142 See Manoly R. Lupul, "The Establishment of the Canadian Institute of Ukrainian Studies at the University of Alberta: A Personal Memoir," *Journal of Ukrainian Studies* 18, nos. 1–2 (Summer-Winter 1993): 1–32; and Petro Savaryn, "Spohady uchasnyka: Polityka, bahatokulturnist, Kanadskyi instytut ukrainoznavstva, abetkova Entsyklopediia Ukrainy-2," in *Zakhidnokanadskyi zbirnyk*, ed. Yar Slavutych (Edmonton: Kanadske naukove tovarystvo im. Shevchenka, Oseredok na Zakhidniu Kanadu, 1998), vol. 3, 317–82.

Bociurkiw's work on the Ukrainian Greek Catholic Church under Soviet rule was as interesting to historians as it was to political scientists.[143]

Meanwhile, at the University of Alberta's Department of History, Rudnytsky structured his courses in Ukrainian history in such a way as to provide in-depth study that was conducive to the research training of students and younger scholars, whom he mentored. He divided Ukrainian history into four timeline-based courses that he rotated to make room for his other offerings. He also created a senior seminar in Ukrainian history. In 1973 Lupul introduced a course on the history of Ukrainians in Canada.[144]

Rudnytsky's own research profile, rather unusual for a Ukrainian historian of his generation, influenced subsequent directions of research on modern Ukrainian history in Canada and beyond. He arrived at the University of Alberta as an established, European-educated scholar who wrote influential essays rather than books.[145] Like his famous mother, Milena Rudnytska, head of the Union of Ukrainian Women in Western Ukraine and a member of the Sejm in interwar Poland, he was critical of radical Ukrainian nationalism.[146] Rudnytsky also approached the Ukrainian nation as a subject of historical research rather than an article of faith and a primordial anthropomorphic organism, unlike many other diasporan Ukrainian patriots of his generation.

---

143 See Bohdan Bociurkiw, *The Ukrainian Greek Catholic Church and the Soviet State (1939–1950)* (Edmonton and Toronto: Canadian Institute of Ukrainian Studies Press, 1996), one of his many publications on religion under Communism.

144 Khymka, "Istoriia Ukrainy," 106.

145 The only book that Rudnytsky published during his lifetime was a collection of essays in Ukrainian: Ivan Lysiak-Rudnytsky, *Mizh istoriieiu ta politykoiu: Statti do istorii i krytyky ukrainskoi suspilno-politychnoi dumky* (Munich: Suchasnist, 1973). His English-language book of selected essays came out posthumously: Ivan L. Rudnytsky, *Essays in Modern Ukrainian History*, ed. Peter L. Rudnytsky (Edmonton: Canadian Institute of Ukrainian Studies, University of Alberta, 1987).

146 For an excellent treatment of Rudnytsky's biography and political views, see Iaroslav Hrytsak, "Ivan Lysiak-Rudnytsky: Narys intelektualnoi biohrafii," *Suchasnist*, no. 11 (1994): 73–96.

In his publications on modern Ukraine, Rudnytsky positioned himself as a historian of political and social thought. But his approach was not a classic history of ideas. A student of the German philosophy of history, he believed in the objective laws of historical development—a belief that required a researcher to take the study of society seriously. Once a given society was properly examined and classified, one could understand the nature of historical change that engendered new political concepts. Of course, one needs a taxonomy of nations in order to classify them, and Rudnytsky evoked the Hegelian distinction between "historical" and "non-historical" nations, according to which Western European nation-states serve as an ideal model. According to Rudnytsky, before the development of its modern national movement Ukraine was a "non-historical" nation characterized by discontinuity in the history of its statehood, the loss of its native elite, and the absence of a native high culture. The loss of elites was of greater importance than the loss of the national polity: "I conclude that the decisive factor in the existence of the so-called historical nations was the preservation, [sometimes even] despite the loss of independence, of a representative upper class as the carrier of political consciousness and 'high' culture.... Conversely, the so-called non-historical nations had lost (or never possessed) a representative class, and were reduced to an inarticulate popular mass, with little if any national consciousness and with a culture of predominantly folk character."[147]

Rudnytsky's intention here was not to belittle the Ukrainian nation, but to establish the essential normality of the Ukrainian historical experience as typical of Eastern Europe. He makes this point at the beginning of his influential article "The Role of Ukraine in Modern History," which was originally published in 1963 in the *Slavic Review*, the leading North American journal of Slavic studies

---

147 Ivan L. Rudnytsky, "Observations on the Problem of 'Historical' and 'Non-historical' Nations," in his *Essays*, 37–48, here 41.

and Eastern European history.[148] Rudnytsky also required this determination in order to formulate the essence of Ukrainian history in the modern period: "The central problem of modern Ukrainian history is that of the emergence of the nation: the transformation of an ethno-linguistic community into a self-conscious political and social community."[149] Before one rushes to criticize this narrow nation-centric view of Ukrainian history, it is worth noting that in Rudnytsky's time the rejection of the primordialist view and the insistence that the contemporary Ukrainian nation was a modern project were both controversial, revisionist ideas.

Patriotic ideas served as the agent of change that completed the construction of the modern Ukrainian nation. Hence Rudnytsky's periodization of the Ukrainian national movement was determined not by social factors but by ideological change, although in the end he came very close to Myroslav Hroch's scheme of national movements among the "small" (another way of rendering "non-historical") Eastern European nations passing through the academic, cultural, and mass-mobilization stages.[150] Rudnytsky mentioned his periodization in several essays, but he provided its fullest explanation in "The Intellectual Origins of Modern Ukraine" (1958). He distinguished between "the Epoch of the Nobility (to the 1840s)," "Populism (1840s to 1880s)," and "Modernism (from the 1890s to the First World War)." The ideological transition from one period to another was that from a local patriotism that could coexist with imperial loyalty to an emphasis on the "people" as constituting the nation, and then to the growth of national consciousness and the idea of independence. At the same time, Rudnytsky matched the first two stages with the social groups that constituted

---

148   Ivan L. Rudnytsky, "The Role of Ukraine in Modern History," in his *Essays*, 11–36; originally published as "The Role of the Ukraine in Modern History," *Slavic Review* 22, no. 2 (June 1963): 199–216.

149   Rudnytsky, "Role of Ukraine," 14.

150   Miroslav Hroch, *Die Vorkämpfer der nationalen Bewegung bei den kleinen Völkern Europas: Eine vergleichende Analyse zur gesellschaftlichen Schichtung der patriotischen Gruppen* (Prague: Universita Karlova, 1968). For the English translation, see *Social Preconditions of National Revival in Europe: A Comparative Analysis of the Social Composition of Patriotic Groups among the Smaller European Nations*, trans. Ben Fowkes (Cambridge: Cambridge University Press, 1985).

their leading force—the nobility and the intelligentsia, respectively. The modernist stage, too, was defined as much by the new ideas as it was by the "breaking down of the artificial walls which tsarism had sought to impose between the Ukrainian intelligentsia and the masses."[151]

Thus, Rudnytsky's analysis of the Ukrainian national movement merged ideological and social criteria to produce a rich and insightful picture. Still, his main emphasis was on the political elites and ideological change. When he writes that "the making of the nation was basically completed during the revolutionary years 1917–20,"[152] one needs to read another of his essays to put these words in their proper context. It was during the Ukrainian Revolution that "the idea of *samostiinist'* … had become a common possession of Ukrainian patriots of all political persuasions."[153] This did not necessarily imply that this idea was endorsed by the masses, especially in the Ukrainian lands of the Russian Empire, but that it had become firmly established in the realm of national politics. This political space could then shrink to the narrow confines of émigré politics or expand again, as it did with the Soviet collapse. But independence remained its defining feature.

Always an original thinker, Rudnytsky did not idealize the nation-state, even though for him the idea of independence marked the highest stage of the national movement. He remained fascinated by the socialist and federalist thought of Mykhailo Drahomanov, the subject of his PhD dissertation. In explaining Drahomanov's preference for a federated Europe, Rudnytsky once wrote that "the existence of a national state does not of itself guarantee either civic freedom or social justice"[154]—a prophetic point that the Orange and Euromaidan Revolutions made only too clear. Likewise, Rudnytsky stood out in his generation by taking seriously the

151 Ivan L. Rudnytsky, "The Intellectual Origins of Modern Ukraine," in his *Essays*, 123–142, here 135.
152 Rudnytsky, "Role of Ukraine," 14.
153 Ivan L. Rudnytsky, "The Fourth Universal and Its Ideological Antecedents," in his *Essays*, 389–414, here 408.
154 Ivan L. Rudnytsky, "The First Ukrainian Political Program: Mykhailo Drahomanov's 'Introduction' to *Hromada*," in his *Essays*, 255–282, here 264.

ephemeral statehood of the Ukrainian SSR. Even though it was accomplished by Stalin's armies, the reunification of almost all the
Ukrainian lands in a single polity was "a tremendous step forward
in the process of nation-building." To be sure, the Ukrainian republic's sovereignty remained a myth but one that could become a la-
tent force, and "Stalin's map might live to be translated, after all,
from the limbo of camouflage into the realm of reality."[155]

Rudnytsky realized that he was revising the national paradigm of Ukrainian history that had been established in interwar
Eastern Galicia and among the majority of postwar Ukrainian émigrés in the West.[156] Moreover he organized a conference with the
telling title "Rethinking Ukrainian History" and edited the conference proceedings.[157] This volume, which included contributions
from North American scholars of different generations, revealed an
important new trend. In answering familiar research questions
about the Ukrainian nation, the profession was increasingly applying new methodological approaches. Urban Studies was one such
innovative aspect in the articles on modern Ukraine, but even the
historians writing about the Ukrainian elites of the early modern
period declared their commitment to the methods of social history.
The volume also included a transcript of a round table on terminology and periodization in the teaching of Ukrainian history, which
actually addressed a much wider set of methodological issues. The
participants discussed the value of ethnic and territorial approaches to Ukrainian history and pondered the ways of incorporating the then new trend of social history. Very telling was John-
Paul Himka's objection to Rudnytsky's proposal to describe the
Ukrainian nineteenth century as "the Age of National Awakening."
The younger scholar argued that doing so would dismiss the
growth of industry and the working class in Ukraine as well as its

---

155 Ivan L. Rudnytsky, "Soviet Ukraine in Historical Perspective," in his *Essays*,
463–76, here 469 and 473.
156 On the national paradigm, see Serhii Plokhy, *Ukraine and Russia: Representations
of the Past* (Toronto: University of Toronto Press, 2008), chaps. 15 and 16.
157 Ivan L. Rudnytsky with John-Paul Himka, eds., *Rethinking Ukrainian History*
(Edmonton: Canadian Institute of Ukrainian Studies, University of Alberta,
1981).

the wider social awakening, all of which were pan-European trends.[158] In other words, social history could not only provide new instruments for studying the nation, but also challenge the nation-centric interpretive frames.

The Nation in Context

Already in the short run, the CIUS proved its importance as a platform for academic forums and publications on the major problems of Ukrainian history. Scholars from other Canadian universities sometimes took the lead in such projects, in particular Peter J. Potichnyj, a political scientist from McMaster University. In retrospect his project of conferences and edited volumes on Ukrainians' relations with their most important historical neighbours — Jews, Poles, and Russians — can be seen as encouraging not just academic dialogue but also what today would be called "transnational history," a concept focusing on interrelations and mutual influences among nations, as well as on common larger historical factors.[159] The three resulting volumes differed somewhat in their approach and coverage, but the fact that the one on Ukrainian-Jewish relations has gone through three editions since 1988 proves the original concept's value.[160]

---

158 Ibid., 253–54.

159 On the potential of transnational history for Ukrainian Studies, see Georgiy [Heorhii] Kasianov and Philip Ther, eds., *A Laboratory of Transnational History: Ukraine and Recent Ukrainian Historiography* (Budapest: Central European University Press, 2009).

160 See Peter J. Potichnyj, ed., *Poland and Ukraine: Past and Present* (Edmonton and Toronto: Canadian Institute of Ukrainian Studies, 1980); Peter J. Potichnyj and Howard Aster, eds., *Ukrainian-Jewish Relations in Historical Perspective* (Edmonton: Canadian Institute of Ukrainian Studies, 1988; 2nd ed., 1990; 3rd ed., Edmonton and Toronto: Canadian Institute of Ukrainian Studies Press, 2010); and Peter J. Potichnyj et al, eds., *Ukraine and Russia in Their Historical Encounter* (Edmonton: Canadian Institute of Ukrainian Studies Press, 1992). Potichnyj also co-edited important source collections on the Ukrainian nationalist underground during and after World War II. Yuri Boshyk, whose 1981 doctoral thesis on the Ukrainian political parties in the Russian Empire remains unpublished, also came to focus on the war and refugee experience co-editing several collections of articles and source material on these topics that were published by the CIUS Press.

With the establishment of the CIUS, two young specialists, Bohdan Krawchenko and (in 1977) John-Paul Himka joined it as research associates. A sociologist by training, Krawchenko eventually wrote an influential dissertation and book on Ukrainian society during the twentieth century that focused on the relationship between social change and national identity.[161] The new focus on society fit well with the Ukrainian-Canadian community's awareness campaign marking fifty years of the 1932–33 famine in Soviet Ukraine. Together with Roman Serbyn, a historian at the Université du Québec à Montréal, Krawchenko co-edited a collection of articles on this topic that appeared before Robert Conquest's *Harvest of Sorrow* and the establishment of the US Commission on the Ukraine Famine.[162] Krawchenko went on to serve as Lupul's successor as CIUS director (1986–91). Himka's PhD dissertation and first book were devoted to the study of Ukrainian and Polish socialism in late nineteenth-century Eastern Galicia, but one of his important conclusions was the role of Ukrainian socialists in formulating the ideas of an independent Ukraine.[163] In Edmonton he applied the methods of social history to the study of the Ukrainian national movement in Eastern Galicia, producing a comprehensive work on Galician peasant society at the time of major social transformations in the nineteenth century. Himka's book emphasized the complex interaction of the social and the national, the significance of print culture, and the role of women in the national movement.[164] (At the University of Manitoba, Stella Hryniuk's contemporaneous re-

161 Bohdan Krawchenko, *Social Change and National Consciousness in Twentieth-Century Ukraine* (London: Macmillan, 1985).

162 Bohdan Krawchenko and Roman Serbyn, eds., *Famine in Ukraine (1932–1933)* (Edmonton: Canadian Institute of Ukrainian Studies Press, 1986).

163 See John-Paul Himka, *Socialism in Galicia: The Emergence of Polish Social Democracy and Ukrainian Radicalism (1860–1890)* (Cambridge, Mass.: Harvard Ukrainian Research Institute, 1983); and idem, "Young Radicals and Independent Statehood: The Idea of Independent Ukraine, 1890–1895," *Slavic Review* 41, no. 2 (Summer 1982): 219–35.

164 John-Pail Himka, *Galician Villagers and the Ukrainian National Movement in the Nineteenth Century* (Edmonton: Canadian Institute of Ukrainian Studies, 1988).

search on the Galician peasantry featured similar methods but different conclusions.[165]) Himka initially shared his time between the CIUS and the History Department, but following Rudnytsky's departure from the CIUS in 1979 he also focused on teaching. After Rudnytsky's death in 1984, Himka was hired as his full-time, tenure-track replacement in East European history. (Replacing Rudnytsky with a Ukrainian specialist was not a foregone conclusion: Peter Savaryn had to apply his influence again, this time as the chancellor of the University of Alberta.)[166]

During the same period, Ukrainian history became established as a regular course at two major universities in Ontario. In 1980 Paul Robert Magocsi was hired as the first holder of the Chair of Ukrainian Studies at the University of Toronto. By then he had a major monograph under his belt—a thick volume on the making of a modern national identity in Subcarpathian Rus'. Although it could be read as a prehistory of Ukrainian Transcarpathia, this book already contained the suggestion that a separate East Slavic ("Rusyn") national identity could have developed in this mountainous region had it not been incorporated into the Soviet Union—an idea Rudnytsky hastened to rebuff in a special article.[167] Magocsi went on to accumulate an impressive publishing record in three main areas: Rusyn history and culture; surveys and atlases of Ukrainian history, and Galicia as both the Ukrainian Piedmont and a multicultural land. In addition to writing about Rusyn identity, he became actively involved in shaping it in the present.[168] In his

---

165 Stella Hryniuk, *Peasants with Promise: Ukrainians in Southeastern Galicia, 1880–1900* (Edmonton: Canadian Institute of Ukrainian Studies Press, 1991).

166 For details, see Khymka [Himka], "Istoriia Ukrainy," 111–15.

167 See Paul R. Magocsi, *The Shaping of a National Identity: Subcarpathian Rus', 1848–1948* (Cambridge, Mass.: Harvard University Press, 1978); and Ivan L. Rudnytsky, "Carpatho-Ukraine: A People in Search of Their Identity," in his *Essays*, 353–74.

168 There is a considerable body of research on Magocsi's role as a modern nation builder. In English, see Chris Hann, "Intellectuals, Ethnic Groups and Nations: Two Late Twentieth-Century Cases," in *Notions of Nationalism*, ed. Sukumar Periwal (Budapest: Central European University Press, 1995), 106–28; Martin Fedor Ziac, "Professors and Politics: The Role of Paul Robert Magocsi in the Modern Carpatho-Rusyn Revival," *East European Quarterly* 35, no. 2 (June 2001): 213–32; and the special section "The Scholar, Historian and Public Advocate:

surveys of the history of Ukraine and his work focusing on Galicia, Magocsi stressed the territorial approach and multicultural character of the lands that formed modern Ukraine.[169]

Given the leading role of the universities of Alberta and Toronto in the renewed institutionalization of Ukrainian Studies in Canada, it made sense that their affiliated academic publishers took the lead in bringing out English-language studies in Ukrainian history. The CIUS published such books from its early years, but in 1989 formally established the CIUS Press as its publishing arm, with its operations now shared between Edmonton and Toronto. The University of Toronto Press also developed a very strong list in Ukrainian Studies in general and Modern Ukrainian History in particular. During 1984–93, the CIUS collaborated with the University of Toronto Press is publishing the five-volume *Encyclopedia of Ukraine*, which became an important resource for the readers not familiar with Ukrainian. A number of Canadian academics wrote entries on Ukrainian history for this major project with Roman Senkus, Krawchenko, and Himka contributing the most. Himka also served as a subject co-editor for the History sections for volumes 3 through 5.

The Academic Contributions of Paul Robert Magocsi" in *Nationalities Papers* in 2011: Taras Kuzio, "A Multi-Vectored Scholar for a Multi-Vectored Era: Paul Robert Magocsi," *Nationalities Papers* 39, no. 1 (January 2011): 95–104; Alexander J. Motyl, "The Paradoxes of Paul Robert Magocsi: The Case for Rusyns and the Logical Necessity of Ukrainians," ibid., 105–9; George G. Grabowicz, ""The Magocsi Problem" (*Problema Magochoho*): A Preliminary Deconstruction and Contextualization," ibid., 111–16; Serhii Plokhy, "Between History and Nation: Paul Robert Magocsi and the Rewriting of Ukrainian History," ibid., 117–24; Dominique Arel, "The Scholar, Historian, and Public Advocate: The Contributions of Paul Robert Magocsi to Our Understanding of Ukraine and Central Europe," ibid., 125–27; Paul Robert Magocsi, "Concluding Observations on the Symposium," ibid., 129–34.

169 See Paul Robert Magocsi, *A History of Ukraine: The Land and Its Peoples* (Toronto: University of Toronto Press, 1987; 2nd ed., 2010; 2nd rev. ed., 2013); idem, *Ukraine: An Illustrated History* (Toronto: University of Toronto Press, 2007); idem, *The Roots of Ukrainian Nationalism: Galicia as Ukraine's Piedmont* (Toronto: University of Toronto Press, 2002); Chris Hann and Paul Robert Magocsi, eds., *Galicia: A Multicultured Land* (Toronto: University of Toronto Press, 2005).

The University of Toronto Press also published the first in Canada original survey of Ukrainian history in English. It was authored by Orest Subtelny, who had taught Ukrainian and East European history at York University since 1982. His *Ukraine: A History* (1988) became an academic bestseller in North America and made an enormous impact on the formation of new historical concepts in independent Ukraine, where it was first published in 1991.[170] A specialist on the Cossack period, Subtelny relied on the then fashionable concept of modernization in his treatment of Ukrainian society during the nineteenth and twentieth centuries. Because of its similarity to Soviet historical models, this concept seemed intuitively familiar to the Ukrainian historical profession, which also adopted from Subtelny the periodization of the Ukrainian national movement based on Hroch's scheme. But it was the overall framework of Subtelny's history as it was interpreted in Ukraine — the story of the ethnic Ukrainians' struggle for their own state — that had the greatest impact there. In the late Soviet dogmatic version, the essence of Ukrainian history had been portrayed as a continuous struggle of the Ukrainian *narod* to "reunite" with its Russian elder brother; now the simplistic interpretation in Ukraine of Subtelny's more complex argument provided the profession there with a new dogma that fit conveniently into the old methodological mold.[171] At least, this was true of the early Ukrainian post-independence textbooks and general surveys.

At the same time, Ukrainian researchers working on the history of modern Ukraine discovered a new range of topics and methodological tools after the channels of academic communication opened up between Canada and Ukraine in the late 1980s. The research profile of the CIUS changed somewhat with the arrival of two authorities on the early modern period: Frank E. Sysyn (acting director, 1991–92) and Zenon E. Kohut (director, 1993–2012). Both of them, as well as Serhii Plokhy, a specialist on the Cossack period,

---

170 Orest Subtelny, *Ukraine: A History*, 4th ed. (Toronto: University of Toronto Press, 2009; first edition published in 1988); in Ukrainian: Orest Subtelny, *Istoriia Ukrainy*, trans. Iurii Shevchuk (Kyiv: Lybid, 1991).

171 See chap. 2 of this book.

who moved from Dnipropetrovsk University to work at the CIUS, also wrote on Ukrainian historiography. Such work was, in part, an outgrowth of the Hrushevsky Translation Project, the main project of the Petro Jacyk Centre for Ukrainian Historical Research (directed by Sysyn since its establishment at the CIUS in 1989, with Plokhy occasionally filling in as acting director). This is certainly true of Sysyn's and Plokhy's work on Hrushevsky. Kohut and Plokhy also wrote important articles on Russian-Ukrainian historiographical controversies; and Plokhy and Sysyn, on religion in modern and contemporary Ukraine.[172] In 1994 the new leadership of the CIUS also co-organized a major international conference on Russian-Ukrainian relations, which indicated the profession's growing interest in cultural identity and representation.

Informed by the concepts of historical myth and national memory as the tools that patriotic intellectuals developed in their struggle against imperial grand narratives, the contributions of Kohut, Plokhy, and Sysyn displayed conceptual synergy with the work being done by such Canadian historians as Thomas M. Prymak, Stephen Velychenko, and Johannes Remy.[173] Olga Andriewsky's subtle analysis of the Ukrainian national intelligentsia before

---

172 Considerations of space preclude an exhaustive list. The following works are representative samples: Serhii Plokhy, *Unmaking Imperial Russia: Mykhailo Hrushevsky and the Writing of Ukrainian History* (Toronto: University of Toronto Press, 2005); Serhii Plokhy and Frank E. Sysyn, *Religion and Nation in Modern Ukraine* (Edmonton and Toronto: Canadian Institute of Ukrainian Studies Press, 2003); Frank E. Sysyn, "Introduction to Mykhailo Hrushevsky's *History of Ukraine-Rus'*," in *Historiography of Imperial Russia: The Profession and Writing History in a Multinational State*, ed. Thomas Sanders (Armonk, N.Y: M. E. Sharpe, 1999), 344–72; and Zenon E. Kohut, *Making Ukraine: Studies on Political Culture, Historical Narrative, and Identity* (Edmonton: Canadian Institute of Ukrainian Studies Press, 2011).

173 See Thomas M. Prymak, *Mykhailo Hrushevsky: The Politics of National Culture* (Toronto: University of Toronto Press, 1987); idem, *Mykola Kostomarov: A Biography* (Toronto: University of Toronto Press, 1996); Stephen Velychenko, *National History as Cultural Process: A Survey of the Interpretations of Ukraine's Past in Polish, Russian, and Ukrainian Historical Writing from the Earliest Times to 1914* (Edmonton: Canadian Institute of Ukrainian Studies Press, 1992); and idem, *Shaping Identity in Eastern Europe and Russia: Soviet and Polish Accounts of Ukrainian History,1914–1991* (New York: St. Martin's Press, 1993). In the twenty-first century Velychenko went on to write a well-researched work of institutional

the Revolution of 1917 and Bohdan Klid's work on Volodymyr Antonovych also dovetailed with the focus on how the nation was imagined. In general, the "historiographic turn" of the 1990s and 2000s
indicated the field's reaction to the new understanding of how
modern nations develop on the basis of earlier communities, with
the intelligentsia providing some crucial myth-making assistance.
It also revealed the growing influence of cultural history and the
impact of the late Soviet and post-Soviet debates in Ukraine about
what should constitute national memory.[174]

One can see a similar evolution, if from a very different starting point, in the distinguished research career of David R. Marples,
one of Ivan L. Rudnytsky's MA students, who went on to obtain a
PhD (1985) from the University of Sheffield with a specialization in
Soviet social and economic history. While a CIUS associate in the
late 1980s, he established himself as a leading authority on the social and environmental impact of the Chornobyl nuclear accident.
After Marples accepted a tenure-track appointment (as a Soviet specialist) in the Department of History at the University of Alberta in

---

and social history — a study of continuity in the Ukrainian government bureaucracy, *State Building in Revolutionary Ukraine: A Comparative study of Governments
and Bureaucrats, 1917–1922* (Toronto: University of Toronto Press, 2011); and an
imaginative work restating the thesis of the Ukrainian Social Democrats of the
revolutionary period about Russian colonialism in Bolshevik garb, *Painting Imperialism and Nationalism Red: The Ukrainian Marxist Critique of Russian Communist Rule in Ukraine, 1918–1925* (Toronto: University of Toronto Press, 2015). Velychenko then continued his book series on the Ukrainian Revolution with volumes on propaganda and violence in Ukraine during this period. The most
recent Canadian contribution to the history of the nineteenth-century Ukrainian
movement is Johannes Remy, *Brothers or Enemies: The Ukrainian National Movement and Russia from the 1840s to the 1870s* (Toronto: University of Toronto Press,
2016).

174 It is worth noting here that Prymak was the first PhD graduate in Ukrainian
history at the University of Toronto (1984) and Bohdan Klid was the first such
graduate at the University of Alberta (1992). Both wrote their dissertations on
great Ukrainian historians and nation builders — Hrushevsky and Volodymyr
Antonovych, respectively. The mandate of the CIUS's newest program, the Holodomor Research and Education Consortium (est. 2013) is also closely related
to the issues of national memory. Led by Sysyn, the research staff of this program has included trained historians — Klid, the late Andrij Makuch, and, in
Ukraine, Liudmyla Hrynevych.

1991, he continued his collaboration with the CIUS until 2014, serving as director of the institute's Stasiuk Program for the Study of Contemporary Ukraine. He also wrote widely on the Soviet Union, Russia, and Belarus, but his books on Ukraine show an evolution from his interest in the workers', ecological, and national movements of the late 1980s to the controversies about national memory in the first two decades of independence and to the analysis of Ukraine's popular revolutions, focusing on their political symbols.[175]

John-Paul Himka was moving in a similar direction. In the process of transitioning from his earlier work on the social history of Galicia to a book project on the Ukrainian Catholic Church in the same region, which was somewhat similar in methodology but more engaged with the cultural sphere, he wrote an influential article on the identity choices opened to nineteenth-century Ruthenian patriots. An example of a mature and well-contextualized "constructivist" approach to national identity, Himka's paper gave careful attention to the possibility of either a regional Galician or a wide Ruthenian (Ukrainian and Belarusian) identity developing into a modern nation.[176] In the previous generation, Ivan L. Rudnytsky would be the first to criticize Himka's approach, but now an

---

175 Marples's books on Ukrainian subjects include *Chernobyl and Nuclear Power in the USSR* (New York: St. Martin's Press and Edmonton: Canadian Institute of Ukrainian Studies, 1986); *Ukraine under Perestroika: Ecology, Economics and the Workers' Revolt* (New York: St. Martin's Press, 1991); *Stalinism in Ukraine in the 1940s* (New York : St. Martin's Press, 1992); *Heroes and Villains: Creating National History in Contemporary Ukraine* (Budapest: Central European University Press, 2007); *Holodomor: Causes of the 1932–1933 Famine in Ukraine* (Saskatoon : Heritage Press, 2011); co-ed., with Frederick V. Mills, *Ukraine's Euromaidan: Analyses of a Civil Revolution* (Stuttgart: Ibidem, 2015); and *Ukraine in Conflict: An Analytical Chronicle* (Bristol, UK: E-International Relations, 2017), www.e-ir.info/wp-content/uploads/2017/05/Ukraine-in-Conflict-E-IR.pdf.

176 John-Paul Himka, *Religion and Nationality in Western Ukraine: The Greek Catholic Church and the Ruthenian National Movement in Galicia, 1870–1900* (Montreal and Kingston: McGill-Queen's University Press, 2000); and idem, "The Construction of Nationality in Galician Rus': Icarian Flights in Almost All Directions," in *Intellectuals and the Articulation of the Nation*, ed. Ronald G. Suny and Michael D. Kennedy (Ann Arbor: University of Michigan Press, 1999), 109–64. Himka also continued Peter Potichnyj's project by co-organizing a conference with Hans-

academic from Ukraine, Yaroslav Hrytsak, wrote a most interesting, English-language critique of Himka's argument.[177] Then
Himka moved decisively into new conceptual terrain in his studies
of two very different chronological periods. On the one hand, he
became involved in the debates about historical memory, focusing
in particular on the controversial World War II record of Ukrainian
radical nationalists.[178] On the other, he wrote a fascinating study of
continuity and change in Last Judgment icons in the Carpathian
Mountain region, in which he questioned not just modern concepts
of this region and its culture but even the research optics of a modern historian. National history became the first victim of this imaginative, postmodernist foray into the cultural past of what is now
part of Ukraine.[179]

Just as in the previous generation, there was notable conceptual cross-pollination and joint work on various projects among the
historians of modern Ukraine and Canadian literary scholars and
anthropologists, whose work was closely related to the new methodology of cultural history. In varying degrees this is true of such
Canadian scholars as Danylo Husar Struk, Oleh Ilnytzkyj, Natalie
Kononenko, Andriy Nahachewsky, Natalia Pylypiuk, Myroslav
Shkandrij, and Maxim Tarnawsky, among others. Canadian research on modern Ukrainian history also benefitted from close contacts with specialists on Ukrainians in Canada such as Jars Balan,
Radomir Bilash, Serge Cipko, Robert Klymasz, Lubomyr Luciuk,

Joachim Torke and co-editing with him the resulting volume of conference papers, *German-Ukrainian Relations in Historical Perspective* (Edmonton: Canadian
Institute of Ukrainian Studies Press, 1994).

177 Yaroslav Hrytsak, "'Icarian Flights in Almost All Directions' Reconsidered," in
Andrew Gow, Roman Senkus, and Serhy Yekelchyk, eds., *Confronting the Past:
Ukraine and Its History: A Festschrift in Honour of John-Paul Himka = Journal of
Ukrainian Studies* 35–36 ([2010–11]): 81–89.

178 See John-Paul Himka, *Ukrainian Nationalists and the Holocaust: OUN and UPA's
Participation in the Destruction of Ukrainian Jewry, 1941–1944* (Stuttgart: Ibidem,
2021).

179 John-Paul Himka, *Last Judgment Iconography in the Carpathians* (Toronto:
University of Toronto Press, 2009). See also Liliya Berezhnaya and John-
Paul Himka, *The World to Come: Ukrainian Images of the Last Judgment*
(Cambridge, Mass: Harvard Ukrainian Research Institute, 2014).

Frances Swyripa, and Roman Yereniuk; sociologists Wsevolod W. Isajiw and W. Roman Petryshyn; political scientists Dominique Arel, Marta Dyczok, Bohdan Harasymiw, John Jaworsky, Bohdan Kordan, and Taras Kuzio; geographer Ihor Stebelsky; anthropologists Tanya Richardson and Natalia Khanenko-Friesen; and others. Finally, education specialists such as Orest Cap, Denis Hlynka, and Valentina Kuryliw have helped shape the delivery of knowledge in the field on Ukrainian history.

As interest in new cultural history and the "linguistic turn" was increasing in the profession during the 1990s and 2000s, another notable trend emerged: the increased interconnection between the Canadian and Ukrainian academic worlds. In addition to exchanges of visits and joint conferences, graduate students from Ukraine soon came to constitute a significant share of those accepted into Canadian doctoral programs in history. The Department of History and Classics at the University of Alberta emerged as the national leader in this respect, especially after the appointment to the Canada Research Chair in Imperial Russian History of Heather Coleman, a specialist on religious and cultural history of the Russian Empire, and its Ukrainian lands in particular, during the late nineteenth and early twentieth centuries.[180] Together with David Marples and John-Paul Himka (until the latter's retirement in 2014), Coleman became actively involved in mentoring graduate students, including a growing number of those from Ukraine, in contemporary Western historical methodologies.[181] In 2013 she also took over the CIUS Research Program on Religion and Culture that Serhii Plokhy and then John-Paul Himka had directed previously.

---

180 See Heather J. Coleman, *Russian Baptists and Spiritual Revolution* (Bloomington: Indiana University Press, 2005); and idem and Mark Steinberg, eds., *Sacred Stories: Religion and Spirituality in Modern Russia* (Bloomington: Indiana University Press, 2007).

181 Since the 1990s, Henry Abramson, Karel Berkhoff, Serhiy Bilenky, Svitlana Frunchak, and Oleksandr Melnyk have written PhD dissertations in modern Ukrainian history at the University of Toronto under the supervision of Professors Paul Robert Magocsi, Lynne Viola, or Piotr Wróbel.

In the 2000s graduate students from Ukraine with Canadian Phds, including historians Serhy Yekelchyk and Andriy Zayarnyuk, began obtaining academic appointments in Canada. They inherited the full spectrum of interests that characterized the development of the field — from the foundational interest in the nation to the notion that such interest should be grounded in social history to the understanding that language and representations shape both the subject and the instruments of their research. In studying the blueprints of the nation developed in the imperial context, they looked for the ubiquitous presence of power in everyday life, the significance of vocabularies, and the persistence of informal networks sometimes only noticeable in a microhistorical studies.[182] Serhiy Bilenky used cultural-history approaches in his study of the Romantic imagination as the fertile ground, from which new concepts of the Ukrainian nation grew.[183] He then went on to publish an innovative history of Kyiv during the late Imperial period.[184] Canadian professors in related disciplines, very often also formerly graduate students in North America from Ukraine — in particular Natalia Khanenko-Friesen, Taras Koznarsky, Svitlana Krys, Olga Pressitch, Maryna Romanets, and Irene Sywenky — have enriched research on Ukrainian culture and society.

Since 1999 the Kowalsky Program for the Study of Eastern Ukraine established at the CIUS under Zenon Kohut's directorship

---

182 See Serhy Yekelchyk, *Stalin's Empire of Memory: Russian-Ukrainian Relations in the Soviet Historical Imagination* (Toronto: University of Toronto Press, 2004); idem, *Stalin's Citizens: Everyday Politics in the Wake of Total War* (New York: Oxford University Press, 2014); Andrii Zaiarniuk [Andriy Zayarnyuk], *Idiomy emansypatsii: "Vyzvolni proiekty" i halytske selo v seredyni XIX stolittia* (Kyiv: Krytyka, 2007); Andriy Zayarnyuk, *Framing the Ukrainian Peasantry in Habsburg Galicia, 1846-1914* (Edmonton and Торонто: Canadian Institute of Ukrainian Studies Press, 2013); and John-Paul Himka and Andriy Zayarnyuk, eds., *Letters from Heaven: Popular Religion in Russia and Ukraine* (Toronto: University of Toronto Press, 2006).

183 Serhiy Bilenky, *Romantic Nationalism in Eastern Europe: Russian, Polish, and Ukrainian Political Imaginations* (Stanford: Stanford University Press, 2012). He also edited a related collection of sources, *Fashioning Modern Ukraine: The Writings of Mykola Kostomarov, Volodymyr Antonovych and Mykhailo Drahomanov* (Edmonton and Toronto: CIUS Press, 2013).

184 Serhiy Bilenky, *Imperial Urbanism in the Borderlands: Kyiv, 1800-1905* (Toronto: University of Toronto Press, 2018).

has closely collaborated with Ukrainian historians in this important region close to the Russian border. With its Ukrainian base at Kharkiv National University, there the program developed a Western-style research centre headed by Volodymyr Kravchenko, a specialist on urban and borderland history, whose work has shown an excellent command of Western theoretical approaches.[185] Kravchenko's move to Edmonton as the director of the CIUS after Kohut's retirement in 2012, like Plokhy's earlier move to Harvard as the Mykhailo S. Hrushevsky Professor of Ukrainian History, confirmed that Ukrainian and Canadian historians of the twenty-first century inhabit a common global academic world. Further proof of that trend came in 2008, when the CIUS established a new program based in Ukraine, this time in its western region and led by the prominent Ukrainian historian Yaroslav Hrytsak. The Jacyk family's continued generous support enabled the CIUS to follow up on its long-standing collaboration with at Lviv National University's Institute of Historical Research and its journal *Ukraina Moderna* (Modern Ukraine), both of which were founded on Hrytsak's initiative, by establishing at Lviv's new leading research institution, the Ukrainian Catholic University, the Petro Jacyk Program for the Study of Modern Ukrainian History, also directed by Hrytsak, who moved *Ukraina Moderna* there.

Today, in the third decade of the twenty-first century, it is becoming increasingly difficult to define the "Canadian" part in the notion of Canadian scholarship on modern Ukrainian history. Yet it was the contribution of Canadian-based academics during the previous decades that played a major role in making Ukrainian history a legitimate academic subject in the West. Their efforts to educate the rising generation of historians in Ukraine helped the latter to join this increasingly global field.

---

185 Kravchenko's early work is on Ukrainian historiography. For a representative selection, see Volodymyr Kravchenko, *Narysy z ukrainskoi istoriohrafii epokhy natsionalnoho vidrodzhennia (druha polovyna XVIII–seredyna XIX st.)* (Kharkiv: Osnova, 1996); idem, *Kharkov/Kharkiv: Stolitsa pogranichia* (Vilnius: European Humanities University Press, 2010); idem, *Ukraina, imperiia, Rosiia: Vybrani statti z modernoi istorii ta istoriohrafii* (Kyiv: Krytyka, 2011).

5. Ivan L. Rudnytsky and the Intellectual History of Modern Ukraine

Few diaspora historians of Ukraine have wielded such a significant amount of influence on the establishment of the study of history in independent Ukraine as Ivan Lysiak Rudnytsky (1919–1984). This is partly explained by the fact that in the 1990s the Ukrainian history profession most needed a new conceptual apparatus precisely in those areas in which he was working: the history of the formation of the modern Ukrainian nation and the development of Ukrainian sociopolitical thought. The new models of these two historical processes were designed to replace the orthodox Soviet historical schema with its class-based history, socialist revolution, and the desire to "reunite" with Russia. Rudnytsky was also an accomplished author of historical essays. He knew how to express his thoughts in short essays that were suitable not only for professional historians but also an educated public. Some of these articles, written in Ukrainian, were accessible to readers in Ukraine even before 1994, when Yaroslav Hrytsak and Frank Sysyn prepared the most complete Ukrainian-language edition of Rudnytsky's scholarly legacy, which also includes texts previously published in English.[186]

Today, citing Rudnytsky's works is par for the course in studies devoted to nineteenth- and twentieth-century Ukrainian history, especially in discussions of the problems of nation building and the history of political thought. It is surprising, however, that in Ukraine there are practically no works devoted to Rudnytsky as a historian or his creative method, conceptual principles, and methodological approaches. There is significantly much more literature about Rudnytsky as a thinker.[187] Those works that are related to the

---

186 Ivan Lysiak-Rudnytsky, *Istorychni ese*, ed. Frank Sysyn and Iaroslav Hrytsak, trans. Marta Badik et al, 2 vols. (Kyiv: Osnovy, 1994).

187 See, e.g., Iaroslav Hrytsak, "Ivan Lysiak-Rudnytsky (Narys intelektualnoi biohrafii)," *Suchasnist*, no. 11 (1994): 73–96; N. Badora, "Filosofsko-kulturolohichni idei u tvorchosti I. Lysiaka-Rudnytskoho," *Visnyk Kyivskoho natsionalnoho universytetu im. Tarasa Shevchenka: Ukrainoznavstvo*, no. 4 (2000): 45–49; V. S. Datsenko, "Pryntsypy liberalizmu i problema natsiietvorennia u politychnii

scholar's historical studies usually do not stray beyond the parameters of discussions of his conception and periodization of the
Ukrainian national movement.[188] The paradoxical consequence of
this situation is that, while Ukrainian scholars cite Rudnytsky's
works extensively, they do not apply his methodology. The aim of
this chapter is to outline the theoretical and methodological approaches of Rudnytsky as a historian, in order to facilitate the fuller
use of his legacy by historians of Ukraine around the world.

From the History of Ideas to Intellectual History

In a letter to Roman Rozdolsky dated 26 August 1966, Rudnytsky
defined his area of historical research as the "history of ideas," explaining to his correspondent that in this thematic field he could
work mainly with published sources, because at the time no others
were available to him in the US.[189] We can assume, in fact, that here
Rudnytsky was offering a more elaborate explanation that allowed
him to describe his specialization to his American colleagues. In
North America during the first postwar decades, the history of
ideas was indeed a recognized and even prestigious branch of history. However, there is little that connects Rudnytsky's creative
method to the conceptual elaborations of Arthur O. Lovejoy and his
disciples, who dogmatically reduced the analysis of history to the
identification in them of some unchangeable "unit ideas."[190] The
Ukrainian term, "history of social thought" in and of itself was a

---

filosofii I. P. Lysiaka-Rudnytskoho," *Filosofiia i politolohiia v konteksti suchasnoi kultury*, no. 8 (2014): 184–88.

188 See, e.g., Vasyl Lisovyi, "I. Lysiak-Rudnytskyi—istoryk ukrainskoi politychnoi dumky," *Politolohichni chytannia*, no. 4 (1993): 207–26; S. V. Bondar, "I. Lysiak-Rudnytskyi: Osoblyvosti formuvannia narodu ta natsii," *Visnyk Kyivskoho natsionalnoho universytetu im. Tarasa Shevchenka: Filosofiia, Politolohiia*, nos. 49–51 (2003): 9–14.

189 Ia. Hrytsak [Yaroslav Hrytsak] and I.-P. Khymka [John-Paul Himka], "Lystuvannia Ivana Lysiaka-Rudnytskoho i Romana Rozdolskoho," *Ukraina Moderna*, nos. 2–3 (1999): 376–413, here 384.

190 Lovejoy's own use of this concept has recently been re-evaluated in a more po-sitive light. See John P. Diggins, "Arthur O. Lovejoy and the Challenge of Intel-lectual History," *Journal of the History of Ideas* 67, no. 1 (2006): 181–208.

wider definition because it included a reference to society. Attention to the link between social and intellectual processes may be re-
garded as the defining mark of Rudnytsky as a researcher; it indicates that the parameters of the traditional Western history of ideas
were too narrow for him.

In the 1970s the history of ideas lost supporters in the West,
where it was supplanted by intellectual history, which emphasizes
the broader social and cultural context of philosophical ideas and
political theories. This term appealed to Rudnytsky. In a letter to
Roman Szporluk dated 22 March 1976 he wrote: "I have plans for
some articles in the field of Ukrainian intellectual history and the
history of political thought."[191] In a lecture and a manuscript of an
article about Franciszek Duchiński dated 1983–84, Rudnytsky set
himself the task of ascertaining the role of this Polish ethnographer
and historian in "Ukrainian intellectual history."[192]

In contrast to the Western history of ideas, by the late 1950s
Rudnytsky was already emphasizing the importance of social processes in order to understand the ideological evolution of Ukrainian
society. A superficial reading of his classic text "The Intellectual Origins of Modern Ukraine" may create the impression that the North
American historian was influenced by the well-known Leninist periodization of the history of the revolutionary movement in Russia
(the Decembrists, Herzen, the Narodniks, Social Democrats).[193] For
Rudnytsky, the first stage in the development of modern Ukrainian
consciousness is "the Epoch of the Nobility (to the 1840s)"; this is
followed by "the Populist Epoch," during which "the leadership of
the Ukrainian movement passed into the hands of a new social
group, that of the intelligentsia."[194] It is interesting that into the

---

191 Volodymyr Kravchenko, "Lystuvannia Romana Shporliuka z Ivanom Lysiakom-Rudnytskym i Iuriiem Shevelovym (1962–1982 rr.)," *Skhid-zakhid: Isto-
ryko-kulturolohichnyi zbirnyk*, nos. 9–10 (2008): 208–94, here 231.

192 Ivan L. Rudnytsky, "Franciszek Duchiński and His Impact on Ukrainian Political Thought," in his *Essays in Modern Ukrainian History*, ed. Peter L. Rudnytsky
(Edmonton: Canadian Institute of Ukrainian Studies, 1987), 187–202, here 187.

193 See V. I. Lenin, "Pamiati Gertsena," *Polnoe sobranie sochinenii*, 55 vols. (Moscow:
Politizdat, 1958–66), 21: 255–62, here 261.

194 Ivan L. Rudnytsky, "The Intellectual Origins of Modern Ukraine," in his *Essays*,
123–42, here 123 and 128–29.

middle of this sociological periodization Rudnytsky inserts subdivisions that are not necessarily based on a change of the leading stratum. Whereas the transition from the Ukrainian nobility to the Decembrists may still be linked to the decline of the ideology of Cossack statehood and the emergence of democratic, pan-Slavic federalism, the two stages in the development of Ukrainian thought during the Narodnik era—the "Romantic" generation of the Cyril and Methodius Brotherhood and the "positivist" generation of the Old Hromada—do not differ in terms of their social component but by their connection to various trends of European thought of the time.[195]

The deviation from the Leninist schema is already obvious here; it is only affirmed by Rudnytsky's use of the concept of "generation," which is foreign to Marxist historical thought. In fact, Lenin and Rudnytsky made use of a common source—the achievements of European sociology of the late nineteenth–early twentieth centuries—in different ways. Rudnytsky was markedly influenced by Viacheslav Lypynsky (1882–1931), who emphasized the role of the Ukrainian nobility during the Khmelnytsky Uprising and later. As Rudnytsky himself comments in one of his articles about Lypynsky, the latter was notably influenced by European sociology of the time, particularly by such thinkers as Georges Sorel, Vilfredo Pareto, and Gustave Le Bon.[196] Rudnytsky had a somewhat critical attitude to this school; he saw it as an intellectual milieu that had nurtured the irrationalism and voluntarism of the interwar nationalistic doctrine, but he valued its attention to the social context and the role of elites.[197] In another fragment Rudnytsky affirms the significant influence on him of another leading European sociologist, Max Weber (1864–1920), especially his research on the "links between various religious systems and economic structures."[198]

195 Ibid., 128.
196 Ivan Lysiak-Rudnytsky, "Viacheslav Lypynsky," in Sysyn and Hrytsak, *Istorychni ese*, 2: 131–48, here 139.
197 Ivan Lysiak-Rudnytsky, "Natsionalizm," in Sysyn and Hrytsak, *Istorychni ese*, 2: 247–59, here 249.
198 Ivan Lysiak-Rudnytsky, "Dyskusiini vystupy na mizhnarodnomu istorychnomu kongresi," ibid., 2: 409–18, here 417.

Thus, Rudnytsky's comments about the narrowness of the "social base" of Ukrainian populism or that "the transition to capitalism did not produce a nationalist Ukrainian bourgeoisie" should be read in the context of the European intellectual and scholarly tradition of the early- to the mid-twentieth century.[199] It is telling that in Rudnytsky's writings the third stage in the development of Ukrainian political thought in the modern period (from the 1890s to the outbreak of World War I), when modern national awareness in Dnipro Ukraine under Russian rule began to seep down to the peasant masses, does not acquire a sociological name. This stage could be defined, for example, by the rise of the social stratum of the peasant intelligentsia, but Rudnytsky proposes instead a term borrowed from the history of art, "Modernism," or, in another text, "the Modernist Age."[200] Indeed, among the signposts of this new period Rudnytsky mentions the transition from "popular" to "national" literature, but not just in the sense of national consciousness. With the emergence of such writers as Lesia Ukrainka, Mykhailo Kotsiubynsky, and Volodymyr Vynnychenko, Ukrainian literature had ceased to be a literature for the peasant masses and become "national," that is, it was able "to satisfy the many-sided spiritual interests of a diverse modern society."[201] Although Rudnytsky does not develop this idea, the reader understands that he is also talking about a change of artistic style: Literary modernism was renouncing the preceding critical realism and populist romanticism, and the above-mentioned writers were definitely modernists. Thus, this early work of Rudnytsky's reveals the devices that would become typical of Western cultural history only in the 1980s.

As we learn from the text of a paper delivered in August 1960 at the International Congress of Historical Sciences in Stockholm, Rudnytsky developed his method of conducting historical research on culture and social thought through a critical reading of Oswald

199 Rudnytsky, "Intellectual Origins," in his Essays, 130–31.
200 Ibid., 134. See also Ivan L. Rudnytsky, "The Role of Ukraine in Modern History," in his Essays, 11–36, here 24.
201 Rudnytsky, "Intellectual Origins," in his Essays, 136.

Spengler and Arnold J. Toynbee. He appreciated the rationale behind the general "unity in style" of social and cultural life in a certain period, but he challenged the possibility of understanding cultural influences through the internal dynamics of culture itself. To
his way of thinking, culture did not constitute a "substantive unity"
but consisted of changeable parts that could be variously combined.
Following in the footsteps of Max Weber, Rudnytsky considered
the most productive method to be "research on interdependencies
and, simultaneously, on the relative autonomy of two (or more)
large spheres of human existence."[202] This required a review of aspects of culture and ideological processes in a certain connection
with social processes, but without the simplistic determinism that
reigned supreme in Soviet historical science.

Rudnytsky's creative method developed in the 1960s and
1970s, particularly through the application of microhistorical approaches to research on ideological phenomena, but the emphasis
on the importance of the European intellectual context and dynamic link between cultural phenomena and social processes remained characteristic of his historical works and essays.

A Nation and Its Culture

Long before the constructivist approach to the history of nations
and the concept of "imagined communities" gained wide acceptance among historians in Eastern Europe, Rudnytsky developed a complex and multidimensional understanding of the formation of the Ukrainian nation, and championed it in the postwar
diaspora, where among the reading public there was no lack of so-
called "primordialists," or enthusiasts of the eternal existence of
Ukrainians.

The scholar's initial thesis was that "[t]he emergence of the
modern Ukrainian nation may be understood as the outcome of an
interaction of social forces and ideas."[203] For Rudnytsky, the difference between ethnicity and nationality was key, and he understood

---

202 Lysiak-Rudnytsky, "Dyskusiini vystupy," in Sysyn and Hrytsak, *Istorychni ese*,
2: 417.
203 Rudnytsky, "Role of Ukraine in Modern History," in his *Essays*, 19.

the latter as a political category, "a phenomenon of a different, higher order."[204] The transition from ethnicity to nationality takes place in the process of nation formation, which consists primarily of the assimilation of new ideas: "By 'nation-building' I mean the penetration of all strata of the population by the national idea, the transformation of an ethnic mass into a culturally and politically self-conscious national community."[205] This thesis of Rudnytsky's proved to be one of his most influential during the discovery of his scholarly legacy in independent Ukraine, Unfortunately, it is often understood in the teleological sense, as a linear process that leads inexorably to a certain result.

Rudnytsky's authorial vision was considerably more complex. He insisted that "[t]he development of modern Ukrainian social thought is to be understood not as a single stream, but rather as a process containing several parallel and distinct, although correlated and interdependent, trends."[206] He also advocated the "cultivation of an inclusive vision of history," which would include in the Ukrainian past even opposing ideological tendencies.[207] Rudnytsky's favourite example of such an approach was the coexistence in London of monuments to Charles I and Oliver Cromwell.[208] He himself recognized the concurrent influence on him of two Ukrainian thinkers from opposite sides of the political spectrum: the conservative monarchist/statist Viacheslav Lypynsky and the anarchist-style socialist-federalist Mykhailo Drahomanov, to each of whom he devoted several studies. For Rudnytsky, therefore, the modern Ukrainian nation was formed out of a conflict between opposing ideologies and their interaction.

Furthermore, Ukraine's intellectual history was not limited to the process of nation building. Rudnytsky welcomed the development of "a territorial concept of Ukrainian history – in which

---

204 Ivan L. Rudnytsky, "Carpatho-Ukraine," in his *Essays*, 353–74, here 358.
205 Ivan L. Rudnytsky, "The Ukrainian National Movement on the Eve of the First World War," in his *Essays*, 375–88, here 377.
206 Ivan L. Rudnytsky, "Trends in Ukrainian Political Thought," in his *Essays*, 91–122, here 91.
207 Ibid., 122.
208 Ibid.

Ukrainian history is defined as everything connected with Ukrainian territory as opposed to a narrowly ethnocentric approach."[209] This sentence is taken from the first paragraph of his article about Michał Czajkowski's Cossack project during the Crimean War, one of several studies by Rudnytsky on Polish figures of the mid-nineteenth century who remained on the margins of Ukrainian history but who, in his opinion, deserved attention regardless of their contribution to the project of the modern Ukrainian nation. A reflection of this approach of Rudnytsky's is his controversial article about the fundamental error, as he saw it, made by diaspora researchers and essayists who wrote about the danger of Russification "in the sense of the disappearance of the Ukrainian people as an ethnic group."[210] For Rudnytsky, no less important and, perhaps, even more real was the danger of "Little Russianization," in the sense of the "assimilation of Ukrainians into the all-Russian Soviet imperial system."[211] The explanation for this unorthodox position lies in the particularities of Rudnytsky's concept of nation, according to which language and other ethnic characteristics per se do not create a nation. Most important is the awareness of oneself as a political community and active subject of history: "This is a matter of political subjectness, which makes a people into a nation."[212] Consequently, for Rudnytsky the main question connected with the Ukrainian language is this: "Will independent Ukrainian political thought also be formed in the Ukrainian language?"[213]

Rudnytsky approaches the problem of the scope of Ukraine's intellectual history the same way. In his view, it is not defined by language. Thus, he insisted on the inclusion of prerevolutionary scholars of Ukrainian descent who were published and lectured

---

209 Ivan L. Rudnytsky, "Michał Czajkowski's Cossack Project during the Crimean War: An Analysis of Ideas," in his *Essays*, 173–86, here 173.

210 Ivan Lysiak-Rudnytsky, "Rusyfikatsiia chy malorosiianizatsiia?" in Sysyn and Hrytsak, *Istorychni ese*, 2: 471–76, here 474.

211 Ibid., 474–75.

212 Ibid., 474.

213 Ibid.

only in Russian, but maintained contact with the Ukrainian movement or expressed ideas that demonstrated "their Ukrainian bias,"
especially Pamfil Yurkevich, Volodymyr Lesevych, Mykola Ziber,
Mykhailo Tuhan-Baranovsky, Maksym Kovalevsky, Bohdan
Kistiakovsky, Oleksander Potebnia, Dmitrii Ovsianiko-Kulikovsky,
and even the military theoretician and governor-general of Kyiv,
Podillia, and Volhynia Mikhail Dragomirov.[214] At the same time,
however, Rudnytsky strongly objected to viewing Russian culture
in the Ukrainian SSR as being on the same footing as Ukrainian culture precisely because such a starting point ignored the political
context: "Ukrainian–Russian cultural relations are not, regrettably,
a free, creative reciprocity between equal partners but relations
whereby one side is privileged, while the other's natural rights are
infringed."[215]

Method and Problems

As John-Paul Himka commented at one time, for a historian of
Ukraine, Rudnytsky was exceptionally well read in fields that had
no direct bearing on his research interests: philosophy, world literature, European culture, etc. This allowed him to analyze events in
Ukrainian history "within broader European and universal contexts."[216]

Rudnytsky left behind scattered references to his creative
method, but they are related to his central points. In particular, he
emphasizes the importance of the "comparative method," which allows historians to uncover the commonality of historical processes
in nations or regions unconnected by language or religion; for example, Latvia and Georgia or Bukovyna and Slovenia. Where these
two pairs of examples are concerned, it is the imperial past. In the

214 Rudnytsky, "Role of Ukraine," 18–19.
215 Ivan Lysiak-Rudnytsky, "V oboroni intelektu," in Sysyn and Hrytsak, *Istorychni
ese*, 2: 381–407, here 382.
216 Ivan Pavlo Khymka [John-Paul Himka], "Nash istoryk, nasha epokha: Ivan Lysiak-Rudnytsky," *Krytyka* XVIII, nos. 1–2 (195–96) (November 2014): 4–8, here
8.

former, it is Russian; in the latter — Austrian.[217] This kind of comparison makes allowances for singling out the typical and the distinct in the development of the two compared countries. Another important criterion is social stratification: the preservation or loss of a traditional social structure, as in the case of Poland and Hungary, where "nobiliary social traditions" survived until the age of mass politics.[218]

The historian also emphasizes the value of "case studies," or detailed examples that allow for an in-depth study of broader processes and local conditions. For Rudnytsky, this method is irreplaceable in researching nation-building processes and intellectual history. For example, he viewed Carpatho-Ukraine (Transcarpathia and the Priashiv region) as a brilliant "case study" of nation building precisely because they were "a typical borderland or transitional territory," where the interaction of various social and cultural forces took place over centuries: "Thus it is possible to study there, in an almost laboratory-like fashion, the interaction of factors which have shaped the evolution of that part of the world as a whole."[219]

It could be argued that Rudnytsky's attention to individual thinkers who were often in no way central figures in the pantheon of Ukrainian political thought was a form of "case study," but in the field of intellectual history. It is interesting that he left behind a description of his approach to analyzing the creative legacy of such figures. He found it most productive to start with a writer's vision of "historical perspectives," that is, his or her historiosophy. In the case of his favourite figure, Drahomanov, it was the conviction that until the end of the eighteenth-century Ukraine "constituted part of the European world."[220]

Finally, Rudnytsky emphasizes the need for a researcher's critical self-reflection, which should help rid Ukrainian scholarship

---

217 Ivan Lysiak-Rudnytsky, "Navkolo mizhnarodnoho istorychnoho kongresu u Vidni," in Sysyn and Hrytsak, *Istorychni ese*, 2: 419–35, here 424.

218 Ibid.

219 Ivan L. Rudnytsky, "Carpatho-Ukraine," in his *Essays*, 353–74, here 353.

220 Ivan Lysiak-Rudnytsky, "Iz Drahomanivskykh studii," in Sysyn and Hrytsak, *Istorychni ese*, 1: 289–98, here 289.

of its age-old affliction—the "subjective-romantic treatment" of a research subject, which was expressed stylistically through "'patriotic' emotionality and tendentiousness."[221] This especially concerned the area in which Rudnytsky himself worked: the intellectual history of Ukraine in the nineteenth century and the first half of the twentieth.

Indeed, Rudnytsky's studies are the epitome of critical self-reflection and bold challenge to national mythology when it is buttressed by black-and-white primitivization of the Ukrainian past or the repudiation of Ukraine's democratic future. Let us examine his essays on some forgotten nineteenth-century Polish figures, who were born in Right-Bank Ukraine. The life of Hipolit (Vladimir) Terlecki is practically unrelated to the Ukrainian national movement or the subsequent development of modern Ukrainian identity, but for Rudnytsky he is an example of something that is critical to understanding the Ukrainian movement: the variability of ethnic self-identification, the possibility of taking turns participating in various national projects, and the importance of the external imperial factor. To him, these factors also defined the ambiguity of "the road which nineteenth-century Ukrainian intellectuals had to travel."[222]

Conversely, in the case of the similarly forgotten Franciszek Duchiński, the scholar sees him as "a major influence on the shaping of modern Ukrainian political thought," but considers him to be ambiguous because Duchiński promoted the racial theory of the conflict between "Aryan" Poland and Rus' (Ukraine), lined up on one side, and "Turanian," or Asiatic Muscovy, on the other.[223] Duchiński's idea about a Polish–Ukrainian federation did not meet with a good critical reception among Ukrainian figures, but his theories about the racial otherness of Russians came in handy at the stage of affirming the notion about the ethnic separateness of Ukrainians. In the Russian Empire their biggest champion was Oleksander Konysky, but they were most widely disseminated in

---

221 Ivan Lysiak-Rudnytsky, "Struktura ukrainskoi istorii v XIX stolitti," in Sysyn and Hrytsak, *Istorychni ese*, 1: 193–202, here 196.
222 Ivan L. Rudnytsky, "Hipolit Vladimir Terlecki," in his *Essays*, 143–72, here 143.
223 Rudnytsky, "Franciszek Duchiński," in his *Essays*, 187.

Galicia. These kinds of views were promoted by Lonhyn Tse-
helsky's brochure *Rus'-Ukraina a Moskovshchyna-Rosiia* (Rus'-
Ukraine and Muscovy-Russia), which Galician branches of the
Prosvita Society widely distributed among peasants.[224]
Kostomarov and Drahomanov criticized Duchiński's ideas, but
Dmytro Dontsov included them, directly or indirectly, in the na-
tionalist canon.

Although one of the main topics of Rudnytsky's work was intellectual connections and the mutual influence of the Ukrainian
lands that were part of the Russian and Austro-Hungarian empires,
he also successfully used the comparative method for analyzing differences in the development rate of the Ukrainian national movement on both sides of the border. For example, his article "The
Ukrainian National Movement on the Eve of the First World War"
begins with a comparison of two events that took place in early
1914: the mass protests in Dnipro Ukraine against the ban prohibit-
ing the celebration of Taras Shevchenko's centenary and the adoption by the Diet of Galicia of a new Regional Statute and electoral
law that guaranteed Ukrainians 27.2 percent of seats in the Diet.[225]
Whereas the first event revealed that the national movement in
Dnipro Ukraine "was beginning to assume a mass character," the
second one demonstrated that in Galicia it had already "conquered
a share of political power."[226] In contrast, in another fragment Rudnytsky compares the development of historical research in Soviet
Ukraine in the 1920s and in Galicia, not in favor of the latter—and
not just because of the anti-Ukrainian policies of interwar Poland,
because in point of fact the greatest freedom was to be found precisely in the scholarly field. Rudnytsky denounces the "spirit of narrow utilitarianism (engineerism) and the Philistine-style notion of
'organic work'" among the general Ukrainian populace, and among

---

224 Ibid., 196.
225 Rudnytsky, "Ukrainian National Movement," in his *Essays*, 375–76.
226 Ibid., 376.

nationalistically inclined young people in particular – a "'Romantic'-voluntarist world perception that was fundamentally hostile to
scholarly knowledge."[227]

A brilliant example of the comparative method in the field of
intellectual history is Rudnytsky's juxtaposition of seemingly insig-
nificant phenomena: Volodymyr Vynnychenko's programmatic
vegetarianism in the 1930s and a forgotten brochure by the nationalist essayist Volodymyr Martynets entitled *Za zuby i pazuri natsii*
(For the Nation's Teeth and Claws, 1937). The former underlined
the utopianism of Vynnychenko's ideas of "concordism" (a system
of cooperative economy and the moral renewal of humanity by
means of a "return" to nature). In contrast, the latter serves as an
unexpected but apt symbol of the radical-nationalist program and,
I should add, the anthropomorphic nature of the nationalist imagination, steeped in Social Darwinism (according to which the
Ukrainian nation emerged as a single organism that found itself in
a struggle against other nations). Martynets called upon Ukrainians
to eat as much meat as possible, in order, as Rudnytsky put it, "to
foster among Ukrainians bloodthirsty instincts, which he considered most praiseworthy from the point of view of nationalist ideology."[228]

Even more astonishing yet more important to Rudnytsky was
the comparison between Vynnychenko and Dontsov. He saw a similarity between these two thinkers from opposing ideological
camps, not in content but in the "style of their political culture."[229]
Both of them were natives of Steppe Ukraine and once belonged to
the Ukrainian Social Democratic Workers' Party, but for Rudnytsky
the explanation of the similarity of style lay in something else: "both
were typical Russian intellectuals."[230] In his view, this is precisely

---

227 Lysiak-Rudnytsky, "Struktura," in Sysyn and Hrytsak, *Istorychni ese*, 1: 195.
228 Ivan L. Rudnytsky, "Volodymyr Vynnychenko's Ideas in the Light of His Poli-
     tical Writings," in his *Essays*, 417–36, here 432.
229 Ibid., 433.
230 Ibid. It was Volodymyr Doroshenko who first called Dontsov a "typical Russian
     intelligent" in his 1931 letter to Yevhen Malaniuk, which caused Dontsov's spi-

what defined the ideological, doctrinaire nature and political radicalism of both these figure. This view of Rudnytsky's is closely
linked to his controversial comparison between Ukrainian communism and twentieth-century Ukrainian radical nationalism as
two fundamentally similar but ideologically opposed "Ukrainian
totalitarian trends."[231] Rudnytsky's theory that in the 1920s
"communism had become a Ukrainian political trend" had already
sparked a negative reaction in the diaspora, which the historian
wrote about in a letter to Roman Szporluk dated 16 August 1969.[232]
Of course, Rudnytsky had in mind the Borotbists and members of
the "other" Ukrainian Communist Party (*Ukrainska komunistychna
partiia*, or Ukapisty, 1920–25), as well as the later current of
"national communism," but not the main party line of the then Bolshevik leadership of the Ukrainian SSR. At the same time, he rejected the ideological kinship between the Ukrainian communists
of the 1920s and Drahomanov, which they dearly wished to develop in order to present themselves as part of a long Ukrainian
tradition, for Drahomanov was in fact "a decided opponent" of
Marxism.[233]

Finally, what was important for Rudnytsky was the concepts
of continuity and interruption ("caesura") in Ukrainian intellectual
history. He frequently mentioned the "Mazepist emigration,"
which did not leave behind a long ideological trace, even though
the hypothetical possibility of the continuity of the Mazepist tradition was a fascinating topic for him. In the same way he comments
that the new wave of resistance in the Ukrainian SSR of the 1960s
was "not a direct continuation of former OUN nationalism, from

rited rebuttal, but this correspondence was only published in the 1990s. See Halyna Svarnyk, "Kilka shtrykhiv do ideinoi biohrafii Dmytra Dontsova," *Ukraina
Moderna*, no. 1 (1996): 150–56, here 154–55.

231 Ivan Lysiak-Rudnytsky, "Natsionalizm i totalitaryzm (vidpovid M. Prokopovi)," in Sysyn and Hrytsak, *Istorychni ese*, 2: 489–96, here 489.

232 This thesis appears in Rudnytsky, "Trends," in his *Essays*, 104. Rudnytsky's
1969 letter to Szporluk is published in Kravchenko, "Lystuvannia Romana
Shporliuka," 227. Cf. Rudnytsky's 1972 letter to Marko Antonovych quoted in
"Komentari," in Sysyn and Hrytsak, *Istorychni ese*, 2: 497–540, here 503.

233 Ivan L. Rudnytsky, "Drahomanov as Political Theorist," in his *Essays*, 203–54,
here 225.

which it differs in terms of its human cadres, methods of activity, and ideological orientation."[234] But the lack of continuity in this case was, in his estimation, a positive phenomenon because it opened up the possibility of the emergence of a democratic Ukrainian political platform within Soviet Ukraine. As is generally known, Rudnytsky was one of a handful of thinkers in the political emigration who pleaded for the formal sovereignty of the Ukrainian SSR to be taken seriously because in future it might become filled with real content—which, after all, is what happened when the Soviet Union collapsed.[235]

* * *

The scholarly legacy of Ivan Lysiak Rudnytsky offers marvelous examples of how the intellectual history of modern Ukraine can be written. His creative method included the establishment of a link between ideas and social processes, a broad comparative approach to ideological and cultural phenomena, as well as the microhistorical method of studying ideological currents through biographical "case studies." The historian's critical self-reflection and treatment of national mythology as a research topic, rather than a symbol of faith, determined the longevity of Rudnytsky's original ideas about the Ukrainian past and present.

Translated from the Ukrainian by Marta Daria Olynyk

---

234 Lysiak-Rudnytsky, "Natsionalizm i totalitaryzm," in Sysyn and Hrytsak, *Isto-rychni ese*, 2: 491.
235 On this, see Yaroslav Hrytsak, "Ivan L. Rudnytsky and His Visit to the Soviet Union (1970)," in Alessandro Achilli, Serhy Yekelchyk, and Dmytro Yesypenko, eds., *Cossacks in Jamaica, Ukraine at the Antipodes: Essays in Honor of Marko Pavlyshyn* (Boston: Academic Studies Press, 2020), 543–53.

6. Nationhood and Modernity in North American Surveys of Ukrainian History

Subtelny's History and Its Predecessors

Orest Subtelny's *Ukraine: A History* appeared in 1988, at a most opportune time. The Soviet Union was crumbling, and the political ferment unfolding in Ukraine would soon capture international attention, especially after the republic's declaration of independence in 1991. Subtelny's survey found wide readership in the West, and even more so in Ukraine, where a Ukrainian translation first came out in 1991, appearing in installments in the flagship *Ukrainskyi istorychnyi zhurnal* (The Ukrainian Historical Journal) and, later that year, as a book. During this heady period of political change, the Ukrainian public was craving a non-Soviet version of Ukrainian history, while history instructors were casting about for a new model of national history. Subtelny's work satisfied all these demands both in Ukraine and the West, becoming the yardstick against which all subsequent surveys would be measured.

Subtelny's work succeeded in large part because it was not just a patriotic narrative, but also a modern one that engaged with the then current trends in Western historical scholarship. One can argue that this survey's conceptual foundations also made it relatively easy for post-Soviet Ukrainian historians to adopt Subtelny's central notions of economic and social modernization and the steady development of the Ukrainian national movement. Subtelny's narrative made sense to those who knew by heart the previous framework of the Soviet Union as a modernization project. The "sociological" Soviet approach to the history of the Russian revolutionary movement prepared readers for accepting the historical evolution of the Ukrainian movement from gentry Romanticism to the *hromadas* and the political parties of the early twentieth century. It also underscored the importance of the national intelligentsia and its access to the masses. Lenin's famous dictum about the importance of a party newspaper as a collective propagandist and organizer primed Ukrainian readers for understanding Benedict Anderson's explanation of how modern nations are "imagined." Of course, Subtelny's book often offered interpretations that were diametrically opposed to those found in Soviet Ukrainian scholarship, but the categories it employed were relatively easy to grasp.[236]

In the Ukrainian context, Subtelny's book made such a splash, not (or not simply) because it restored to prominence the national paradigm of Ukrainian history, but because it did so in a way that was explicitly "modern" and intuitively accepted as a "proper" replacement for Soviet historical models. The other alternative was, of course, to revert to the pre-Soviet historical models of Mykhailo Hrushevsky or Dmytro Doroshenko, but their writings belonged to the age before the advances of modern social science came to inform historical research. Both of these luminaries avoided clear engagement with modern sociological theories — or, for that matter, even clear statements of their theoretical arguments. It makes sense that, in independent Ukraine, more theoretically inclined historians found the writings of Viacheslav Lypynsky more interesting than those of Hrushevsky and Doroshenko, particularly with respect to the historical role of the national elites. Lypynsky made a close study of the European sociological concepts of his time and, in his historical works, did not shy away from overarching generalizations.

However, the attempts by Ukrainian scholars to portray him as the father of national "elite studies," whose theories provided a universal cue to Ukrainian history, sometimes resembled their previous efforts to include in every text the Soviet notion of the Communist Party's leading role. The European sociologists whom Lypynsky had been reading have long been out of favor in the West. In contrast, the notions of economic and social modernization remained very much part of the Western liberal discourse; they fit well with the development of civil society, which the West tried to encourage in Ukraine.

---

236 Volodymyr Masliichuk, "Orest Subtelny," *Historians.ua*, 1 August 2016, https://www.historians.in.ua/index.php/en/institutsiji-istorichnoji-nauki-v-ukrajini/1955-volodymyr-masliychuk-orest-subtelnyi.

Although Subtelny's conceptualization incorporated Lypyn-sky's most productive ideas about the role of the national elites in Ukrainian history, it did so within a decidedly modern framework based on the notions of modernization and nation building. This model was far easier to accept for those in Ukraine raised on Soviet narratives, but now seeking to overturn them. In the West, the mod-ernization paradigm made Subtelny's history of Ukraine relatable because most Western history surveys of the 1970s and early 1980s employed it in their conceptualization of world, European, and na-tional history.

When we think of Subtelny's magnum opus, it is easy to forget that it was written, not for the methodological guidance of Ukrain-ian historians, but rather as a textbook for a university-level course on Ukrainian history, possibly with the Ukrainian diaspora in Eng-lish-speaking countries in mind as a secondary market. The book's innovative features are best seen in comparison with the surveys of Ukrainian history in English that were used as textbooks or intro-ductory texts before its appearance in 1988. This chapter will dis-cuss three of them before returning to the analysis of Subtelny's work.

Toward a National History

The first widely used survey of Ukrainian history in English, pub-lished in Canada in 1939, was an international collaborative effort. As mentioned in the previous chapter, the leading Ukrainian histo-rian in the diaspora, Dmytro Doroshenko, who lived in Germany, toured Western Canada in 1936 on the invitation of the theninflu-ential Ukrainian Self-Reliance League (*Soiuz ukraintsiv-samosti-inykiv*, abbreviated in English as USRL). This organization sup-ported efforts to develop Ukrainian Orthodox structures and edu-cational institutions in Western Canada. Following Doroshenko's successful lecture tour, Ukrainian Canadian activists began explor-ing possibilities for creating Ukraine-related courses at universities in Western Canada. These plans did not come to fruition during the 1930s, but community activists managed to establish contacts with some Canadian Slavists sympathetic to the Ukrainian case, most notably Professor George W. Simpson, the influential historian and administrator at the University of Saskatchewan. It was Simpson who advised them to start by preparing textbooks in English.[237]

The USRL agreed to fund the publication of a textbook on Ukrainian history based on Doroshenko's reputable two-volume *Narys istorii Ukrainy* (Survey of Ukrainian History), which came out in Ukrainian in Poland in 1932–33.[238] Thomas M. Prymak, who reconstructed the history of these events, shows that Doroshenko promptly wrote additional chapters covering the events of the Ukrainian Revolution, and the German-based translator and librarian Hanna Chykalenko-Keller translated the book into English in fluid prose.[239] Simpson helped legitimize the book for non-Ukrainian academic audiences by adding an enthusiastic preface. All these factors taken together ensured the success of Doroshenko's survey in English. It was not surpassed by the English edition the following year of Mykhailo Hrushevsky's *Iliustrovana istoriia Ukrainy* (An Illustrated History of Ukraine), once a very popular one-volume work in Ukrainian and Russian, if somewhat outdated by the 1930s. Sponsored by the Ukrainian National Association (*Ukrainskyi narodnyi soiuz*) in the US, this translation included a preface by Professor George Vernadsky of Yale University and an update to the year 1940 by Professor O. J. Frederiksen of Miami University of Ohio, who also edited the translation. Nevertheless, the difficult prose and the truncation of Hrushevsky's long-winded positivist arguments into what contemporary reviewers saw as simplistic nationalist language resulted in this work's not gaining traction in academia.[240]

---

237 See Chap. 5 of this book and Thomas M. Prymak, *Gathering a Heritage: Ukrainian, Slavonic, and Ethnic Canada and the USA* (Toronto: University of Toronto Press, 2015), chaps. 5 and 7.

238 Dmytro Doroshenko, *Narys istorii Ukrainy*, 2 vols. (Warsaw: Ukrainskyi naukovyi instytut, 1932–33).

239 Prymak, *Gathering a Heritage*, 111.

240 Ibid., 107–110. See Michael Hrushevsky, *A History of Ukraine*, ed. O. J. Frederiksen, Preface by George Vernadsky (New Haven: Yale University Press for the Ukrainian National Association, 1941).

In contrast, Doroshenko's *History* was a success. The first two chapters, dealing with historiography, were cut in the English edition; in other respects, the editors did not change the sequence and content of chapters, compared to the Ukrainian original. Instead of being treated to a dense historiographical discussion, readers first encountered Simpson's Introduction legitimizing Doroshenko's narrative by making important ideological claims that could have been dismissed had they originated from a Ukrainian historian. Writing in June 1939, Simpson postulates that contemporary Ukrainians are being moved by a "powerful spirit of nationalism."[241] He speaks of the "Ukrainian movement for independence" reaching its apex in the seventeenth century and warns that, although, as of the summer of 1939, "Ukrainian nationalist hopes have been frustrated in every direction," national movements "are not lightly dissipated when they are rooted in historical tradition."[242]

In the English edition, Doroshenko refers to Kyivan Rus' as a "Ukrainian state" and insists that the Great Russians constitute a "different ethnic type" and are distinguished from Ukrainians by their "national character and political ideals."[243] However, such terminology sounded only somewhat outdated in comparison to the concepts of nationhood that Western historians employed at the time. It did not raise the red flags that the Hrushevsky translation had.

Doroshenko's *History* never discussed the overall framework of Ukrainian national history or its moving forces. Instead, it used two somewhat contradictory concepts of the struggle for Ukrainian independence without fully reconciling them. At the end of the chapter on the period of the Ruin (late seventeenth century), the author steps back from his narrative of events to comment on the historical aims of the Ukrainian nation. In line with his reputation as a historian of the statist school, Doroshenko does not doubt the

---

241 G. W. Simpson, introduction to *History of the Ukraine*, trans. and abridged Hannah Chykalenko-Keller, by D. Doroshenko (Edmonton: The Institute Press, 1939), 3–15, here 3.

242 Ibid., 13 and 15.

243 Ibid., 25 and 57.

Ukrainian instinct for independence, but he appears to lack the social and cultural conceptual instruments for explaining the failure
of Ukrainian efforts, which resulted in the transformation of their
land into a "desert":

> This desert was as a symbolic tombstone on the grave of the Ukrainian peo-
> ple's aspirations for independence, a people who would rather ruin their
> country and strew it with their bones than voluntarily accept an alien polit-
> ical and social order. But at the same time the Ukrainian people had shown
> that they were not sufficiently mature politically nor steadfast enough to
> grasp the aims of their own more far-sighted leaders and support them in
> the struggle for the realization of their lofty ideal. Ukrainians were too im-
> mature to sacrifice their immediate advantage to a remote ideal. In conse-
> quence they remained but the tools of their politically more advanced and
> better organized neighbors and ceased to be lords of their own land.[244]

If, in his discussion of the Cossack period, Doroshenko assumes at
once the Ukrainian people's innate "aspirations for independence"
and their "immaturity," his understanding of the nineteenth-century "national revival" is more in line with modern scholarship on
national movements. He asserts that the "national renaissance" began in the region where the Ukrainian historical tradition (understood as the legacy of "political and cultural autonomy") was
stronger, that is, in the former Hetmanate on the Left Bank of the
Dnipro. Yet he also acknowledges the importance of new ideas arriving from the West, beginning in the late eighteenth century. Like
Subtelny and the Ukrainian historians of the twenty-first century,
Doroshenko emphasizes the new "conception of nationality, of an
ethnic unity and its aspirations and rights," as well as the "rights of
peoples" proclaimed by the French Revolution.[245]

By the mid-nineteenth century, these conceptual innovations
gave rise to the "Ukrainian national movement, now entirely con-
secrated to cultural work among the masses."[246] Moreover, it included very few representatives of the landed elite, who could provide a living link to the tradition of Cossack statehood: "Deprived,

---

244 Ibid., 323.
245 Ibid., 530–31.
246 Ibid., 563.

with but few exceptions, of the support of the most influential and wealthy class in the Ukraine, that of the landowning nobles, the Ukrainian national movement was furthered by the efforts of the 'déclassé intelligentsia.'"[247] Although one might expect from a historian of the statist school and, moreover, former foreign minister under Hetman Pavlo Skoropadsky, to see some historical logic in the creation in 1918 of this short-lived Hetmanate, Doroshenko remains faithful to his emphasis on the Ukrainian intelligentsia's role in the national movement. The Skoropadsky administration "did not consider it necessary to take in the account the feelings of the Ukrainian intelligentsia," but it was the intelligentsia-led "national revival actually leading to the creation of a Ukrainian independent State."[248] Doroshenko's surprisingly modern interpretation is much more persuasive here than in the chapters on the Cossack period, where the notion of "political maturity" functions more like a metaphor than an analytical concept.

Doroshenko's emphasis on the national movement consolidating the modern Ukrainian ethnic nation brings his analysis of the Ukrainian Revolution very close to the interpretations that are widespread in Ukraine today. He refers to the Bolshevik invasion of the Ukrainian People's Republic in 1917 as the "Ukrainian-Russian War." Accordingly, the Bolshevik assault on the Directory in late 1918 and early 1919 becomes the Second Ukrainian-Russian War.[249] The Bolshevik-controlled Ukrainian Socialist Soviet Republic exists, as the section title stresses, "in the Russian Soviet Union."[250]

Instead of ending his narrative either in Soviet Ukraine or by discussing the condition of Ukrainians in Poland, Romania, and Czechoslovakia, Doroshenko does something that subsequent Ukrainian historians will emulate. The final section of his last chapter in the 1939 edition is called "Ukrainian Political Refugees." The

---

247 Ibid., 585.
248 Ibid., 638.
249 Ibid., 623 and 639.
250 Ibid., 647. Soviet Ukraine's official name was changed in 1937 to the Ukrainian Soviet Socialist Republic.

story of Ukraine thus ends not in Ukraine itself, but with politically engaged Ukrainian émigrés who promote the "idea of Ukrainian political independence."[251] Subtelny's survey will use a similar scheme, in which the story of the Ukrainian nation ends with the true keepers of the national cause — the diaspora.

However, for a survey of Ukrainian history published in 1939, Doroshenko's book did not prepare its readers properly for understanding Soviet Ukraine. The relevant section of the last chapter is not even two pages long. The Holodomor, which is not known under this name yet, does not even get a full sentence; the role of the Stalinist authorities remains ambiguous. They wanted to crush the resistance of Ukrainian peasants, but they did no more than "[allow] millions of the population to perish from terrible hunger in 1932."[252] Doroshenko briefly covers the cultural policies of the 1920s and the repressions against the Ukrainian intelligentsia during the 1930s, but the economic and social transformations of this period are not mentioned at all. However, this is not unexpected of a work produced during the interwar period.

Modernization and Modern Ukraine

During the postwar decades Doroshenko's survey remained a standard North American textbook and reference source in English. It was only in the 1980s that the *Encyclopedia of Ukraine* (5 vols., 1984–93) and Subtelny's *Ukraine: A History* provided updated and more modern accounts of Ukraine's past. By that time, Doroshenko's account already existed in an updated version. In 1975 Professor Oleh W. Gerus of the University of Manitoba published Doroshenko's survey, which included additional chapters written by Gerus, bringing the book's coverage to 1975.[253]

Gerus succeeded in updating Doroshenko's text while preserving his overall interpretation of Ukrainian history. This was

---

251 Ibid., 654.

252 Ibid., 648.

253 Dmytro Doroshenko, *A Survey of Ukrainian History*, ed., updated (1914–75), and with an introduction by Oleh W. Gerus (Winnipeg: Humeniuk Publication Foundation, 1975).

made easier by the fact that the two historians shared some research interests, such as the history of the Orthodox Church and the Ukrainian diaspora in Canada. At the same time, Gerus made Doroshenko sound more familiar for the new generations of patriotic Ukrainians abroad – politically engaged postwar refugees and their children. The 1939 edition of Doroshenko lacked chapter titles; like in the Ukrainian original, chapter numbers were followed by a short list of topics covered therein. Gerus supplied chapter titles that articulated the overall scheme of Ukrainian history as a struggle for national statehood. For example, the chapter on the late seventeenth century acquired the title "Struggle for Unity," and the one about Hetman Ivan Mazepa was entitled "An Attempt to Obtain Independence." This trend fit with the names of chapters that Gerus authored: The events of 1917 became framed as "The Road to Independence," and the chapter on Hetman Pavlo Skoropadsky was titled simply "The Ukrainian Statehood." Chapter titles did not impose on Doroshenko's text an alien interpretive scheme, but removed the ambiguities one could find in chapters featuring little or no historical analysis. Interestingly, Gerus's decision to rewrite the chapters on World War I and the Ukrainian Revolution appears fully justified. Doroshenko was a contemporary and active participant of these events, but for that very reason his narrative was unbalanced – privileging the topics he knew best because of his personal involvement – and lacking the conceptual apparatus for the study of the revolutionary period that became developed in English between the late 1950s and early 1970s. In other words, Doroshenko did know Richard Pipes's study about the formation of the Soviet Union or the early works of social historians about the role of the peasantry in the "Russian" Revolution, but the text Gerus added was already informed by these trends.[254]

Gerus's chapters on Soviet Ukraine retained Doroshenko's general focus on political history and national culture; a detailed

---

254 See, e.g., Richard Pipes, *The Formation of the Soviet Union: Communism and Nationalism, 1917–1923* (Cambridge, Mass.: Harvard University Press, 1954) and Moshe Lewin, *Russian Peasants and Soviet Power: A Study of Collectivization*, trans. John Biggart and Irene Nove, Preface by Alec Nove (London: Allen and Unwin, 1968).

treatment of the collectivization is a notable exception. Gerus does not use the term "Holodomor," but he classifies it as a "form of genocide" with between two and seven millions victims.[255] In the chapters on the postwar period, Gerus returns the locus of contemporary Ukrainian history from the diaspora to Soviet Ukraine. It was the dissident movement there during the 1960s and early 1970s that offered new hope to the diaspora. But acknowledging the potential of Ukrainian dissidents also meant the need to re-examine Soviet Ukraine in a search for the social and cultural processes that made the dissident movement possible. In his quest for an explanation, Gerus zeroes in on de-Stalinization, which allowed Soviet Ukrainian intellectuals to reclaim the national culture that Stalin had destroyed. He does not focus on the concept of modernization, which will offer such an explanation to Orest Subtelny or Bohdan Krawchenko. However, this term appears in Gerus's text one time, in a sentence about the "socio-economic ramifications of industrialization and modernization."[256] Gerus connects the "change in the sociological fabric of Ukraine" to the successes of Ukrainization during the late 1920s.[257] Social change is very much present in Gerus's narrative, although its connection to the Ukrainian national movement is often implied rather than clearly articulated. Gerus points to social mobility as potentially contributing to cultural assimilation, but at the same time he hypothesizes that the competition for jobs between ethnic Ukrainians and Russians in the Ukrainian republic resulted in "economically stimulated national tensions," which he sees as potentially more dangerous to the Soviet regime than intellectual dissent.[258]

The Gerus update ends on a high note. Although he includes a discussion of émigré communities in the final chapter on "Contemporary Ukraine," it ends with a section entitled "Prospects for the Future," returning the center of Ukrainian history back to

---

255 Doroshenko, *Survey*, 698.
256 Ibid., 811.
257 Ibid., 692.
258 Ibid., 813.

Ukraine. Gerus endows Soviet Ukrainians with agency: "Concerned with their survival as a distinct nation, they have insisted on a stricter adherence to the federal provisions."[259] He compares the leaders of Soviet Ukraine to the eighteenth-century Cossack hetmans who recognized Russian domination, but "resented excessive centralization and struggled to preserve Ukrainian autonomy."[260] He also believes that Ukrainian youth "are opposed to assimilation and do sympathize with the dissenters."[261]

For a Western reader of the late 1970s and early 1980s, the period following the removal of Petro Shelest as first secretary of the Communist Party in Ukraine and the nearly complete suppression of the dissident movement, such optimism might appear unjustified. Nevertheless, the story of Ukraine's road to independence between 1985 and 1991 confirmed that, for better or worse, thet next stage in Ukrainian history stemmed directly from the Soviet Ukrainian experience.

The focus on Soviet Ukraine is even more pronounced in a short survey of Ukrainian history by Roman Szporluk, then professor of East European History at the University of Michigan Ann Arbor. This pocket-size book did not receive wide distribution in North America or internationally; the Detroit Festival Committee published the first edition in 1979 and the second in 1982, both in small print runs.[262] Nevertheless, the author generously handed out copies to his colleagues, many of whom became influenced by this small book. As late as 2022, the prominent Ukrainian historian Yaroslav Hrytsak referred to Szporluk's pocketbook as one of the two best histories of Ukraine, the second being Andreas Kappeler's brief survey in German.[263]

---

259 Ibid., 808.
260 Ibid., 810.
261 Ibid.
262 Roman Szporluk, *Ukraine: A Brief History*, 2nd ed. (Detroit: Ukrainian Festival Committee, 1982).
263 Iaroslav [Yaroslav] Hrytsak, *Podolaty mynule: Hlobalna istoriia Ukrainy* (Kyiv: Portal, 2022), 14. The other history mentioned is Andreas Kappeler, *Kleine Geschichte der Ukraine* (Munich: C. H. Beck, 1994), which appeared in a Ukrainian

Szporluk starts his survey with the unambiguous statement that "Ukraine today is politically constituted as the Ukrainian Soviet Socialist Republic."[264] His focus on Soviet Ukraine's promise is only reinforced by the decision not to include any treatment of the Ukrainian diaspora. Szporluk also states early on his main thesis, which Subtelny eventually borrowed: Ukrainians are similar to the Latvians, Finns, Czechs, and Croats in that they "experienced the major sociocultural transformations of the modern period within larger political structures, which were dominated by people of different ethnic identity."[265] Since Ukrainians had not fully assimilated and, according to Szporluk, had preserved their political aspirations, their modern history logically becomes that of the Ukrainian national movement. To study it, Szporluk introduces the model created by the Czech scholar Miroslav Hroch, who divided such movements of "stateless" nations in East-Central Europe into academic, cultural, and political phases.[266] Hroch's sociological scheme accounted for the type of patriotic activity and activists' access to the masses. Together with the concept of modernization under alien rule, Subtelny would use it prominently in his survey. Through his and Szporluk's mediation, this model of the national movement was introduced in Ukraine during the early 1990s.

Given the focus on the national movement, it is not surprising that Szporluk's Chapter 3, devoted to "The Making of Modern Ukraine," begins with the events of the late eighteenth century. It is equally logical that the final chapter, "Contemporary Ukraine: Problems and Prospects," is by far the longest of those covering the twentieth century. Szporluk's sociological approach is obvious in this chapter, which begins with a section on "Population Data," but

---

translation as Andreas Kappeler, *Mala istoriia Ukrainy*, trans. O. Blashchuk (Kyiv: K. I. S., 2007).

264 Szporluk, *Ukraine*, ix.

265 Ibid., xi.

266 Ibid., 41. See Miroslav Hroch, *Die Vorkämpfer der nationalen Bewegung bei denkleinen Völkern Europas* (Prague: Universita Karlova, 1968), published in English as Miroslav Hroch, *Social Preconditions of National Revival in Europe: A Comparative Analysis of the Social Composition of Patriotic Groups among the Smaller European Nations*, trans. Ben Fowkes (Cambridge: Cambridge University Press, 1985).

later includes separate sections on "Demographic Developments" and "Population and Politics." In the second edition, the author repeatedly brings up the Polish experience of 1980–81: the creation of the independent trade union "Solidarity" and mass social protests acquiring a political dimension. Szporluk leaves open the question of whether something similar might happen in Soviet Ukraine, but he does suggest that the social problems underlying the Polish protests are present in Soviet Ukraine as well.[267] In any case, the Polish example validates Szporluk's emphasis on contemporary Ukrainian society. The next page of Ukrainian history, whatever it would be, was to be written in Soviet Ukraine.

Orest Subtelny's *Ukraine: A History* (1st ed., 1988) further developed the application of Hroch's concepts to the Ukrainian case, but combined them with notions of Ukraine as a "borderland," which could be found in the works of Hrushevsky and his followers. At the same time, Subtelny borrowed from Doroshenko and the statist school the idea of the Ukrainians' constant strivings to establish their own polity.

Subtelny stresses in the Preface to the first edition the two main themes of his book —"statelessness" and "modernization."[268] According to him, the fact that modernization in Ukraine "occurred largely under the aegis of non-Ukrainians" had a major impact on Ukrainian history: "To this day a crucial dichotomy still exists between things Ukrainian and modern."[269]

However, the author's "Introduction: The Earliest Times" brings into the discussion another major factor: Ukraine's geographical and, subsequently, cultural position as a "borderland" located "on the southeastern edge of Europe, on the threshold of Asia, along the fringes of the Mediterranean world, and astride the once important border between sheltering forests and the open steppe."[270] The influence of Hrushevsky and his school is obvious in this definition, but in Subtelny's Introduction the notion of

---

267 Ibid., 131–32, 135, and 140.
268 Subtelny, *Ukraine: A History* (Toronto: University of Toronto Press, 1988), xv.
269 Ibid.
270 Ibid., 3.

Ukraine at the crosscurrents of cultures appears to be less significant than the interpretation of Ukraine's geographical position as
leading to "devastating foreign invasions and conquests." This connection is important for him as a segue to the thesis that "foreign
domination and the struggle against it is a paramount theme in
[Ukrainian] history."[271]

As his narrative unfolds, Subtelny keeps fine-tuning his idea
of what constituted the most important trend in Ukrainian history.
In the short opening of Chapter 4 ("Under Polish and Lithuanian
Rule") he elaborates on what foreign domination meant: "No
longer dominant but dominated, the natives of Ukraine would have
to struggle not only for their political self-determination but also for
their existence as a separate ethnic and national entity. This effort
became — and remains to this day — one of the major themes of
Ukrainian history."[272] Indeed, the presence in some form of the
Ukrainian nation as a conscious subject of history with clearly defined national aims marks Subtelny's narrative of Ukrainian history
from the fourteenth century to post-Soviet Ukraine. By so doing,
the Canadian historian fused the notions of the Hrushevsky school
with those found in the writings of Lypynsky and Doroshenko —
and arrived at an interpretation that perfectly fit the demand of the
diaspora and post-communist Ukrainian audiences.

Chapter 13, "The Growth of National Consciousness," with its
opening section entitled "The Modern Idea of Nationhood," might
seem to contradict the book's overall argument, inasmuch as it discusses the reinvention of the nation according to Hroch's model.
However, Subtelny's insistence on statelessness as one of the book's
two main themes saves the day: The nation needed to be reconstructed because it has lost its state tradition and native elite.

The treatment of Soviet Ukraine and the diaspora presents a
greater challenge for Subtelny, in part because of the way the University of Toronto Press dealt with the design of the subsequent
editions. The publisher chose to leave unchanged the chapters from
the first edition, while adding new chapters at the end. This meant

---

271 Ibid., 5.
272 Ibid., 69.

that subsequent editions were still discussing the Soviet period in the present tense. In subsequent editions, Chapter 26, which brought the coverage to the spring of 1987, also ends with the concluding statement that "a cloud of uncertainty hangs heavily over Ukraine and the Ukrainians."[273] It is followed by two chapters dealing with Ukrainians abroad, which end with the conclusion that a major function of the Ukrainian diaspora "has been to preserve the political and cultural values and traditions of non-Soviet Ukraine," as well as to "speak up for Ukrainian interests, when compatriots in Soviet Ukraine were forced to be silent."[274] Yet, the stories of Soviet Ukraine and the diaspora are never reconciled; their relations as of 1987 are identified as "antagonistic."[275] This definition is generally correct if one means the leadership of Soviet Ukraine and the leading political forces of the diaspora. Still, the chapters dealing with the independence period never really delve into the diaspora's important role in the shaping of post-communist Ukraine.

The unintended effect of this omission is that the issue of agency in the development of a new Ukraine does not receive full treatment. Gorbachev's reforms enabled the educational and mobilization efforts of Ukrainian intellectuals, but the global context of their activities and the origins of their notion of "Ukraine" remain unclear. At some level, this misbalance also enabled a more simplistic reading of Subtelny's argument, the primordialist one, which assumes that the striving for an independent *soborna* Ukraine – encompassing all the Ukrainian ethnolinguistic territories – is inherent to all ethnic Ukrainians.

Subtelny's survey proved such a success because each segment of the audience found in it confirmation of their own views. Historians welcomed the effort to write Ukraine into the story of modernization, specialists on Eastern Europe appreciated the application of the Hroch model, and general readers embraced the notions of statelessness as responsible for any problems in contemporary Ukraine. The concept of a permanent struggle against foreign

273   Ibid., 537.
274   Ibid., 572.
275   Ibid.

domination and for Ukrainian statehood also dovetailed with the attitudes in the diaspora and newly independent Ukraine, in part because they had been formed by the older non-Soviet surveys of Ukrainian history, and Doroshenko's book in particular.

* * *

In this chapter I have shown that the predecessors of Subtelny's survey were surprisingly modern. Although Doroshenko never elaborates on his understanding of the Ukrainian nation or the meaning of its history before the late eighteenth century, his analysis of the Ukrainian national movement during the nineteenth and twentieth centuries is very similar to that of present-day historians. Doroshenko's survey also established the tradition of including coverage of the Ukrainian diaspora at the end of histories of Ukraine, thus depicting the political refugees abroad as the true carriers of the national tradition. In his 1975 updated edition of Doroshenko's history, Gerus established the importance of the Soviet experience for understanding Ukraine's national tragedies and the promise one could see in the manifestation of autonomism and dissent. He also introduced the notion of modernization as a factor shaping the development of twentieth-century Ukraine. In his pocketbook history (1979/1982), Szporluk clearly stated a thesis that would become the major argument of Subtelny's survey—that Ukraine underwent modernization as a stateless nation under foreign domination and that this circumstance explains much about the political, social, and cultural processes in modern Ukraine. Finally, Subtelny's history (1988) successfully combined the notion of the Hrushevsky school, such as Ukraine as a borderland, with the concept of Ukraine's modernization taking place during the stateless period in its history. In other words, Subtelny's greatest achievement was fusing the arguments of various historical schools and striking the right balance between scholarly conceptualization and popular understanding of strivings for independence as the main feature of Ukrainian history.

Part III

New Historical Methodology and the Ukrainian Intellectual Tradition

7. The Ukrainian Tradition of Spatial History

In the West in recent decades spatial history has evolved into a powerful interdisciplinary field of historical research. It is based on theoretical propositions about the complex symbiosis between landscape and social life, which rely on the works of Henri Lefebvre. In *The Production of Space*, Lefebvre formulated an important theory, according to which space is neither empty nor simply decorations of the historical process. Instead, people create it and constantly change their relationship with the environment. In this way, space becomes simultaneously a product and a participant in the historical process.[276] Lefebvre's disciples developed these theses by pointing out that the environment also constantly affects social life. It makes certain things more possible or impossible and prescribes goals for people. After all, the consequences of a previous interaction between society and landscape determine their future relations.[277]

This conceptual apparatus in and of itself presented an opportunity to reinterpret many historical processes that are crucial in the history of Ukraine, from the settlement of the South in the late eighteenth century to the space of social protest in the urban revolutions of the early twenty-first century. However, the potential and popularity of spatial history markedly increased after the emergence of a new methodological instrument — the technologies known as the Global Positioning System (GPS) and Geographic Information System (GIS), both of which enable the visualization of complex spatial processes as well a more thorough study of the history of society in its spatial dimension.

The aim of this chapter is to offer a survey of new possibilities that spatial history is opening up for Ukrainian humanities, as well as to discuss some examples of the reception of spatial methods in

---

276 Henri Lefebvre, *The Production of Space* (Oxford: Blackwell, 1991).
277 See, e.g., Edward W. Soja, *Postmodern Geographies: The Reassertion of Space in Critical Social Theory* (London: Verso, 1989); Karl Schlögel, *Im Raume lesen wir die Zeit: Über Zivilisationsgeschichte und Geopolitik* (Munich: Carl Hanser, 2003).

Ukrainian historical writing in recent decades. I argue that the experience of the Hrushevsky school of the 1920s, and the powerful tradition of Ukrainian regional studies are creating favourable conditions for the development of Ukrainian spatial history. The second part of the chapter demonstrates that Ukrainian history offers a plethora of topics, the study of which would benefit from the methods of spatial history.

The Space of History

Even though the conceptual and methodological apparatus of spatial sistory is new, historians of Ukraine have dealt with tangential issues over the centuries. Concepts that are central to traditional historical narratives, like the role of the trade route "from the Varangians to the Greeks" in the emergence of the ancient Rus' state or the rise of the Ukrainian Cossack Host on the southern steppe border, are an excellent fit for reinterpretation in the framework of contemporary spatial history. At the same time, however, we must bear in mind the essential difference between the contemporary understanding of the interaction between humans and nature and the geographic determinism of older scholarship that reflected the then-prevalent ideas about nature as a space for human conquest. The notion of human society and the environment being part of a single ecosystem, as well as special attention to ecological questions, only came to prominence in recent decades.

However, new directions in the study of Ukraine's regions, which could have led to the formulation of innovative concepts of historical space, were already developing in Ukrainian historical science in the mid-to-late 1920s, until its forcible Stalinist dogmatization. Worth mentioning here is Mykhailo Hrushevsky's research project on Ukraine's historical regions, which was suspended before the publication of a fascinating collection of articles on the history of the Ukrainian steppe and the South. It has been established that, as of 1929, it contained 24 articles totalling almost 900 typed pages and was entitled *"Poludneva Ukraina"* (Southern Ukraine).[278] In his extant introduction to the collection entitled "The Steppe and the Sea in the History of Ukraine," Hrushevsky occasionally goes beyond the framework of the traditional tasks of "acquiring knowledge about the general social process in given physical and geographic conditions," as it was also his intention to research the reciprocal influence, both economic and demographic, of various regions and "how these relations changed in connection with colonizing, cultural, and political changes."[279]

Hrushevsky also underscored the importance of a new approach to so-called historical regions, which would focus on the experience of migration and the reciprocal influence of life and work in various geographic and economic conditions. After all, "until recently and, one can say, even today 'Novorossiia' and 'Ukraine' were thought of as separate, disparate concepts not connected organically."[280] Instead, he proposed to investigate not only the "constancy, spontaneous invincibility, and organicity" of the process of the South's Ukrainian colonization, but also to determine the reverse influences of steppe colonization on the life of the population inhabiting the forest and forest-steppe zone.[281] Hrushevsky also rejected the traditional view of the steppe as an antagonist in Ukrainian history, and pushed for seeing the "Ukrainian population in symbiosis with it."[282] In addition, he proposed applying the historical method to the cultural identification of regions, inasmuch as the "colonizing mass of both Novorossiia and the Crimea and the Donets Basin and the Caucasian Riviera, with all the changes of external regimes and forms, remained mostly Ukrainian," and the national mosaic of these regions that "were covered by single-hued

---

278 Nadiia Shvaiba, "Komisiia Poludnevoi Ukrainy VUAN (1926–1930 rr.)," *Naukovi zapysky Instytutu ukrainskoi arkheohrafii ta dzhereloznavstva im. M. S. Hrushevskoho NANU* 12 (2006): 328–38, here 335.

279 Mykhailo Hrushevsky, "Step i more v istorii Ukrainy: Kilka sliv shchodo plianu i perspektyv tsoho doslidu," *Ukrainskyi istoryk*, nos. 3-4 (1991–92): 54–68, here 54.

280 Ibid., 58.

281 Ibid., 58–59.

282 Ibid., 64.

Russification" from above should also be viewed as part of the history of Ukraine.[283]

Western historians, and I am one of them, have written about the way that in our time the so-called "national paradigm," although historically progressive during the period when it emerged, can impoverish historical accounts and make them teleological.[284] This especially concerns local and regional history, during the work on which historians must constantly check themselves to see whether they are writing with an end result in mind, that is, the admittance of a given locale to one modern state or another. But, in the case of Ukrainian scholarship of the 1920s, we are dealing with the moment of deconstruction of the imperial narrative, which makes national history a more critical and more creative conceptual fulcrum.

Regrettably, this potential of Ukrainian historiography of the 1920s, like its openness to Western influences and to a political — not just cultural-ethnographic — understanding of nation, was not fully realized because of the Stalinist turn to a dogmatic, simplistic version of Marxist social science. In the *Short Course on the History of the Communist Party of the Soviet Union (Bolsheviks)*, the environment is treated as a part of nature, and nature as an external factor that can "speed up or slow down the development of society" but does not exert a "definitive influence" on this process.[285] Obviously, Stalin, who wrote the subsection on "Dialectical and Historical Materialism," was primarily concerned with the critique of geographic determinism, not with the consequences of human activities.[286]

In the 1960s the attempts of some Soviet geographers, first and foremost, Vsevolod Anuchin, to propose a more complex Marxist

283   Ibid., 67.
284   See Serhii Plokhy, *Ukraine and Russia: Representations of the Past* (Toronto: University of Toronto Press, 2008), 288–89 and chap. 1 of this book.
285   *Istoriia Vsesoiuznoi kommunisticheskoi partii (bolshevikov): Kratkii kurs* (Moscow: OGIZ, 1946), 113.
286   On Stalin's authorship of this section, see David Brandenberger and Mikhail Zelenov, "Editors' Introduction," in *Stalin's Master Narrative: A Critical Edition of the History of the Communist Party of the Soviet Union (Bolsheviks), Short Course*, ed. David Brandenberger and Mikhail Zelenov (New Haven: Yale University Press, 2019), 1–85, here 51–52.

definition of the environment as "materialized labor" (Rus. *ovesh-chestvlennyi trud* or the Ger. *vergegenständlichte Arbeit* in Marx's writings), that is, as the result of historical interaction with society, were criticized by the scholarly establishment.[287] One way or another, they did not leave any discernible mark on historical scholarship of that period, let alone in the Ukrainian SSR.

The History of Space

It is telling that, after the Soviet collapse, the revival of research on space as a historical and social category began practically at the point where Hrushevsky and his associates left off, although this time around the theoretical push came from the West. Anton Kotenko, who published an article in 2010 about the spatial turn in the social sciences in *Ukrainskyi humanitarnyi ohliad* (Ukrainian Humanities Review), defended his English-language doctoral dissertation at the Central European University about the formulation of a concept of Ukrainian national territory from the nineteenth century to the early twentieth.[288] Ukrainian readers were thus acquainted with spatial history in its current Western variant (founded on the works of Lefebvre and his disciples) by a scholar who studied the spatial dimension of the Ukrainian national project at a time when European multinational empires were in crisis and national movements within them sought to claim their ethnolinguistic territories. Kotenko's article was in fact a survey of tangential Western theoretical literature, which was supplemented in 2012 by Olena Betlii's response article with its emphasis on historical research.[289] Whereas Kotenko came to spatial studies from the field of "mental map-

---

287 On this, see Iurii Gladkii, *Gumanitarnaia geografiia kak nauchnoe znanie* (Moscow: Direkt-mediia, 2016), 398–401.

288 Anton Kotenko, "The Ukrainian Project in Search of National Space, 1861–1914" (PhD diss., Budapest: Central European University, 2013).

289 Anton Kotenko, "Povernennia prostoru," *Ukrainskyi humanitarnyi ohliad*, no. 15 (2010): 45–60; Olena Betlii, "Istoryk na pozovakh iz prostorom, abo Chy mozhlyva sinkhronizovana istoriia," *Ukrainskyi humanitarnyi ohliad*, nos. 16–17 (2012): 132–51; Anton Kotenko, "Space Oddity," *Ukrainskyi humanitarnyi ohliad*, no. 18 (2013): 172–76.

ping," which now has its own respectable history, Betlii is a researcher of urban history, a field in which the spatial approach developed earlier than in others — and with the most revealing results. The exchange of ideas between these two researchers not only in-formed readers about the achievements of Western spatial history, but also provided the research agenda for Ukrainian scholars. In particular, Betlii proposed the possible application of the spatial approach to the history of Kyiv by using the geographical stratification method for medieval, early modern, and modern strata.[290]

At the time of this discussion the spatial approach has already begun to be introduced to Ukrainian historical scholarship by several enterprising research centers that could react more swiftly to the new global trends. In 2005 the Center for Urban History of East Central Europe in Lviv, an independent, privately-funded research institute, began implementing various programs to study the urban space of Lviv and other regions. In recent years these have included the Internet-based "Interactive Lviv," a project aimed at researching the landscapes of the Russian Empire's industrial South, and a project to study planned residential neighbourhoods of the late Soviet period.[291] The results of these multi-year projects include several important books, notably, one that explores the Lviv district of Sykhiv, which was constructed as a cohesive, planned project beginning in 1979, and another, devoted to the industrial "mono-towns" (company towns) of the Donbas.[292] In 2010 a group of young researchers in Kyiv devoted the second issue of the left-leaning journal of social criticism *Spilne* (Common Cause) to the transformation of the urban space, and in 2015 a group of young scholars and curators from the independent Visual Culture Research Center

---

290 Betlii, "Istoryk na pozyvakh," 143.
291 See "Doslidnytski proekty," Tsentr miskoi istorii Tsentralno-Skhidnoi Ievropy, http://www.lvivcenter.org/uk/researchprojects.
292 Volodymyr Kulikov and Iryna Sklokina, eds., *Pratsia, vysnazhennia ta uspikh: Promyslovi monomista Donbasu* (Lviv: FOP Shumylovych, 2018); Natalia Otrishchenko, ed., *Sykhiv: Prostory, pamiati, praktyky* (Lviv: FOP Shumylovych, 2018).

published a bilingual alternative guidebook entitled *The Book of Kyiv/Kyivska knyzhka*.[293]

Meanwhile, in the 2010s the Harvard Ukrainian Research Institute (HURI) launched "MAPA: Digital Atlas of Ukraine," which was initially aimed at producing a detailed map of the Holodomor. This map became not only a visualization tool but also a scholarly instrument that has allowed researchers to highlight the particular brutality of the Holodomor in Kyiv and Kharkiv oblasts, regions that were not so much agricultural as politically important for the Stalinist regime in its struggle against Ukrainian "nationalists."[294] Hereafter, the MAPA project, in collaboration with various scholarly institutions in Ukraine, added new research areas, for example, a linguistic mosaic of independent Ukraine, "Leninfall" (the mass toppling of Lenin statues), the Revolution of Dignity, the environmental and human impact of Chornobyl, the toponyms of medieval Podillia, etc.[295]

Throughout the 2010s spatial history gradually became part of the academic mainstream in Ukraine, and is now being studied at leading universities and research institutes based at the National Academy of Sciences of Ukraine (NANU). At the same time, we can further trace the already familiar ways of implementing this method: through contacts with the West, thanks to the development of urban history, and through regional studies. Thus, as early as 2011 Natalya Yakovenko began her article about the burial sites of princely families of Volhynia from the fifteenth to the seven-

---

293 *Transformatsii   miskoho   prostoru*   (=   *Spilne*,   no.   2   [2010]), https://commons.com.ua/uk/zhurnal-spilne-2-transformatsiyi;   Kateryna Mishchenko, ed., *The Book of Kyiv/Kyivska knyzhka* (Kyiv: Medusa, 2015).

294 "Newly Mapped Data Leads to New Insights," Harvard Ukrainian Research Institute, 11 June 2018, https://huri.harvard.edu/news/newly-mapped-data-leads-new-insights.

295 "The MAPA Digital Atlas of Ukraine Program Aims to Advance Ukrainian Studies Using GIS," Harvard Ukrainian Research Institute, https://gis.huri.harvard.edu/about.

teenth century with a discussion of spatial history's theoretical un-
derpinnings, Lefebvre's views in particular.[296] In 2016 a group of
researchers from the Institute of the History of Ukraine under the
umbrella of the National Academy of Sciences and Taras
Shevchenko National University of Kyiv launched an electronic
journal of Urban Studies called *Misto: Istoriia, Kultura, Suspilstvo*
(City: History, Culture, Society).[297]

Finally, a stellar example of the return, on a new methodological level, to the research tasks set by Hrushevsky, is the first volume of the collective monograph *Skhid i Pivden Ukrainy: Chas,
prostir, sotsium* (The East and South of Ukraine: Time, Space, Society), published in 2014 by a group of authors from the Institute of
the History of Ukraine and other institutions as part of the Regional
History Studies series.[298] Although this book is based on conference
proceedings, its structure and the internal relationships between
the texts justify its inclusion in the genre of collective monograph.
In the opening chapter, Yaroslava Vermenych offers a detailed survey of Western theories of the "spatial turn" in the social sciences
and their possible application to Ukrainian studies. As regards the
latter, the chapter emphasizes above all the concept of "periphery"
and the potential for reviving regional studies.[299] Vermenych's contribution establishes the theoretical framework for the other chapters, and even those authors who do not mention spatial history fit
well into the book's overall framework.

Very important for the development of Ukrainian urban studies, although not yet translated into Ukrainian, is the recent book in
English by a Ukrainian-born scholar working in Canada, Serhii Bilenky. His innovative history of Kyiv considers this city between

296 Nataliia Iakovenko, "'Pohreb tilu moiemu vybyraiu s predky moiemy': Mistsia
    pokhovannia volynskykh kniaziv u XV–seredyni XVII stolit," *Ukraina: Kulturna
    spadshchyna, natsionalna svidomist, derzhavnist*, no. 20 (2011): 784–808.
297 *Misto: Istoriia, kultura, suspilstvo: E-zhurnal urbanistychnykh studii*,
    http://mics.org.ua/?p=41.
298 Iaroslava Vermenych, ed., *Skhid i Pivden Ukrainy: Chas, prostir, sotsium*, 2 vols.
    (Kyiv: Instytut istorii Ukrainy NANU, 2014–16).
299 Iaroslava Vermenych, "Prostorove modeliuvannia istorii: Zmina paradyhm,"
    in Vermenych, *Skhid i Pivden Ukrainy*, 1: 16–53.

WRITING THE NATION 147

1800 and 1905 as the Russian Empire's urban outpost in the border-lands, which played equally important but very different roles in the "mental geography" of the empire builders and the region's many ethnic groups. Bilenky also examines the debates about ur-ban planning and the city's changing social composition in the light of Lefevbre's notions of "perceived," "conceived," and "living" spaces.[300]

The Spaces of Ukraine

What are the promising areas for the development of Ukraine's spa-tial history? Both the historical development of Ukrainian regions and the current war suggest numerous projects for specialists in ge-opositioning. For example, one excellent research tool could be a multilayered, district-level map of national and linguistic identifi-cation correlated with the results of elections, and the emergence of the "anti-Maidan in Ukraine's east and south. The Harvard-based MAPA project, which is being conducted in collaboration with spe-cialists from Ukraine, is already beginning to study these issues.

It is worthwhile examining several case studies that demon-strate the usefulness of the spatial research method for historians who are not necessarily skilled in computer technologies or familiar with the conceptual apparatus of spatial history. For example, the historical development of the Podil district of Kyiv was linked to the circumstance that natural conditions allowed for the construc-tion there of a port on the Dnipro River; in this case, it seems that the pre-existing environment is structuring social designation. However, the Dnipro regularly flooded the Podil, necessitating the construction in the 1770s of a canal, known as Probytets, on the other side of Trukhaniv Island. Shipping then moved there – to the Desenka Strait (known at the time as Chortoryi, or "The Devil's Whirlpool"). But everything changed during the steamboat era. Owing to the deep draft of steamboats, in the mid-nineteenth cen-tury the need arose to restore the full volume of water of the Dnipro's main channel, and in 1851 a weir was constructed at

---

300 Serhiy Bilenky, *Imperial Urbanism in the Borderlands: Kyiv, 1800–1905* (Toronto: University of Toronto Press, 2018).

Probytets and in the 1880s — a dam. Among other things, this led to flow deceleration of the Desenka Strait, thanks to which its banks were already a popular beach area by the twentieth century and Kyivites began rethinking the role of this great river in their daily life.[301] The complex interaction between people and the environment thus determined the unique historical spiral of mutual influence.

No less interesting is the example of Savur-Mohyla, located in the eastern part of Donetsk oblast. From this height, which dominates the steppe (227 m above sea level), you can see for thirty to fifty kilometers in all directions. For that very reason, it was an important strategic point during the Cossack era. It is mentioned in the *duma* about "The Escape of the Three Brothers from Azov," who are fleeing Turkish captivity via Savur-Mohyla. A Cossack watchtower once stood there. However, the Second World War rewrote the history of this natural monument. From a site of memory of the Cossack period it was transformed into a "hill of glory" of Red Army soldiers, countless numbers of whom were killed — first, while defending it from the Germans in 1941–42, and later, while trying to recapture it from the Germans in the summer of 1943. In 1963 a large memorial complex was built on the hill. During the late Soviet period countless delegations from Donetsk and Luhansk oblasts, as well as from Rostov oblast in the RSFSR, the border with which is situated very close by, visited every year on 9 May to lay flowers..[302] In 2014 Savur-Mohyla still preserved its importance as a strategic position overlooking the steppe, but for Russian and pro-Russian forces it also has a symbolic meaning as a site of memory, where their "granddads" fought against the fascists, because it fits in well with their official model of the current war's interpretation. In the summer of 2014 the Ukrainian army expelled them with great difficulty but later was forced to abandon Savur-Mohyla. During

---

301 I. Iu. Parnikoza, "Kyivski ostrovy ta pryberezhni urochyshcha na Dnipri — pohliad kriz viky," *Myslenne drevo,* http://www.myslenedrevo.com.ua/ uk/Sci/Kyiv/Islands.html.

302 M. Ia. Oleinikov, *Saur-Mogila: Putevoditel* (Donetsk: Donbass, 1976).

this period nearly all the Soviet-era monuments on the hill were destroyed. The first to fall was the figure of a soldier, then the stela.[303]

It is interesting to compare Savur-Mohyla with Donetsk airport, which has no such history and was not built as a defensive structure, yet became an important symbol for Ukrainian patriots, thanks to the feats of the "cyborgs." At first, these "superhuman" Ukrainian defenders of the airport tried to hold out there because it was an airport and therefore a strategically important facility, and later, when the airport began to be destroyed by shelling — because of this Ukrainian stronghold's proximity to the city of Donetsk.[304] But, in terms of geography, it could have been anywhere in that steppe; the environment was not a determining factor here.

The Carpathian Mountains are another good example of the productiveness of spatial thinking, as recent English-language publications about the role of this mountain range in the formation of modern Polish and Ukrainian identities have proved.[305] Today we regard them as the heart of Ukraine. In 2004 the pop singer Ruslana won the Eurovision Song Contest with her song "Wild Dances," which is based on the image of the Carpathians as the wild, primeval place where Ukraine came into existence.[306] In fact, the Carpathians were an obstacle to creating the modern Ukrainian nation. In the 1870s Mykhailo Drahomanov risked his life travelling to Transcarpathia along the narrow mountain roads.[307] The very term "Transcarpathia" points to the spatial location of the narrator on

---

303 "Savur-Mohyla Left without Obelisk Because of Shelling: Photo," *Tsenzor.net*, 21 August 2014, https://censor.net/en/p299092.

304 See Iryna Shtohryn, ed., *AD 242: Istoriia muzhnosti, braterstva ta samopozhertvy* (Kharkiv: KSD, 2016).

305 Anthony J. Amato, *The Carpathians, the Hutsuls, and Ukraine: An Environmental History* (Lanham, Md.: Lexington Books, 2020); Patrice M. Dabrowski, *The Carpathians: Discovering the Highlands of Poland and Ukraine* (Ithaca, N.Y.: Cornell University Press, 2021).

306 See Marko Pavlyshyn, "Ruslana, Serduchka, Jamala: National Self-Imaging in Ukraine's Eurovision Entries," in *Eurovisions: Identity and the International Politics of the Eurovision Song Contest since 1956*, ed. Julie Kalman, Ben Wellings, and Keshia Jacotine (London: Palgrave Macmillan, 2019), 129–50.

307 Mykhailo Drahomanov, "Avstro-ruski spomyny," in Mykhailo Drahomanov, *Literaturno-publitsystychni pratsi*, 2 vols. (Kyiv: Naukova dumka, 1970), 2: 263–74.

this side of the Carpathians; on the other side, Transcarpathia could have been called — and, indeed, was called — Subcarpathian Rus' or Carpatho-Ukraine.[308] Thus, the national idea — the cornerstone of contemporary Ukrainian historiography — is also essentially a kind of spatial perspective of history.

* * *

As we can see, the history of Ukraine offers an extraordinarily broad range of opportunities for applying spatial approaches and geopositioning methods. The introduction of Spatial Studies in Ukraine hinges on a hallowed tradition of Regional Studies and the popularity of Urban Studies. Although new Spatial History is grounded in the study of the Western theoretical and methodological apparatus, in a certain sense it continues the directions of research that were established in the 1920s, before the forcible Stalinization of Ukrainian historical science.

Translated from the Ukrainian by Marta Daria Olynyk

---

308   Andrew Wilson, *The Ukrainians: Unexpected Nation* (New Haven: Yale University Press, 2000), 111.

8. Histories of Ukrainian Culture
From 1918 to the Orange Revolution

Historians have long thought that the formation of modern national identities involves the creation of codified and full-fledged national cultures. Ernest Gellner has argued that patriotic intellectuals construct modern "high" cultures for their nations by selecting and developing certain components of folk tradition. Benedict Anderson and Eric Hobsbawm analyzed the cultural mechanisms involved in the "invention" of modern nations — traditions, museums, novels, newspapers, etc.[309] Ukrainian specialists, like historians elsewhere, have published works applying these conceptual models to their country's case. Yet they — and students of nation building in general — have focused on social practices, such as the transformation of a peasant costume into a national symbol, the national cult of the bard, the use of ancient first names, and the spread of reading rooms throughout the countryside.[310] National cultures and national identities, however, have also been constructed discursively, and never in more coherent form than in histories of a national culture.

---

309 See Ernest Gellner, *Nations and Nationalism* (Oxford: Blackwell, 1983); Benedict Anderson, *Imagined Communities: Reflections on the Origin and Spread of Nationalism*, rev. ed. (London: Verso, 1991); Eric J. Hobsbawm and Terence Ranger, eds., *The Invention of Tradition* (New York: Cambridge University Press, 1983).

310 See, e.g., John-Paul Himka, *Galician Villagers and the Ukrainian National Movement in the Nineteenth Century* (Edmonton: Canadian Institute of Ukrainian Studies Press, 1988); John-Paul Himka, "The Construction of Nationality in Galician Rus': Icarian Flights in Almost All Directions," in *Intellectuals and the Articulation of the Nation*, ed. Ronald Grigor Suny and Michael D. Kennedy (Ann Arbor: University of Michigan Press, 1999), 109–66; Iaroslav Hrytsak, "Iakykhto kniaziv buly stolytsi u Kyievi? Do konstruiuvannia istorychnoi pamiati halytskykh ukraintsiv u 1830–1930-ti roky," *Ukraina Moderna*, no. 6 (2001): 77–95; Serhy Yekelchyk, "The Body and National Myth: Motifs from the Ukrainian National Revival in the Nineteenth Century," *Australian Slavonic and East European Studies* 7, no. 2 (1993): 31–59; Ostap Sereda, "From Church-Based to Cultural Nationalism: Early Ukrainophiles, Ritual-Purification Movement and Emerging Cult of Taras Shevchenko in Austrian Eastern Galicia in the 1860s," *Canadian-American Slavic Studies* 40, no. 1 (2006): 21–47.

Notable interest in folk culture and historical tradition was present in East European national movements from their origins in the age of Romantic nationalism during the late eighteenth and early nineteenth centuries. One can argue that the historical approach to the study of Ukrainian folk culture was outlined already in Mykhailo Maksymovych's introduction to his collection of Ukrainian folk songs (1827).[311] This short text emphasized that the national culture was produced by the common folk and that the contrast between the Ukrainian folk culture and the Russian became the starting point for modern Ukrainian humanities. A century later Mykhailo Hrushevsky called Maksymovych's introduction "a manifesto of our populism."[312] Systematic narratives of how a national culture developed, however, appear late in the nation-building process, at an advanced stage of popular mobilization when patriotic intellectuals have more or less completed the codification of national culture and need textbooks to help with "nationalizing" the masses.

Gellner focused on the general fallacy of patriotic cultural imagination. He pointed out that, although national high culture is a relatively recent invention, nationalists always insist on its primordial character and folk roots.[313] Getting national culture wrong, presenting it as ancient, authentic, and cohesive is, therefore, a common trait of modern nation builders. However, a more productive way of looking at the historical narratives of national culture could be to view them in the context of decolonization, that is, the efforts to reclaim the people's cultural heritage from oppressive empires. Rather than criticizing a national cultural framework from a supranational position, which is perfectly compatible with the cultural logic of imperialism, one could focus on how national discursive strategies undermined imperial cultural hierarchies. In this light, the insistence on the ancient national cultural tradition appears in

---

311   Mikhail Maksimovich [Mykhailo Maksymovych], "Predislovie," in Mikhail Maksimovich [Mykhailo Maksymovych], ed., *Malorossiiskiia pesni* (Moscow: Avgust Semen, 1827), i–xxxviii.

312   Mykhailo Hrushevsky, "'Malorosiiskiia pesni' Maksymovycha i stolittia ukrainskoi naukovoi pratsi," *Ukraina*, no. 6 (1927): 1–13, here 2.

313   Gellner, *Nations and Nationalism*, 57.

its proper context of critical engagement with what one might call imperial temporality.

In this chapter I will briefly analyze the most important surveys of the history of Ukrainian culture published in Ukraine between 1918 and 2005 — from the first modern survey defining the fate of Ukrainian ethnic culture under imperial rule to the end of neo-imperial hybridity, which characterized much of Ukrainian culture until the Orange Revolution (2004–5). The Orange Revolution ushered in a new Ukrainian identity and cultural narratives that wedded the notions of a multiethnic Ukrainian civic nation and the Ukrainian language and culture as symbols of that democratic choice.

This chapter treats these surveys of Ukrainian culture as texts in which national identity is negotiated through interpretation of the country's rich cultural past. The present-day Ukrainian state, which gained independence with the Soviet Union's collapse in 1991, brought home this topic's significance by introducing in all colleges and universities obligatory courses on the history of Ukrainian culture (in the faculties of Arts and Humanities) or the history of world and Ukrainian culture (for students of other faculties). The hybrid version of Ukrainian cultural history, which prevailed between the early 1990s and 2005, is an important factor in understanding the cultural and identity processes that culminated in the Revolution of Dignity and Russia's war on Ukraine.

Neither Russia nor Poland

It is significant that the oldest surveys of Ukrainian culture analyzed in this chapter, those published in 1918 and 1937, have been reprinted in independent Ukraine and are still widely used as textbooks or supplementary texts. Although their coverage and interpretations may appear outdated, their ethnic notion of Ukrainian identity established the model that re-emerged in the 1990s as an important component of post-imperial hybrid cultural narratives. These earliest systematic surveys focused on separating Ukrainian culture from those of Ukraine's former imperial masters, Russia and Poland, which saw themselves as Slavic cultural powerhouses.

In contrast, the histories published in the age of post-Soviet hybrid-ity often obscured the anti-imperial pathos of Ukrainian culture or combined anti-imperial declarations with justifications of the em-pire's cultural legacy.

For Ivan Ohiienko, the author of the 1918 survey *Ukrainian Culture*, Ukraine's principal "other" is Russia. This short book ap-peared in the Ukrainian People's Republic (UNR), an independent state that emerged after the Russian Empire's collapse and existed until the Bolsheviks established their control late in 1920. A former instructor in Slavic languages at the University of Kyiv and soon-to-be UNR education minister, Ohiienko delivered the lectures on which this text is based in the fall of 1917, after the proclamation of Ukrainian autonomy but before the declaration of independence. The question of Ukraine's cultural separateness and its right to self-rule is central to the book, which the UNR's Minister of War or-dered printed in 100,000 copies as a reader for his soldiers.[314] Ohiienko begins his survey with two questions that for him are re-lated: "Do we have the right to live in freedom and the right to au-tonomy, which we have been demanding staunchly for more than two centuries? Do our people constitute a separate nationality; do they have their own original and distinctive culture?"[315] Ohiienko's answer is, not surprisingly, affirmative, but more interesting is his book's structure.

Unlike present-day historians of Ukrainian culture, Ohiienko deemphasizes the nineteenth century, when a modern Ukrainian culture developed based on the peasant vernacular. His focus is in-stead on the sixteenth to eighteenth centuries, when, as he shows, Ukrainian culture was superior to Russian. The first part of the book begins with the exaltation of Ukrainian folk songs, which even

---

314 See Mykola Tymoshyk, *"Lyshus naviky z chuzhynoiu..." Mytropolyt Ilarion (Ivan Ohiienko) i ukrainske vidrodzhennia* (Kyiv: Nasha kultura i nauka, 2000), 53–59; Halyna Hrinchenko and Valentyna Kudriashova, "Pedahohichna diialnist Ivana Ohiienka," in *Ivan Ohiienko i utverdzhennia humanitarnoi nauky ta osvity v Ukraini*, ed. M. V. Levkivsky (Zhytomyr: Zhurfond, 1997), 11–12.

315 Ivan Ohiienko, *Ukrainska kultura* (Kyiv: Nasha kultura i nauka, 2002), p. 54. The original edition was subtitled *A Short History of the Ukrainian People's Cultural Life*. See Ivan Ohiienko, *Ukrainska kultura: Korotka istoriia kulturnoho zhyttia ukra-inskoho naroda* (Kyiv: Ie. Cherepovskyi, 1918).

Muscovites love; the Ukrainian language, which is said to be the richest and most expressive of all the Slavic languages; and even Ukrainian handwriting of the Cossack period, which was much prettier than the Russian one and which the Muscovites adopted in the eighteenth century.[316] Ohiienko claims for Ukrainian culture the literature of medieval Kyivan Rus' that had long been presented as "Russian." He then traces the continuous development of the Ukrainian cultural tradition to the seventeenth century, "the golden age of our literature and our culture," when among the Slavic nations Ukraine was second to Poland in terms of cultural development. As Ohiienko's main "other" is Russia, he glosses over Polish social oppression and cultural assimilation that nineteenth-century Ukrainian historians emphasized to claim that, unlike Russia, "Ukraine has never been afraid of Western culture, and Western influences have flown to us like a broad river."[317] Not only does Ohiienko challenge the Russian imperial cultural narratives by claiming higher status for Ukrainian culture, he also presents Ukraine as a part of Europe in an implicit opposition to Russia.

Much of the first part and the entire second part of the book, entitled "The Influence of Ukrainian Culture on Muscovite Culture," are devoted to proving Russia's cultural inferiority before the nineteenth century. Ukrainian scholars brought modern orthography, theater, singing, and syllabic poetry to Russia. Muscovites traveled to Ukraine to study at Kyiv's Mohyla Academy, and transplanted Ukrainians created Russia's modern educational system. Ohiienko argues that even the Russian literary language was based on the "Slavonic-Rus" bookish language that had developed in Ukraine during the sixteenth and seventeenth centuries.[318] This line of argument helps explain why Ohiienko gives short shrift to the nineteenth century, when writers using the peasant vernacular laid the foundations of present-day Ukrainian culture. For him, switching from a Slavonic literary language to peasant speech undermined claims of cultural continuity from Kyivan Rus and cultural

---

316 Ohiienko, *Ukrainska kultura* [2002], 61, 69–70, and 73.
317 Ibid., 85 and 89.
318 Ibid., 166 and 317–18.

superiority over Russia. Indeed, the first published work in the Ukrainian vernacular, Ivan Kotliarevsky's *Eneida* (1798) was, for Ohiienko, "a cross on the grave of our old literary language."[319]

The author thus devotes only two pages to the development of Ukrainian literature during the nineteenth century — a period that most present-day cultural historians of Ukraine would consider central to their subject. The long fourth part of the book is instead entitled "On a Thorny Path (About the Injustices Committed against the Ukrainian People)." It deals in great detail with tsarist repressions against Ukrainian culture during the eighteenth and nineteenth centuries. Ohiienko does not reflect on the nature of Russian imperial rule, but simply states that "Moscow hated everyone who was not Russian."[320] His choice to frame nineteenth-century Ukrainian culture as a story of persecution rather than perseverance fits well with his stated intention — to prove with cultural arguments Ukraine's right to self-rule.

The publication of Ohiienko's *Ukrainian Culture* provoked an interesting response from a prominent Ukrainian patriot of the older generation, Volodymyr Naumenko. Interestingly, he would also serve as Ukraine's education minister — in his case, in November and December 1918 in the last cabinet of the conservative and, at that point, pro-Russian regime of Hetman Pavlo Skoropadsky. A representative of the so-called Ukrainophiles, who for decades conducted semi-legal cultural work under the tsarist regime without openly challenging it, Naumenko attacked Ohiienko's survey in a longer review, which appeared as a separate booklet under the title *How the History of Ukrainian Culture Should Not Be Taught*. The older Ukrainian activist found many faults with the book, most of them related to what he saw as Ohiienko's exaggeration of the nation's achievements: the claims that Ukrainian language (and not Polish, Czech, or Russian) is the richest Slavic language, that modern Russian is based on a literary language developed in Ukraine, and that nineteenth-century Ukrainian literature was "on par with the great literatures of the world." Ultimately, though, most of Naumenko's

---

319 Ibid., 319.
320 Ibid., 189.

critiques relate to his stated uneasiness about "irritation and hatred" towards Russian culture displayed in Ohiienko's text: "Unfortunately, there is no objectivity in the author's book and instead
everywhere you will find minor and often uncertain proofs of Russian oppression against Ukrainians, and even more often, quotations about how savage and uncultured Muscovites were."[321] Naumenko's harsh appraisal reflects his generation's apprehension of
an open break with Russia and Russian culture. The Ukrainophiles
did not extend their vision beyond a regional status for Ukrainian
culture in a Russian-dominated federation — which indeed was the
very reason why their generation did not produce a history of
Ukrainian culture.

Ohiienko's survey, meanwhile, reflected the cultural policies
of a Ukrainian state born during the revolutionary turmoil of 1917–
20. After the UNR fell, the Bolsheviks and the restored Poland divided the Ukrainian ethnolinguistic territories, with smaller parts
ending up in Romania and Czechoslovakia. *Ukrainian Culture* became a popular textbook among Ukrainians living outside the Soviet Union, although its anti-Russian focus did not fully reflect the
cultural concerns of readers. For most Ukrainians in interwar East-
Central European states, the cultural past was represented by the
Austro-Hungarian Empire, which allowed education and publishing in Ukrainian, while the present was marked by assimilationist
pressures in Poland and Romania. (In the Ukrainian ethnolinguistic
territories within Hungary, the situation had been just as difficult
before 1918.) Ohiienko's work, however, all but ignored cultural developments in these western Ukrainian lands.

In 1937 Ohiienko's book was superseded by a much more detailed and balanced survey, *The History of Ukrainian Culture*, which
was published in Lviv (then part of Poland) under the editorship of
the prominent historian Ivan Krypiakevych. Originally appearing
as a series of fifteen separate booklets, this collection featured a thematic approach to Ukrainian culture, with areas such as everyday
life, literature, art, theater, and music assigned to different authors.

---

321 Volodymyr Naumenko, *Iak ne treba vykladaty istoriiu ukrainskoi kultury* (Kyiv:
Petro Barskyi, 1918), 1–9. The longer quote is on 9.

In contrast to Ohiienko, Krypiakevych and his collaborators were not concerned with establishing the separateness of Ukrainian culture from Russian. In Poland during the 1930s this question was decisively passé. The cultural borders in need of demarcation included those with Polish culture and with socialist Ukrainian culture inside the Soviet Union. Conveniently separated by a different religion and alphabet, Polish culture was nonetheless based on a related Slavic language and was historically an attractive imperial culture for Ukrainians. In Soviet Ukraine during the 1930s, the state's attacks on Ukrainian cultural figures marked the end of the "Executed Renaissance" and the advent of the doctrines of "Russian guidance" and Socialist Realism.

The collection's authors answered these challenges by stressing the combination of Western and Eastern influences in Ukraine's past—the symbiosis separating Ukrainian culture from Polish, which, due to the dominant role of Roman Catholicism, was seen as belonging fully to the "West." In writing about the twentieth century, they, on the contrary, emphasized the common dynamics of cultural processes in western Ukrainian lands outside the Soviet Union and those in Western Europe—thus making Soviet Ukrainian culture look like an aberration. Finally, to remove any doubts about Ukraine's distinctiveness from Russia, the authors clearly claimed Kyivan Rus for Ukrainian culture by calling it "ancient Ukraine" and discussing the earliest chronicles under the very modern subheading "Scholarship and Ukrainian Studies."[322] After the fourteenth century, the narrative focuses more on the western Ukrainian lands, thus making the book more relevant for its potential readership.

Typical of the book's general approach is its appraisal of the seventeenth-century Mohyla Academy in Kyiv, a great cultural center for Ohiienko and most of today's historians. Because the academy was modeled on Polish Jesuit colleges and emphasized the study of Latin, Krypiakevych sees its cultural role as largely

---

322 Ivan Krypiakevych, "Pobut," in *Istoriia ukrainskoi kultury*, ed. Ivan Krypiakevych, 4th ed. (Kyiv: Lybid, 2002), 36 ("ancient Ukraine") and 48 ("Ukrainian Studies").

negative: "The Academy opened the doors wide to Western, Catholic, influences, but at the same time did not continue Ukraine's old
links with the East, with Byzantium. Even the study of the Greek
language decreased with every decade. Because of this, Ukrainian
culture began losing the comprehensiveness that distinguished it in
ancient times, as well as its originality and distinctiveness; instead,
it fell under the overwhelming influence of Western Europe represented for us by Poland."[323] In this scheme of things, the Cossack
revolt of 1648 and the liberation of eastern Ukraine from Polish
domination restored Ukraine's traditional role as a cultural media-
tor and heir to both Eastern and Western traditions. Although it increasingly controlled Ukraine politically after 1654, Muscovy was
no competitor on the cultural scene: "When Moscow, stagnating in
its religious formalism, covered up its cultural backwardness with
an artificial foreign veneer, Ukraine, this true and worthy heir of
ancient eastern and Greek culture, accepted only those Western
forms and only in such an application that did not contradict its
established aesthetic worldview."[324]

    With Ukrainian culture's separateness from Polish and Rus-
sian established, the collection's authors had to position themselves
in relation to Soviet Ukrainian culture and especially its Stalinist
version, which had been emerging during the 1930s. Volodymyr
Radzykevych, who contributed the chapter on literature, stresses
that all major Ukrainian writers in the late nineteenth and early
twentieth century, including Ivan Franko, Lesia Ukrainka,
Mykhailo Kotsiubynsky, and Olha Kobylianska "based their work
on modern Western European literary trends and implanted in
Ukrainian soil new artistic achievements of Western European
writers."[325] Such a strong statement can be seen as devaluing

---

323 Ibid., 125.
324 Mykola Holubets, "Mystetstvo," in Krypiakevych, *Istoriia ukrainskoi kultury*,
     500.
325 Volodymyr Radzykevych, "Pysmenstvo," in Krypiakevych, *Istoriia ukrainskoi
     kultury*, 411 and 423. Mykola Khvylovy was a leading prose writer in Soviet
     Ukraine, who during the 1920s advocated a cultural orientation toward Wes-
     tern Europe or, as he put it in his famous slogan, "Away from Moscow." After

Ukrainian authors' originality, but Radzykevych needed it as a lead-in to his conclusions: "Ukrainian culture should part company with the Muscovite one. Mykola Khvylovy gave his life for this idea. If Ukrainian literature is to serve the people, it should follow in the footsteps of Western Europe."[326]

Since this is a political position as much as an aesthetic one, it comes as no surprise that the western Ukrainian authors disapprove of certain "European" avant-garde artistic trends that were associated with the Bolsheviks. The prominent Ukrainian writer Volodymyr Vynnychenko, whose work featured Nietzschean motifs, is criticized for justifying "savage" human instincts—an approach that the critics see as being "far removed from the psychology and thinking of Ukrainian society."[327] Although Vynnychenko fit nicely into "Western European" cultural trends of the early twentieth century, what made him less acceptable was his long association with the extreme political left, which included periods of closeness to the Bolsheviks. In painting too, Cubism and Futurism receive a negative evaluation because of their prominence in early Soviet art—although they were on the rise elsewhere in Europe as well. Mykola Holubets, who wrote the chapter on art, speaks warmly of the resistance from Ukrainian postimpressionists and expressionists to officially sponsored early Soviet "Cubo-Futuro-Primitivism." Only the turn to Socialist Realism in Soviet Ukrainian art during the early 1930s removes the need for western Ukrainian commentators to sort out modernist trends into "safe" European and not-so-European. From then on, Soviet Ukrainian art parts ways with modernist Europe and is dominated by "illustrators, who with greater or lesser success imitate the old and forgotten [Russian] Wanderers."[328]

---

a prolonged campaign of denunciation in the official press, he committed suicide in 1933.

326 Ibid., 423.

327 Ibid., 414.

328 Holubets, "Mystetstvo," 575–76. The Wanderers were a Russian school of realist painting during the last third of the nineteenth century.

Yet the Soviet model of Ukrainian culture was soon imposed on Western Ukrainians when Stalin absorbed their territories into the Soviet Union in 1939-40. Ohiienko's survey and Krypiak-evych's collection continued to be used by the Ukrainian diaspora in Western Europe, North America, and Australia, but were withdrawn from public circulation in Soviet Ukraine. Both books were continually reprinted abroad, as was a similar but somewhat less influential survey, which did not have a chapter on literature — *Ukrainian Culture*, edited by Dmytro Antonovych and first published in 1940 in Czechoslovakia, then under Nazi occupation.[329] In 1985, a more up-to-date survey appeared in the Ukrainian diaspora. The book by Myroslav Semchyshyn was written along the same lines as its interwar predecessors and ended the story of Ukrainian culture with an examination of cultural processes in the diaspora, rather than in Soviet Ukraine.[330]

Stalinist bureaucrats did not replace the Ohiienko and Krypiakevych surveys, which they branded "bourgeois nationalist," with ideologically sound Soviet accounts of Ukrainian culture, because they saw no need for such books. Previous popular narratives of the history of Ukrainian culture were written as textbooks for the general reader and moreover, for a readership discovering or affirming its sense of Ukrainian identity either during the revolutionary turmoil or under oppressive Polish rule. In Soviet Ukraine, where the only permitted narrative of Ukrainian culture was the Soviet one, Ukrainian language, literature, and history were taught as separate disciplines and from "proletarian" positions, which in reality meant saturating these subjects with crude sociological analysis. There was no academic niche for a standalone introduction to Ukrainian culture. Perhaps more important, beginning in the early 1930s Stalin's regime abandoned the promo-

---

329 For a modern edition, see Dmytro Antonovych, ed., *Ukrainska kultura* (Kyiv: Lybid, 1993).

330 See Myroslav Semchyshyn, *Tysiacha rokiv ukrainskoi kultury*, 2nd ed. (Kyiv: Druha ruka/Feniks, 1993); originally published in New York in 1985.

tion of non-Russian cultures characteristic of the 1920s "nativization" policy in favor of a renewed Russification drive.[331] Under the
circumstances, a patriotic history of the Ukrainian culture would be
inappropriate because it inevitably involved an ethnic definition of
the national culture.

Thus, there was no replacement for a brief survey published
on the eve of the state's attack on "nativization," Antin
Kozachenko's *Ukrainian Culture: Its Past and Present* (1931). In any
case, the author interprets cultural processes in coarse class-analy-
sis terms typical of Soviet social science during the 1920s. He insists
on class labels for each epoch, which results in Shevchenko, for example, being stuck in the middle of the "gentry" period. Modernism in Ukrainian architecture is qualified by the term "bourgeois,"
and contemporary Ukrainians could fully identify only with
"Ukrainian proletarian culture," best represented by the "proletarian poets" of the 1920s — Vasyl Elan-Blakytny, Vasyl Chumak, and
Volodymyr Sosiura.[332] What made Kozachenko's book outdated,
however, was not so much its unsophisticated sociological labels,
which went out of fashion by the mid-to-late 1930s, as its harsh critique of tsarist policies in Ukraine. Statements about Muscovy's
"colonial oppression" and cultural repression resulting from the
Russian government's drive "to fully absorb Ukraine"[333] were beginning to sound odd after the mid-1930s. As Soviet ideologues embraced the concept of the "friendship of peoples," they also increasingly rehabilitated the tsarist regime, and rewrote the history of
Russo-Ukrainian relations.[334]

---

331 See Terry Martin, *The Affirmative Action Empire: Nations and Nationalism in the
       Soviet Union, 1923–1939* (Ithaca: Cornell University Press, 2001).

332 Antin Kozachenko, *Ukrainska kultura: Ii mynuvshchyna i suchasnist* (Kharkiv:
       Proletar, 1931), 42, 76, 96, and 122.

333 Ibid., 14 and 59.

334 On the ideological change in the Soviet Union in general, see David Branden-
       berger, *National Bolshevism: Stalinist Mass Culture and the Formation of Modern
       Russian National Identity* (Cambridge, Mass.: Harvard University Press, 2002).
       On the implications for Russian-Ukrainian relations, see Serhy Yekelchyk, *Sta-
       lin's Empire of Memory: Russian-Ukrainian Relations in the Soviet Historical Imagi-
       nation* (Toronto: University of Toronto Press, 2004).

With the partial and temporary rehabilitation of Ukrainian patriotic rhetoric as a mobilization tool during World War II, scholars at the Ukrainian Academy of Sciences planned the preparation of a survey of the history of Ukrainian culture, but this project was abandoned after the Kremlin denounced "nationalist deviations" in Ukrainian culture in 1944, 1946, and again in 1951.[335] The next Soviet history of Ukrainian culture appeared only during Khrushchev's "Thaw." In 1961, Mykhailo Marchenko published his *History of Ukrainian Culture: From Ancient Times to the Mid-Seventeenth Century*, intended as a supplementary text for teachers and university students specializing in history. The author criticizes Ohiienko's and Krypiakevych's texts as "bourgeois falsifications" — without, however, naming Krypiakevych, who had repented for his past indiscretions and emerged after the war as a prominent Soviet academic. Marchenko also devotes due attention to the contacts between the "fraternal" Ukrainian and Russian cultures during the sixteenth and early seventeenth centuries.[336] But at the same time he stresses Ukrainian national culture's cohesiveness over class distinctions: "The class character of a culture does not contradict the fact that a people's culture reflects the unity of the psychological makeup of this given tribe, nationality or nation."[337] Moreover, he obliquely repeats the point about the innate democratic character of Ukrainian culture, determined by the fact that the upper classes were mostly foreign—an idea found in the works of nineteenth-century Ukrainian patriotic historians and in Ohiienko's book, but considered a nationalist heresy in the Soviet Union. According to Marchenko, "The culture of those peoples and nations that experienced oppression by foreign conquerors is the one that is penetrated by the spirit of the common people."[338]

---

335 See V. A. Smolii, ed., *U leshchatakh totalitaryzmu: Pershe dvadtsiatyrichchia Instytutu istorii NAN Ukrainy (1936–1956 rr.)* (Kyiv: Instytut istorii Ukrainy, 1996), vol. 1: 119 and 121.

336 M. I. Marchenko, *Istoriia ukrainskoi kultury: Z naidavnishykh chasiv do seredyny XVII st.* (Kyiv: Radianska shkola, 1961), 6 and 270–75.

337 Ibid., 4.

338 Ibid.

Yet no sequel treating the period after the seventeenth century ever appeared. The short-lasting Thaw gave way to the Brezhnev period, when patriotic non-Russian intellectuals were reined in, often dismissed from their posts and arrested, and studies of cultural contacts with Russia became more important than analyses of Ukrainian culture as such.[339]

The Universal and the National in Culture

The situation changed with the disintegration of Soviet ideological controls during the late 1980s. In 1989 the Ukrainian Ministry of Higher Education began cancelling the previously obligatory social-science courses at the university level: History of the Communist Party, Marxist-Leninist Philosophy, Scientific Communism, etc. Among their replacements was a required course on "The History and Theory of World and Ukrainian Culture," which was phased in during the academic year 1990–91. Reforms in higher education continued after Ukraine became independent in 1991, as the young state was searching for a new official ideology. Most political leaders in the republic simply changed colors in 1990–91 by switching from communism to superficial patriotic rhetoric; college departments underwent a similar transformation. The Ministry of Higher Education first renamed the departments of Communist Party history as departments of political history, but late in 1990 recommended their conversion into departments of Ukrainian Studies. Thus, former historians of the Communist Party ended up teaching the history of Ukrainian culture. At some smaller or specialized colleges, however, instruction in cultural history was assigned to departments of philosophy, previously known as departments of Scientific Communism, while former party historians took responsibility for Ukrainian history.[340] The last significant reorgan-

339 See, e.g., A. D. Skaba, ed., *Vinok druzhby*, vol. 3: *Dukhovnyi rozkvit ukrainskoho narodu* (Kyiv: Politvydav, 1972) and Iu. Iu. Kondufor, ed., *Druzhba i bratstvo russkogo i ukrainskogo narodov* (Kyiv: Naukova dumka, 1982), 2 vols.
340 See B. A. Holovko, "Spetsyfika vykladannia filosofskykh dystsyplin u natsionalnomu ahrarnomu universyteti," in *Humanitarna osvita: Dosvid i problemy*, ed. M. I. Bletskan (Uzhhorod: Grazhda, 1999), 97–98; E. P. Polishchuk, "Pro mistse

ization during the early 1990s came in 1993, when the ministry introduced an obligatory course entitled the History of Ukrainian Culture for students in faculties of Arts and Humanities, while all others studied the History of World and Ukrainian Culture.[341]

To support these courses, within a decade Ukrainian academics published dozens of textbooks. Most of them were in Ukrainian, but some were in Russian, as many institutions of higher education in eastern Ukraine continued to offer instruction in this language until the mid-2010s. The majority of textbooks cover both world and Ukrainian culture, but many are devoted only to Ukrainian. Of the former, a significant number is tailored towards the specific profile of the college where the authors teach—for example, Aviation University, Institute of Military Engineers, Academy of Internal Affairs—with special emphasis on the history of aviation, military technology, or social order. Yet all textbook authors during that period shared the same conceptual and methodological problems, none of them more challenging than defining Ukrainian culture.

The textbook on world and Ukrainian culture used during the 2000s at the University of Kyiv is a good illustration of the nature of this difficulty. Written by fourteen academics, most of them former instructors of Communist Party history, the text begins with a section on theory and methodology, in which old, dogmatic Marxism and equally outdated nationalistic interpretations of ethnic nations having their unique psychological makeup blend into a confusing theory of national culture. The Marxist interpretation of history was based on so-called Historical Materialism emphasizing the

kursu istorii kultury v systemi humanitarnoi osvity," idem., 486–88; L. V. Kuznetsova, "Problemy vykladannia teorii ta istorii natsionalnoi kultury v osvitnikh zakladakh Ukrainy," in *Ukrainska kultura: Zmist i metodyka vykladannia*, ed. A. K. Bychko (Kyiv: Navchalno-metodychnyi kabinet vyshchoi osvity Ministerstva osvity, 1993), 100; and A. I. Pavko, "Chy potribno vyvchaty politychnu istoriiu Ukrainy u vyshchii shkoli?" *Ukrainskyi istorychnyi zhurnal*, no. 2 (2005): 204–7, here 205.

341 S. M. Klapchuk and V. F. Ostafiichuk, eds., *Istoriia ukrainskoi kultury: Zbirnyk materialiv i dokumentiv* (Kyiv: Vyshcha shkola, 2000), 5; L. M. Malyshko, "Pro deiaki aspekty vykladannia ukrainskoi natsionalnoi kultury v tekhnichnomu vuzi," in Bychko, *Ukrainska kultura*, 122.

evolution of the means of production, while nationalist theoreti-
cians defined the ethnic nation in terms of psychological unity. As
already noted in Chapter 2, this textbook's authors claim to be able
to combine the two methodologies into a "psychological approach
based on the principle of Historical Materialism."[342] In reality, like
in most other surveys, the forces of production and production relations are replaced in the role of the history's moving force by an
organic development of an ethnic nation – with the nation's struggle for its own state often understood as dogmatically as the class
struggle or the Communist Party's leading role had been in Soviet
times.

Most textbooks published during the 1990s and early 2000s
define Ukrainian culture as the sum of material and spiritual values
produced by the Ukrainian people, including the diaspora.[343] The
last qualification indicates that this understanding of culture is
based on the ethnicity and language of cultural producers rather
than on territory or a sense of belonging to the same political and
cultural community. In this understanding, "Ukrainian culture"
would not include the rich cultural heritage of Ukraine's historically significant national minorities, such as the Crimean Tatars,
Poles, and Jews or much of the mass culture in Ukraine, which at
the time functioned mostly in Russian. The latter exclusion can be
seen as logical, but it really constituted a lack of engagement with
this complex issue or even mass culture in general; Ukrainophone
mass culture was usually ignored as well. Even the sophisticated
textbook on the history of Ukrainian culture, written by top specialists from the Ukrainian Academy of Sciences, features the concept
of Ukrainian culture as a "system of thought and creativity" generated by the Ukrainian people and reflecting their "ethical ideals"

---

342 S. M. Klapchuk and V. F. Ostafiichuk, eds., *Istoriia ukrainskoi ta zarubizhnoi kultury*, 4th ed. (Kyiv: Znannia-Pres, 2002), 12. As is the case with many other textbooks published in Ukraine, it remains unclear who wrote which chapter(s),
because the fourteen authors are not listed in the table of contents.

343 Ibid., 10; M. M. Zakovych, ed., *Ukrainska ta zarubizhna kultura: Navchalnyi posibnyk*, 3rd ed. (Kyiv: Znannia, 2002), 296–97.

together with the specific features of "national mentality."[344] To better explain what "mentality" is, one of the collection's authors reaches back to the conceptual apparatus of nineteenth- and early twentieth-century scholarship: "This notion had as its historical predecessors the spirit of the people, the nation's spiritual makeup, and the national character."[345]

During the late 1990s and early 2000s, such an understanding of Ukraine's culture as the traditional folk and modern "high" culture of ethnic Ukrainians was allowed to coexist with the textbooks published in southern and eastern Ukraine, where most of Ukraine's sizeable Russian minority lived and where a significant share of ethnic Ukrainians also embraced Russian culture. Indeed, many of these textbooks were even published in Russian. Their authors often preferred to speak of the "history of culture in Ukraine" defining their subject, for example, as the "historical conditions of spiritual life of the population of contemporary Ukraine."[346] Another writer from the same region observes (in Russian) that "today, the culture of each ethnic group is characterized by a combination of components specific to the national culture in question and those common to all humankind."[347] One can see in this example the implicit identification of Russian culture as global or international, in opposition to "local" Ukrainian culture — an understanding that the Soviet authorities encouraged from in the 1950s.

Irrespective of how authors define their subject matter, however, all of them face the same methodological problem — how to structure their narratives of Ukrainian cultural history. This issue, of course, is not simply a structural question, but relates to defining the inner dynamic of Ukrainian culture. Did it go through the same

---

344 M. V. Honcharenko, "Kultura i natsiia," in *Kultura ukrainskoho narodu: Navchalnyi posibnyk*, ed. V. M. Rusanivsky (Kyiv: Lybid, 1994), 5 and 7.

345 M. P. Kozak, "Rytmy kultury i arytmiia epokhy," in Rusanivsky, *Kultura ukrainskoho narodu*, 214.

346 Ie. T. Ievseev, S. A. Kanavenko, V. I. Kovalov, and V. V. Hrebeniuk, *Istoriia kultury Ukrainy* (Kharkiv: Kharkivskyi natsionalnyi avto-dorozhnyi instytut, 2001), 4.

347 K. V. Zablotskaia, ed., *Istoriia mirovoi i ukrainskoi kultury: Uchebnoe posobie* (Donetsk: Ukrainskii kulturologicheskii tsentr, 1999), 218–19.

change of styles and schools as Western Europe or was its development determined by political events specific to this corner of Eastern Europe, such as foreign domination, assimilation, and attempts
to regain statehood? The first decision authors have to make, however, *is* structural. In surveys of Ukrainian culture, it is the division
into chapters, and in surveys of world and Ukrainian culture, it is
the division, if any, between the two.

In the overwhelming majority of textbooks on the history of
world and Ukrainian culture these two subjects are treated separately: world culture first and Ukrainian second. An obvious theoretical difficulty that authors encounter is where to discuss Russian
culture, both the one produced in Russia (but consumed in
Ukraine) and the one produced in Ukraine by ethnic Russians and
Russian-speaking Ukrainians. One solution popular with textbook
authors from eastern Ukraine is to feature Russian culture prominently in the section on the world. Thus, the reader sees Russian
culture as equal to the best achievements of the West, with the
names of Russian writers and artists mentioned next to those of
Western cultural figures. Fedor Rokotov appears next to Francisco
Goya, Denis Fonvizin follows Gotthold Ephraim Lessing, Vasily
Zhukovsky is in the same sentence as Lord Byron, Petr Tchaikovsky
is grouped with Giuseppe Verdi, Vladimir Favorsky is paired with
Pablo Picasso, and Andrei Tarkovsky follows Ingmar Bergman.
Ukrainians who wrote in Russian or worked in Russia are also
listed there: Nikolai Gogol is discussed together with Honoré de
Balzac, Ilia Repin on the same page as the Impressionists, and the
Ukrainian-born Russian writer Mikhail Bulgakov is mentioned on
par with Thomas Mann and James Joyce. The Winter Palace in St.
Petersburg is a popular example of Baroque architecture, while one
author calls Moscow "one of Europe's architectural centers during
the twentieth century."[348] Although later chapters in such textbooks

---

348 See Zablotskaia, *Istoriia mirovoi*, 157, 178, 183, and 206; A. M. Vorobev, G. A.
Lisovik, et al., *Ukrainskaia i zarubezhnaia kultura: Uchebnoe posobie* (Kyiv: Natsionalnyi aviatsionnyi universitet, 2002), 145, 150, 152, 163, 170, 183, and 185 (the
quote about Moscow).

duly discuss the development of Ukrainian culture, in such a context its separate treatment makes the culture of ethnic Ukrainians
sound less prestigious and less developed. Such narratives reproduce the cultural hierarchies developed in the Russian Empire and
the Soviet Union.

The majority of textbook authors realize the danger of exclud-
ing Ukrainian culture from world culture, but their ways of getting
around this problem differ. Most prefer to keep separate the narratives of world and Ukrainian culture because of the different criteria employed in periodization — world culture develops from primitive art to postmodernism, while Ukrainian culture proceeds from
this ethnic group's origins to state independence. (This contradiction is discussed below.) Such periodization can be seen as emphasizing independence and decolonization, but in reality it reflected
the Soviet conventions of analyzing culture according to the so-
called socioeconomic formations. For those (usually Ukrainophone) authors who were uncomfortable with this division the easy
solution is to include some Ukrainian examples — together with
Russian ones — in the story of world culture, while treating Ukrainian culture fully in the second part of the book. Thus, the reader
finds Pavlo Rusyn and Stanislav Orikhovsky listed among the Renaissance writers, Taras Shevchenko's paintings discussed as examples of Romanticism in art, and the poetry of young Pavlo Ty-
chyna mentioned in the same sentence as that of Paul Verlaine and
Rainer Maria Rilke.[349]

Ironically, Ukrainian inserts into universal cultural history,
apparently written by specialists on Western culture, are sometimes
more sophisticated than the discussion of the same topics in
"Ukrainian" chapters penned by narrow specialists on Ukraine,
many of whom had been trained as Soviet propagandists. One textbook intended for the education of military engineers features in its

---

349   See A. Iartys and V. Melnyk, eds., *Lektsii z istorii svitovoi ta vitchyznianoi kultury*,
2nd ed. (Lviv: Svit, 2005), 233 and 286; V. Hrechenko, I. Chornyi, V. Kushneruk,
and V. Rezhko, *Istoriia svitovoi ta ukrainskoi kultury* (Kyiv: Litera, 2005), 162 and
233; V. T. Zhezherun and V. H. Rybalka, eds., *Ukrainska ta zarubizhna kultura*
(Kharkiv: Slobozhanshchyna, 2003), 191 and 285.

world-culture section a discussion of differences between the European and Ukrainian Enlightenment during the eighteenth century—as a consequence of Russian cultural controls, in Ukraine philosophy was not yet separate from theology, and natural sciences were slow to develop—which is superior not just to its Ukrainian sections, but to other surveys of Ukrainian culture for Humanities students.[350]

Another, less popular, solution is to combine in a single chapter a discussion of world and Ukrainian culture during the same period. The difficulties there, illustrated well in the survey edited by S. M. Klapchuk and V. F. Ostafiichuk, include incorporating Ukrainian material into early chapters and synchronizing the development of Ukrainian and Western cultures in later chapters. Some patriotic Ukrainian scholars—perhaps, recent converts from the Soviet school of myth-making—cannot resist the temptation to claim that the ancient Slavs built Stonehenge, the prehistoric Trypillians (who lived in what is now Ukraine in 4,000–2,500 BC) spoke Ukrainian, the famous Sumerian civilization (in the Middle East) was possibly Ukrainian, and the proto-Ukrainians brought Sanskrit to ancient India.[351] It is easier to fit the history of Ukrainian culture into chapters on "Medieval Culture," "The Age of the Renaissance," and "The Age of the Enlightenment," although the Ukrainian section of the latter is called "Ukrainian Culture during the Period of National Revival" and has little to do with the European Enlightenment either thematically or chronologically. In the titles of later chapters, artistic styles and philosophical trends give way to simple chronology: mid-nineteenth to early twentieth centuries (encompassing Realism, Modernism, and the national school in Ukrainian culture), the interwar period, and—in a throwback to the awkward-sounding Soviet term for the period from the late 1950s to the early 1980s—"Foreign and Ukrainian Culture during the Development of the Scientific-Technological Revolution."

350 Ibid., 256–65.
351 Klapchuk and Ostafiichuk, *Istoriia*, 39, 53, and 60.

The problem of matching developments in Ukraine with the established periodization of Western culture is not limited to textbooks that do not divide world and Ukrainian culture. Rather, it is a theoretical difficulty apparent both in double-bill textbooks and in separate surveys of Ukrainian culture. Most authors do not address this problem directly, although it is not new and may be traced back to Dmytro Chyzhevsky, who in his *History of Ukrainian Literature* divided his material into periods that correspond almost exactly to Western literary styles.[352] Yet the authors of present-day textbooks do not follow in Chyzhevsky's footsteps, opting instead for the history of ethnic Ukrainians as a basis of periodization. The period of Kyivan Rus' — which is interpreted as "Ukrainian" in some textbooks but as "East Slavic" in most, and especially in those published in eastern Ukraine — is followed by the cultural stage to which all authors apply the adjective "Ukrainian" — the fourteenth to the sixteenth centuries — when the Ukrainian language developed. The seventeenth and eighteenth centuries can be lumped together or treated separately, but their main theme is the Cossacks. The nineteenth and early twentieth centuries, even when split into two or three chapters, focus on the development of modern high culture based on the peasant vernacular. Independent Ukraine is almost always discussed in a separate chapter.

In one textbook, the entire period from the late eighteenth century to the 1980s is divided into the following two phases: "From the Destruction of the [Cossack] Hetmanate to the Early Twentieth Century" and "Ukraine's Renewed, Interwar and Postwar Subjugation by Her Eastern and Western Neighbors."[353] The vision of the entire nineteenth and early twentieth century as a single cultural stage is common, but when authors want to break it up into smaller time periods, they follow the periodization of the Ukrainian national movement, not that of artistic movements. Thus, they speak of stages of academic interest in folklore, development of literature

---

352 See D. I. Chyzhevsky, *Istoriia ukrainskoi literatury* (Kyiv: Akademiia, 2003) and Hryhorii Hrabovych [George Grabowicz], *Do istorii ukrainskoi literatury: Doslidzhennia, ese, polemika* (Kyiv: Osnovy, 1997), 453–542.
353 Zakovych, *Ukrainska ta zarubizhna kultura*, 298–304.

172 HISTORIES OF UKRAINIAN CULTURE

and education, and political mobilization, or, according to another
book, the cultural-educational period (until the 1890s), the political
period (1890s–1910s), and the period of state building (1910s and
1920s).[354] As explained in previous chapters, this periodization is
ultimately based on Miroslav Hroch's model of national movements in stateless East-Central European states, which reached
Ukraine in the 1990s.

Of course, Ukrainian scholars do not completely ignore the
history of worldwide literary styles and artistic trends, but for them
these are secondary analytical tools, unless they are seen as related
to the development of a distinctive Ukrainian national identity. The
latter is true, in particular, of the Cossack Baroque and Romanticism with its interest in folklore. In some cases, however, authors
apparently see finding a certain period in Ukrainian cultural history as a matter of national prestige, which is particularly true of
the Renaissance. Some authors claim the existence of a fully-fledged
"Ukrainian Renaissance" between the fifteenth and mid-seventeenth century, complete with the "formation in Ukrainian culture
of a humanistic worldview putting humans' earthly lives and work
at the center of attention."[355] Others agree that Italian architects
working in the part of Poland that is now western Ukraine left numerous examples of Renaissance buildings, but acknowledge that
Renaissance humanism did not develop in Ukrainian literature,
dominated as it was by ecclesiastical writings. Instead of "Renaissance humanism," they find "Renaissance classicism" with its renewed interest in antiquity in the work of Ukrainian authors writing in Latin (again, in what was then Roman Catholic Poland).[356]
Yet others realize that the use of Latin and references to classical
humanistic tradition were at best marginal in Ukrainian culture,
based as it was on Church Slavonic as the language of scriptures
and learning. If they want to apply the term Renaissance (meaning

354 Iartys and Melnyk, *Lektsii z istorii*, 473–78 and Zhezherun and Rybalka, *Ukrai-
    nska ta zarubizhna kultura*, 321–30.
355 Iartys and Melnyk, *Lektsii z istorii*, 416 and 419.
356 S. O. Cherepanova, ed., *Ukrainska kultura: Istoriia i suchasnist* (Lviv: Svit, 1994),
    134–35 and 227.

"revival" of ancient learning and humanism) to Ukrainian culture, such authors rethink it as "our national Renaissance."[357] This "Renaissance" refers to the revival of the legacy of Kyivan Rus' and covers the flourishing of Ukrainian education, religious thought, and publishing during the sixteenth and early seventeenth centuries. Ultimately, such creative use of terminology confirms the primacy of Ukrainian nation building over pan-European artistic trends as the basis for cultural periodization.

More interesting yet is the evaluation in Ukrainian textbooks from that period of more recent cultural phenomena, such as mass culture and postmodernism. The divergence between narratives of foreign and Ukrainian cultures is at its greatest in the discussion of the contemporary period. The survey edited by Klapchuk and Ostafiichuk once again provides the most telling illustration of general trends, with its last chapter, "Culture at the Turn of the Century," featuring two sections: "Western Relativism" and "The Cathedral of Ukrainian Spirituality." The first denounces the propaganda of violence in Western mass culture and uncovers postmodernism's "commercial bent," while the second features a rather declarative account of Ukrainian patriotism, state support for Ukrainian culture, and the restoration of the Ukrainian language's proper position in society.[358] Such a juxtaposition is easy to interpret as a reflection of Ukrainian nationalism but, in reality, it is an extension of a recognizably Soviet anti-Western narrative privileging folk and high culture over mass culture and Socialist Realism over the Western decadence and postmodernism. In the world-culture sections of other textbooks, there are occasionally detailed and sophisticated treatments of postmodernism and Western pop-art. One author notes perceptively that today's mass culture is a direct successor of "low culture" that has always existed parallel to "high culture."[359]

---

357 Zhezherun and Rybalka, *Ukrainska ta zarubizhna kultura*, 190.

358 Klapchuk and Ostafiichuk, *Istoriia*, 331–44.

359 See Zhezherun and Rybalka, *Ukrainska ta zarubizhna kultura*, 342–59 and Iartys and Melnyk, *Lektsii z istorii*, 319–38. The comparison with "low culture" is in Hrechenko et al., *Istoriia svitovoi*, 251–52.

But both "low" and "high" culture of the postmodern age re-
ceives largely negative evaluations in surveys of Ukrainian cultural
history published during the 1990s and early 2000s. Chapters on the
late Soviet and post-communist periods focus so much on the re-
versal of assimilation, the (insufficient) state support for Ukrainian
culture, and the return of forbidden works that the reader is left
wondering whether there is a Ukrainian postmodernism. For some
reason, the Ukrainian-born theater director Roman Viktiuk was
mentioned time and again as a native representative of cutting-
edge trends, who has gained worldwide fame — even though he
grew to prominence while working in Russia and is usually known
as a Russian cultural figure.[360] This is probably because his belonging to "high culture" makes him more acceptable to Soviet-trained
cultural historians, in contrast to Ukrainian postmodernists of the
time, such as the literary group Bu-Ba-Bu and its most famous
member, the poet and novelist Yuri Andrukhovych. Perhaps postmodernism, with its subversion of cultural certainties and hierarchies, was not understood by textbook authors during that period
as a strength of Ukrainian culture in its decolonizing struggle
against the still-dominant Russian one, but seen instead as a threat
to a cohesive narrative of Ukrainian culture that these authors believed they were creating.[361] Of course, none of these texts mentioned Ukraine's Russophone writers, such as Andrei Kurkov, who
clearly positioned themselves as members of the Ukrainian political
community.

The same Soviet legacy explains the diatribes against mass
culture found in the majority of surveys, sometimes even in Ukrainian sections of books that in their world-culture sections approve of
mass culture and pop-art. One should not be misled by the fact that
the authors justify their hostility by arguing that mass culture in

---

360   Volodymyr Bokan and Leontii Polovyi, *Istoriia kultury Ukrainy*, 2nd ed. (Kyiv:
MAUP, 2001), 233; Cherepanova, *Ukrainska kultura*, 286.

361   On the liberating potential of postmodernism in Ukrainian culture, see the influential text that would have been accessible to textbook authors: Marko Pavlyshyn, "Ukrainska kultura z pohliadu postmodernizmu," in his *Kanon ta iko-
nostas* (Kyiv: Chas, 1997), 213–22.

Ukraine is primarily of foreign derivation. According to one text-book, "Americanization, Westernization, and the assault of mass-culture kitsch have resulted in their almost complete conquest of our national film distribution network, as well as television."[362] The domination of Western mass culture "began suppressing the inter-est for national culture that has only just woken up" and, moreover, the ideas that universal mass culture propagates "are often alien to our morals and our mentality."[363] Some textbooks see the threat of mass culture to Ukrainian national identity as emanating from both the West and Russia — they speak of the "dominance on television and in mass-media of low-quality and openly hostile output (*vidverto vorozhoi produktsii*) from the US, Western Europe, and Rus-sia."[364] The failure to distinguish between the heritage of Russian colonialism and globalizing cultural trends is notable here. Even the authors of Russian-language textbooks, who typically are not opposed in principle to cultural products generated in Russia, sometimes denounce mass culture in general as "based on sex, ad-venture, and thoughtless enjoyment."[365] Apparently, they do not see such culture as fulfilling the traditional role of the foundation of national identity, regardless of what this identity is.

In fact, open acknowledgement, let alone defense, of the de facto bilingualism that existed in Ukraine at the time is extremely rare in the textbooks under consideration. Only in one textbook published in Ukrainian in Kharkiv in eastern Ukraine do the au-thors criticize the official rhetoric about forced assimilation of Ukrainians in Soviet times and decry the alleged breakup of cul-tural ties with Russia in contemporary Ukraine.[366] But equally as rare are balanced and informed discussions of what modern Ukrainian mass culture is and why much of it functions in Russian. Only one textbook in our sample explains that some "foreign" au-thors of fantasy and romance (popular in Ukraine) whose books are

362 Zakovych, *Ukrainska i zarubizhna kultura*, 541.
363 Ibid.
364 Klapchuk and Ostafiichuk, *Istoriia*, 344.
365 Vorobev et al., *Ukrainska ta zarubizhna kultura*, 196.
366 Ievseev at al., *Istoriia kultury Ukrainy*, 147–48.

published in Russian in Russia actually live in Ukraine: D. Hromov and O. Ladyzhensky write as Henry Lyons Oldi, while N. Havrylenko uses the pen name Simona Vilar. Market forces, namely, access to a large Russian-speaking market common with Russia and the general public's fascination with foreign fantasy and romance, are responsible for the choices these Ukrainian writers have made.[367] The overall lack of discussion in textbooks of Ukrainian popular culture is even more conspicuous because an excellent collection of articles on this topic, *Essays on Ukrainian Popular Culture*, edited by Oleksandr Hrytsenko, was published in 1998 and widely discussed among in Ukrainian intellectual circles. This book is structured as an encyclopedia and features entries on subjects as diverse as Anecdote, Bazaar, Poetry, Female Ideal, Soap Opera, Song, Advertisement, Sport, and Dance.[368]

Yet, by the turn of the century there were signs in Ukrainian scholarship of overcoming the distrust of popular culture and the obsession with identity-shaping function of high culture. Philosophers and literary critics have long presented in specialized publications a much more complex view of culture as a system combining diverse elements.[369] In 2001 the Ukrainian Academy of Sciences launched the publication of a fundamental five-volume *History of Ukrainian Culture* that would not be completed until 2013; some volumes came out in two or more books — as many as four in the case of Volume 5. The bulky multi-authored volumes offer a much too detailed narrative to be used as textbooks, and they are priced out of the reach of most students and professors, yet the project is very promising in certain respects. Although superficial patriotic rhetoric occasionally spoils the conclusions to this or that volume, the Introduction to Volume One specifies that the authors did not agree on any common concept or methodology, deciding instead "to be

367 Hrechenko et al., *Istoriia svitovoi*, 461–62.

368 See Oleksandr Hrytsenko, ed., *Narysy ukrainskoi populiarnoi kultury* (Kyiv: Ukrainskyi tsentr kulturnykh doslidzhen, 1998).

369 See V. Shynkaruk and Ie. Bystrytskyi, eds., *Fenomen ukrainskoi kultury: Metodolohichni zasady osmyslennia* (Kyiv: Feniks, 1996); Oksana Zabuzhko, *Dvi kultury* (Kyiv: Znannia, 1990); Ivan Dziuba, "Chy usvidomliuiemo natsionalnu kulturu iak tsilisnist?" *Ukraina: nauka i kultura* 22 (1988): 309–25.

guided in their texts by the philosophical and methodological principles each of them considered appropriate."[370] Such an open declaration of methodological pluralism may sound strange but is actually refreshing for the Ukrainian reader who has grown tired of the strange mixture of Soviet concepts and those that essentialize ethnic nations. Precisely because the volumes are so large and the narrative so detailed, the authors pay much more attention to material culture and everyday life than histories of Ukrainian culture usually do. The five-volume *History* can serve as an excellent reference tool and a source base for well-informed and balanced textbooks.

Another source of optimism during that period could be found in the popularity in Ukrainian colleges and universities of a textbook that was excluded from the preceding analysis: Myroslav Popovych's *Survey of the History of Culture in Ukraine* (1999; 2nd edition, 2001). Written by a leading philosopher and public figure, this book defies the stereotypes of a Ukrainian cultural history. The book's title promises an analysis of cultural life in Ukraine as opposed to the development of ethnic Ukrainian culture, but Popovych also makes his readers think of the latter in inclusive terms. He reaches this aim by asking provocative questions about whether the Bible and Beethoven's music are part of modern Ukrainian culture.[371] Alone among textbook authors from that period, Popovych refuses to define Kyivan Rus' in ethnic terms as Ukrainian, Russian, or East Slavic. He sees it as a society in which there could be no "ethnic" consciousness because the common high culture functioned in Old Church Slavonic (shared with Bulgarians and Serbs), while the population spoke a host of dialects. Popovych also stands out in not applying the term "Renaissance" to Ukrainian culture, denying any conflict between the Ukrainian and Russian aspects of Gogol's identity as a writer, honestly discussing anti-Semitism in nineteenth-century Ukraine, and emphasizing — in-

370 Editorial Board, "Peredmova do piatytomnyka," in *Istoriia ukrainskoi kultury u piaty tomakh*, ed. B. Ie. Paton (Kyiv: Naukova dumka, 2001), vol. 1:19.

371 Myroslav Popovych, *Narys istorii kultury Ukrainy*, 2nd ed. (Kyiv: ArtEk, 2001), 3–4.

stead of the Ukrainian movement's unity — an artistic conflict between modernists and realists in fin de siècle Ukrainian literature.[372]

According to Popovych, ethnic Ukrainian culture functions in independent Ukraine as a center of gravity in a cultural system that also includes the layers of Russian-language Ukrainian culture and what he calls imperial, or common post-Soviet culture.[373] This is precisely the understanding of the modern Ukrainian identity and the role of Ukrainian culture therein, which made its political debut with the Orange Revolution of 2004-5 and became mainstream after the Revolution of Dignity of 2013-14.

* * *

Ever since the appearance of Ivan Ohiienko's survey in 1918, histories of Ukrainian culture have served as important ideological statements on what Ukraine was or should be. Unlike the Western discipline of "cultural history" with its focus on texts and their readings, the history of national culture has functioned in Ukraine as a discursive site, where the debate about modern Ukrainian identity has taken place. During the 1990s and early 2000s, the emphasis on ethnic cultures allowed for the continued presence of imperial hybridity. The distrust of mass culture and postmodernism went hand in hand with the failure to acknowledge the elephant in the room: the still-dominant role of Russian "high" and mass culture. Post-Soviet hybridity also allowed for the coexistence of patriotic Ukrainian and pro-Russian textbooks, each group predominating in different parts of Ukraine and both working with the ethnic understanding of national culture. True decolonization of a Ukrainian cultural narrative could only begin with the appearance of innovative surveys like the one by Myroslav Popovych, followed by the two Ukrainian revolutions and Russia's war on Ukraine. These new narratives and political events have established a new definition of a Ukrainian identity fit for the postmodern age — a civic, multiethnic community anchored in the ethnic cultures of Ukrainians and Crimean Tatars but at home in the global world.

---

372 Ibid., 66, 160–190, 362, 413–17, and 505.
373 Ibid., 723–24.

Part IV

Locating the Nation in European and Global History

9. Postcolonial Studies and Ukrainian Historical Debates of the Late Twentieth Century

The two revolutions in the early twenty-first century and Russia's subsequent war against sovereign Ukraine brought the notion of decolonization to prominence in Ukrainian media and public debates. It is curious that this happened many decades after Ukraine's proclamation of independence in 1991. The global discipline of Postcolonial Studies had made limited inroads in the Ukrainian academy, primarily in literary scholarship, but did not extend to social sciences or become notable in public discourse until the start of the war in 2014, if not until six years later, when Putin openly denied the existence of Ukraine as separate from Russia and launched a full-scale invasion. The discipline of Postcolonial Studies and the concept of decolonization could have been established in Ukraine much earlier, but this chapter will attempt to show that some prominent debates in the Ukrainian historical profession during the 1980s and 1990s were in fact about the decolonization of historical knowledge about Ukraine, even if their participants were not articulating this point clearly.

In 1995 *Slavic Review*, the leading North American journal, published American historian Mark von Hagen's provocatively-named think piece, "Does Ukraine Have A History?", accompanied by responses from six other scholars. This discussion in *Slavic Review* raised many important topics, such as the place occupied by Ukrainian Studies in North American academia, the transition of Ukrainian historical scholarship to Western models, and the role of historians in creating or deconstructing the national myth. Von Hagen's initial question, however, might have encouraged the rethinking of some deeper problems of Easter European history. For those who have been following the rise of the Postcolonial paradigm in historical writing, and especially for readers of the 1994 landmark Forum on the Subaltern Studies group in *American Historical Review*, the question "Does X have a history?" would signal interest in a

181

group of closely connected problems. The question might have suggested a debate about the field's liberation from grand narratives privileging colonial powers. It could involve the issues of agency and autonomy in Eastern European history; the functioning of the dominant discourses of progress, modernity, and "legitimate" nation-states; the questioning of the universal narrative of "European" history; and the invention and marginalization of the "Other" in this capital-H History.

Such a discussion did not happen at the time. However, this chapter will show that the issue of decolonizing Ukrainian history was implicitly present in the 1994 forum in the *Slavic Review*, if not articulated by its participants. Like some earlier discussions in the profession, it can be understood best in connection with the ongoing global debates about power, knowledge, agency and the functioning of dominant narratives that, in the field of professional historical writing, were initiated by the Subaltern Studies project.

As Gyan Prakash, Robert Young, and others have argued, postcolonial criticism seeks to undo the Eurocentrism produced by the institution of the West's trajectory—a task seemingly opposite to that of Ukrainian intellectuals during the late twentieth century. Postcolonial criticism deconstructs the peculiar way in which all other histories become variations of a master-narrative that could be called "(Western) European History"—or simply its provincial/colonial subplots. From this perspective, Marxism, nationalism, and other ideologies of modernity with their universalist stories of reason, progress, nation-state, or mode of production, are also variations of a Eurocentric master-narrative.[374] The Soviet version of history is very similar, in that it assigns the role of a modernizing force to the Russian people.

---

374 Dipesh Chakrabarty, "Postcoloniality and the Artifice of History: Who Speaks for 'Indian' Pasts?" *Representations* 37 (Winter 1992): 1–26; Veena Das, "Subaltern as Perspective," in *Subaltern Studies VI: Writings in South Asian History and Society*, ed. Ranajit Guha (Delhi: Oxford University Press, 1989): 311–24; Gyan Prakash, ed., *After Colonialism: Imperial Histories and Postcolonial Displacements* (Princeton: Princeton University Press, 1995); Gyan Prakash, "Postcolonial Criticism and Indian Historiography," *Social Text* 31/32 (1992): 8–19; idem, "Subaltern Studies as Postcolonial Criticism," *American Historical Review* 99, no. 5 (December 1994): 1475–90; Gayatri Chakravorty Spivak, "Subaltern Studies:

The original historiographic rebellion of the Subaltern Studies group against imperial historical narratives was inspired by Gramsci's concept of the subaltern and the desire to rewrite history from the perspective of the subaltern, on whom the various programs of modernity were imposed. However, this intention to retrieve the subaltern's autonomy was frustrated precisely because the after-the-fact restoration of autonomy contradicted the very essence of subalternity. Thus, the Subaltern Studies collective, which was concentrated on research into South Asian history, and subsequently its followers in other parts of the world, turned to the deconstruction of dominant discourses of modernity, colonialism, and nationalism with the aim of showing how they subordinate other forms of knowledge and agency. Ranajit Guha and other historians seemed to show the way to recovering the subaltern's resistance, myths, and ideologies through the analysis of blind spots, silences and anxieties of the dominant colonial or nationalist narratives.[375]

The limitations of this project became instantly obvious. It was impossible to recover the subaltern's voice where the subaltern was not given a subject-position from which to speak and remained an object of either imperial or nationalist-paternalistic discourse. Here, postcolonial historiography reached and recognized the limits of historical knowledge, when all the researcher can extract from the archive is, to use Spivak's expression, "a pregnant silence."[376] In truth, the questions raised by the Subaltern Studies group and other postcolonial theorists pressed for a radical re-thinking and re-formulation of accepted forms of knowledge.

Although Mark von Hagen did not say so, the "absence" of Ukrainian history in both meanings of this term — as an established narrative and a legitimate academic field — had much in common

---

Deconstructing Historiography," in *Subaltern Studies IV: Writings in South Asian History and Society*, ed. Ranajit Guha (Delhi: Oxford University Press, 1985): 338–63; Robert Young, *White Mythologies: Writing History and the West* (London: Routledge, 1990).

375 Cf. Ranajit Guha, *Elementary Aspects of Peasant Insurgency in Colonial India* (Delhi: Oxford University Press, 1983) and the articles in *Subaltern Studies* I–VII.

376 Gayatri Chakravorty Spivak, "The Rani of Sirmur: An Essay in the Reading of the Archives," *History and Theory* 24, no. 3 (1985): 247–72.

with the "silence" of the subaltern, the notion that was already in use by the 1990s. This chapter will demonstrate how postcolonial perspectives on history can illuminate several of the most important debates and controversies in Ukrainian historiography of the late twentieth century.

The Splendors and Miseries of Grand Narratives

One of the traditional organizing themes of modern universal historical narrative has been the Western European model of "national history," which usually ignores the fact that the paradigmatic Western European nation-states were in fact empires that had successfully assimilated their minorities while building up their overseas colonial possessions. As Robert Young notes perceptively, History with a capital-H simply cannot tolerate Otherness or leave it outside its economy of inclusion; the Other is necessarily appropriated as a form of knowledge within a totalizing system of universal history.[377] The "nation-state" of the Western European type became a fundamental category that shaped historical thinking. All "Other" communities were marginalized, understood either in terms of a lack, a deflection from the ideal type of Western European nation-state, or dismissed as being "without history."

Owing to the fact that the autonomous Ukrainian Cossack state within the Russian Empire ceased to exist in the late eighteenth century and the Western Ukrainian principalities lost the last vestiges of their statehood by the sixteenth century at the latest, Ukrainians did not fit into that universal criterion of "historicity." And although the debate about the "non-historical" character of the Ukrainian people still appeared in the pages of *Harvard Ukrainian Studies* and occupied the attention of Ukrainian scholars in the 1980s, its roots go back to the late eighteenth century.

In the last decade of the eighteenth century, when an authoritative collective of British and continental historians planned the

---

[377] Young, *White Mythologies*, 4. For insightful remarks on "Europe" as a silent referent in modern historical knowledge, see Chakrabarty, "Postcoloniality and the Artifice of History."

publication of a corpus of universal history in separate monographs, they allotted to Ukrainian history an entire volume. It was
written by the Austrian historian Johann Christian Engel and published in Halle in 1796. The first part of the book contained the history of the Ukrainian Cossacks, and the second dealt with the history of the (Western Ukrainian) Kingdom of Galicia and Volodymyr.[378] Thus, for the compilers of this book series entitled
*Fortsetzung der Algemeinen Welthistorie durch eine Gesellschaft von
Gelehrten in Teutschland und Engeland ausgefertiget,* Ukrainian history was a legitimate part of universal history, of a master-narrative
of development of nation-states. But soon enough, by the 1820s and
1830s, the compilers of the next authoritative corpus, Gotha Universal History, did not bother to include Ukrainian history, which had
been "consumed" by the grand narratives of Russian and Austrian
imperial histories.[379] The decisive intellectual impetus behind their
decision was Hegel's.

For Hegel, the essence of history is the development of Reason, and the purpose of history is to bring Reason to its ultimate
incarnation, the "absolute idea." On its way to self-realization,
however, Hegelian Reason follows the familiar path of the establishment and development of the nation-state. The state is the pin-
nacle of this march of Reason in history, the "hieroglyph of reason."
Peoples without independent statehood or who enjoyed it briefly
and before modern times are therefore "non-historical," or "his-
tory-less." For Hegel, the explanation lies in these people's "spirit":
It is the *Volksgeist* (spirit of the people) that realizes Reason in history. Hegel's three historical civilizations, with their corresponding
Volksgeister, are the Oriental, the Greco-Roman, and the Germanic.
The Slavic peoples, agricultural and mostly stateless at the turn of

---

378 See Dmytro Doroschenko, *Die Ukraine und Deutschland: Neun Jahrhunderte
Deutsch-Ukrainischer Beziehungen* (Munich: Ukrainische Freie Universitat, 1994),
70–74.

379 Omeljan Pritsak's observation. See Omeljan Pritsak, Taras Hunczak, Ivan L.
Rudnytsky, et al., "Problems of Terminology and Periodization in the Teaching
of Ukrainian History: Round-table Discussion," *Rethinking Ukrainian History,*
ed. Ivan L. Rudnytsky with the assistance of John-Paul Himka (Edmonton: Canadian Institute of Ukrainian Studies, 1981), 233–68, here 234.

the nineteenth century, says Hegel, have "not appeared as an independent element in the series of phases that Reason has assumed in the world."[380]

Hegel's description of the Slavs displays rich colonialist connotations: "The *Sclavonic nations* were *agricultural*. This condition of life brings with it the relation of lord and serf. In agriculture the agency of nature predominates; human industry and subjective activity are on the whole less brought into play in this department of labor than elsewhere. The Sclavonians therefore did not attain so quickly or readily as other nations the fundamental sense of pure individuality — the consciousness of Universality — that which we designated above as 'political power', and could not share the benefits of dawning freedom."[381]

The universalist nature of Hegel's philosophy of history deeply influenced the European intellectual tradition. All principal universal historical narratives of the nineteenth and twentieth centuries came out of it: the dynastic-monarchist master-narrative of the state and reason, the liberal master-narrative of nation-state and progress (which competed with the former and finally absorbed it), and the Marxist master-narrative of the mode of production and class struggle. However, the attempts of all these universal narratives to discover their "major" trends of history in Ukraine's past and thus satisfactorily accommodate Ukrainians into a unified world history, if undertaken at all, were repeatedly frustrated. To appropriate the Ukrainian past within the totalizing systems of knowledge, these master-narratives used two basic tools: marginalizing the Ukrainian experience as not clearly reflecting the most salient trends of history and inventing special accommodating devices to compensate for their failure, like the "non-historical" character of the Ukrainian nation in the liberal master-narrative of nation-state and "backwardness and underdevelopment" in the Marxist master-narrative.

380   Georg Wilhelm Friedrich Hegel, *The Philosophy of History* (New York: Dover, 1956), 350.

381   Ibid., 420.

In the 1970s and 1980s, when chairs and research institutes of Ukrainian studies were established in North America, émigré intellectuals and the post-war generation of scholars became involved in a debate over the "non-historical" character of the Ukrainian nation. The debate was an expression of concern for intellectual legitimization of the field and a desire to place it in the context of dominant universal narratives, periodizations, and terminologies. The round table on the "Problems of Terminology and Periodization in the Teaching of Ukrainian History" at the Ukrainian Historical Conference in London, Ontario, in 1978 expressed these concerns in a coherent form. There, one of the most influential representatives of the postwar émigré generation, Ivan L. Rudnytsky, opted for the traditional master-narrative of the nation, while a scholar of the 1970s generation, John-Paul Himka, opposed him from the position of the Marxist master-narrative. Himka, in particular, refused to see the nineteenth century in Ukraine only as "the Age of National Awakening" and pointed out the importance of the growth of industry in southern Ukraine, the social awakening of the peasantry and, "where there were actual industrial workers," the growth of their class consciousness.[382]

In 1981 *Harvard Ukrainian Studies* published a discussion between Ivan L. Rudnytsky and George G. Grabowicz. In an attempt to apply the general "laws" of European history to Ukrainian history and to enable comparative analysis, Rudnytsky evoked the Hegelian distinction of "historical" and "non-historical" nations. Rudnytsky's ultimate aim was to include Ukraine in European history. The price for doing so was the recognition of the "marginality" of Ukrainian experience: "The Ukraine is undeniably a member of the European cultural community, albeit a somewhat marginal one."[383] What Rudnytsky saw as the difference between "historical" and "non-historical" nations was basically that of the character of the

---

382 Pritsak et al., "Problems of Terminology," 253–54.

383 Ivan L. Rudnytsky, "Observations on the Problem of 'Historical' and 'Non-Historical' Nations," *Harvard Ukrainian Studies* 5, no. 3 (September 1981): 358–68, here 361.

elite and high culture: "I conclude that the decisive factor in the existence of the so-called historical nations was the preservation, despite the loss of independence, of a representative upper class as the carrier of political consciousness and 'high' culture.... Conversely, the so-called non-historical nations had lost (or never possessed) a representative class, and were reduced to an inarticulate popular mass, with little if any national consciousness and with a culture of predominantly folk character."[384] This distinction implied the essential "normality" of the social structure of the (Western) European nation-state and modern (European) "high" culture, with the notion of "national consciousness" substituting for the Hegelian *Volksgeist*. Accordingly, Rudnytsky classified Ukrainians as a "non-historical" nation.

A representative of the next generation of academics of Ukrainian background who had grown up in North America, the structuralist historian of literature George G. Grabowicz, opposed this concept by stressing the specificity and uniqueness of all cultural phenomena and the pointlessness of measuring them against some absolute standard. He also questioned the core category of modern universal narratives. According to him, the meaning of "nation" itself is "polysemous and often amorphous and thus precisely requiring a pluralistic, model approach." Grabowicz went on to show that in Rudnytsky's classification "political consciousness and power is [sic] made into *the* criterion for determining degree and quality of nationhood, and the state... remains the ultimate yardstick."[385] The debate, however, was also a generic misunderstanding between a practicing historian, who looked for the laws of development of humankind and their application to concrete societies, and a literary scholar, who stressed the intrinsic value of all cultures and societies. Until the 1990s, the concept of a "non-historical" nation remained a major methodological tool of Ukrainian historiography in the diaspora. This included Marxist historians as

---

384 Ibid., 362–63.
385 George G. Grabowicz, "Some Further Observations on 'Non-historical' Nations and 'Incomplete' Literatures: A Reply to Ivan L. Rudnytsky," *Harvard Ukrainian Studies* 5, no. 3 (September 1981): 369–80, here 379.

well. For example, Himka also used this concept in his first book, which came out in 1983.[386]

In this context, one observation that Mark von Hagen made during the 1995 discussion in *Slavic Review* seems most perceptive. He noted that Ukrainian historians "have tried valiantly but ultimately in vain to configure Ukraine's past in line with the once conventional but increasingly outdated narrative of the formation of the nation-state."[387] In fact, the Ukrainian past may be best interpreted within a new framework that questions the established models: "Ukraine represents a case of a national culture with extremely permeable frontiers, but a case that perhaps corresponds to postmodern political developments... In other words, what has been perceived as the 'weakness' of Ukrainian history or its 'defects' when measured against the putative standards of west European states such as France and Britain, ought to be turned into 'strengths' for a new historiography. Precisely the fluidity of frontiers, the permeability of cultures, the historic multi-ethnic society is what could make Ukrainian history a very 'modern' field of inquiry."[388] Von Hagen concluded his discussion piece with a statement connecting the dichotomy of the empire and the nation-state, the latter based on the Western European model, to the marginalization of Ukrainian history: "... Ukrainian history can serve as a wonderful vehicle to challenge the nation-state's conceptual hegemony and to explore some of the most contested issues of identity formation, cultural construction and maintenance, and colonial institutions and structures."[389]

Unfortunately, many readers saw the main focus of von Hagen's essay as being placed on the connected, but not theoretical, problem of the marginal status of Ukrainian studies in Western academia. Some participants of the debate concentrated precisely on

---

386 See John-Paul Himka, *Socialism in Galicia: The Emergence of Polish Social Democracy and Ukrainian Radicalism (1860–1890)* (Cambridge, Mass.: Harvard Ukrainian Research Institute, 1983), 4–7.

387 Mark von Hagen, "Does Ukraine Have a History?" *Slavic Review* 54, no. 3 (Fall 1995): 658–73, here 670.

388 Ibid.

389 Ibid., 673.

the latter. The representative of post-communist Ukrainian academic scholarship, Academician Yaroslav Isaievych, plainly announced without further elaboration: "I do not agree that the nation-state model of historical process is out-dated and should be left
to patriotic history teachers and state-building politicians."[390] The
question as to how Ukrainian history could be shaken loose from
the domination of categories of the universal narrative of Western
European modernity was lost in the debate on the "legitimacy" of
the subject in North American academia. The very fact of the primacy of "legitimacy" over methodology in this debate shows the
relevance of the postcolonial view of contemporary Ukrainian historiography. Its most significant social function in post-communist
Ukraine remains the location of the nation in time and space.

Can the Subaltern Imagine a Nation?

One of the most influential contributions to the study of nations and
nationalism has been Benedict Anderson's argument that modern
nations are not the determinate products of given sociological conditions (for example, race, religion, language), but are "imagined
communities" maintained by a wide variety of discursive institutions, ranging from national literatures and languages to national
curricula in education.[391] Two other powerful interventions, those
by Gayatri Chakravorty Spivak and Partha Chatterjee, introduced
several disturbing and creative postcolonial tensions modifying
Anderson's basic model. Spivak's celebrated essay, "Can the Subaltern Speak?" poses radical questions to both colonialist and anti-
colonialist forms of historical narratives. The subaltern is allowed
no subject-position and is continuously rewritten as the object of
imperialism (in Western narrative) or nationalism and patriarchy
(in the narrative of an imperial-educated nationalist elite).[392]

---

390 Iaroslav Isaievych, "Ukrainian Studies—Exceptional or Merely Exemplary?"
    Slavic Review 54, no. 3 (Fall 1995): 702–8, here 706.
391 Benedict Anderson, *Imagined Communities: Reflections on the Origin and Spread of
    Nationalism*, rev. ed. (London: Verso, 1991). The first edition appeared in 1983.
392 Gayatri Chakravorty Spivak, "Can the Subaltern Speak?" in *Marxism and the
    Interpretation of Culture*, ed. Cary Nelson and Lawrence Grossberg (Urbana:

The best example for applying the notion of subaltern agency to Ukrainian history is, perhaps, the so-called Kyivan Cossack movement of 1855. (Coincidentally, this peasant rebellion happened in the same year as the Santal *hool*, the rebellion of Indian peasants, which was the subject of an exemplary analysis by the members of the Subaltern Studies group[393]). That year, when the Crimean War was approaching its humiliating (for the Russian Empire) end, the tsarist government announced the formation of a volunteer militia. Close to 200,000 Ukrainian peasants, construing the militia to mean a renewal of Cossackdom, rushed to form "Cossack" units. Later Ukrainian historians made the case that the national sentiments and traditions of the Ukrainian autonomous Cossack state of the seventeenth-eighteenth centuries were alive among the peasantry, which, because it was Ukrainian, used every opportunity to rebel against hated Russian rule. The sources reveal, however, that, according to the rumors circulating among the peasantry, those new "Cossacks" would receive their freedom from serf obligations; the rebels did indeed end up refusing to serve their landowners. As far as one can reconstruct the rebels' idea of the Cossack past, it was a rather vague utopian myth of "ancient freedom,"[394] something quite different from the understanding of Ukraine that modern patriotic citizens would have. Parallels with the historiography of the Indian peasant rebellions, as studied by Guha, are, of course, striking. There, too, modern historical writing sought to appropriate the subaltern's myths and community bonds by ascribing to the subaltern full-fledged national consciousness and hatred of the foreign oppressors.

University of Illinois Press, 1988), 271–313 and idem, "Subaltern Studies: Deconstructing Historiography," in *Subaltern Studies IV: Writings on South Asian History and Society*, ed. Ranajit Guha (Delhi: Oxford University Press, 1985): 338–63.

393 See Ranajit Guha, "The Prose of Counter-insurgency," in *Subaltern Studies II: Writings on South Asian History and Society*, ed. Ranajit Giha (Delhi: Oxford University Press, 1983): 1–42.

394 Compare Serhii Shamrai, *Kyivska kozachchyna 1855 r. (Do istorii selianskykh rukhiv na Kyivshchyni)* (Kyiv: Vseukrainska Akademiia nauk, 1928) with Stepan Tomashivsky's "national" interpretation in his *Kyivska kozachchyna 1855 r.* (Lviv: NTSh, 1902).

The modern Ukrainian nation was first "imagined" in the nineteenth century by the patriotic intelligentsia, which had a typical middle-class, liberal imagination and was not prepared to challenge imperial rule openly.[395] One of the central concerns of the nineteenth-century Ukrainian liberal imagination was the location of Ukraine (the imaginary one, since the Ukrainian state did not come into existence until 1917) between West and East, Europe and Asia, Poland and Russia.

As Partha Chatterjee has shown, if we think in Andersonian terms, non-European (and one could add, non-Western European) peoples do not have much choice in their national imagination: nationalisms in the rest of the world had to build their imagined communities from the intellectual bricks already made available to them by Europe.[396] Chatterjee qualifies Anderson's theory by exploring the difference between the material and the spiritual domains of anti-colonial nationalism, but the following discussion will restrict itself to Chatterjee's notion of the inescapable secondary character of national imaginations.

The implicit or explicit desire for association with the reason and progress identified with the nation-states of Western Europe, as opposed to the despotism typifying "Asiatic" Russia, was a prominent presence in the modern Ukrainian liberal national imagination. Even radical Ukrainian thinkers on the left of political spectrum sought association with the reason and progress of the "Europe" of political, civil and national liberties, as illustrated by the 1896 manifesto penned in the Habsburg province of Galicia by Ivan Franko and Volodymyr Hnatiuk, "And We in Europe: The Protest

---

395 To date, there has been no study of the nineteenth-century Ukrainian national imagination. Some preliminary observations are offered in my articles "The Body and National Myth: Motifs from the Ukrainian National Revival in the Nineteenth Century," *Australian Slavonic and East European Studies* 7, no. 2 (1993): 31–59, and "The Nation's Clothes: Constructing a Ukrainian High Culture in the Russian Empire, 1860–1900," *Jahrbücher für Geschichte Osteuropas* 49, no. 2 (2001): 230–39.

396 Partha Chatterjee, *The Nation and Its Fragments: Colonial and Postcolonial Histories* (Princeton: Princeton University Press, 1993), 5–6; idem, *Nationalist Thought and the Colonial World – A Derivative Discourse* (London: Zed Books, 1986), Chap. 1.

of the Galician Ruthenians Against the Magyar Millennium."[397] While the "European" dimensions of the nineteenth-century Ukrainian national imagination have yet to be explored, the Ukrainian Revolution of 1917–20 marked a decisive political and cultural break with the previous line of accepting Russia as somehow more modern. The Ukrainian national communists of the 1920s carried forward that legacy of rejecting the empire's superiority. The best-known exposition of this position was provided by the writer and critic Mykola Khvylovy in his appeal for the rejection of Russian cultural influences and an orientation toward the West, coined in his famous slogan "Away from Moscow!"[398]

Of course, the "Europe" that Ukrainian patriots were longing for was in no hurry to accept Ukraine as its constituent part because it continued thinking in colonial terms and was not prepared to let every "non-historical" nation into the club.

Between Europe and Its Elusive "Other"

The question of the nation's location between East and West has haunted Ukrainian historical thought since at least the mid-nineteenth century. Travels in imaginary national(ist) geography became particularly intense after World War II, when Europe became divided by a powerfully imagined "iron curtain" and a significant group of Ukrainian intellectuals found themselves on its western side, teaching in Western Europe and Northern America. The location of Ukraine "between East and West" has developed into one of the major concerns in postwar theoretical and methodological debates among Ukrainian academics in North America.

One of the most influential contributions proved to be Ivan L. Rudnytsky's celebrated essay "Ukraine between East and West"

---

397 Ivan Franko [and Volodymyr Hnatiuk], "I my v Ievropi: Protest halytskykh rusyniv proty madiarskoho tysiacholittia," in *Zibrannia tvoriv*, 55 vols. (Kyiv: Naukova dumka, 1986), 46, bk. 2: 339–50.

398 See James E. Mace, *Communism and the Dilemmas of National Liberation: National Communism in Soviet Ukraine, 1918–1933* (Cambridge, Mass.: Harvard Ukrainian Research Institute, 1983); Myroslav Shkandrij, *Modernists, Marxists, and the Nation: The Ukrainian Literary Discussion of the 1920s* (Edmonton: Canadian Institute of Ukrainian Studies Press, 1992).

(1963; Ukrainian translation, 1976; Polish translation, 1988). Although operating from the nineteenth-century idealist premise of "national character," which was supposedly stable and able to reject "disruptive influences," Rudnytsky makes several insightful observations. First, although the archetypal "West" is represented by the Atlantic, or Western European, zone in Ukrainian political thought and culture, "West" refers to "Europe as a whole." Rudnytsky argues that, in the eyes of Ukrainians, historically "the West" was actually represented by the Germans and, to a stronger degree, by the Poles.[399] Accordingly, this was not the "real" West but, rather, the easternmost representatives of Europe's "common cultural and social heritage." Since Rudnytsky does not develop this promising point about the relative, elusive, and all-marginalizing character of the "West" (were Germany and Poland not struggling with their own imaginary "Easternness"?), it would be helpful to pause here for a moment and examine his interpretation of the East.

The concept of the East, or "Orient," says Rudnytsky, is used in Ukrainian political and cultural texts to refer to two "completely different historical entities": the world of Eastern Christianity and the Byzantine cultural tradition on the one hand, and "the world of Eurasian nomads," on the other.[400] This dismemberment of the East is not without purpose. The raids of the nomads, Rudnytsky writes, were "a powerful retarding factor" in Ukrainian history, and the struggle with them elicited "a strong defensive reaction by the Ukrainian people."[401] The nomadic element, thus, "acted on the Ukrainian people from the outside, without becoming internalized, without becoming a constituent element of the Ukrainian national

---

399   Ivan L. Rudnytsky, "Ukraine between East and West," in Ivan L. Rudnytsky, *Essays in Modern Ukrainian History*, ed. Peter L. Rudnytsky (Edmonton: Canadian Institute of Ukrainian Studies, 1987): 1–10, here 2–3.

400   Ibid., 3.

401   Ibid., 5 and 6.

type."[402] The Byzantine religious and cultural tradition, on the contrary, acted "from the inside, by shaping the very mind of the society."[403]

To paraphrase this representation, the "real" Orient, nomadic and destructive, acted from the outside and was fought with, while the "not quite" Oriental Byzantium, the legitimate heir of ancient Greece and the Roman Empire, influenced Ukraine from the inside. This absolute demarcation may, of course, be challenged by considering the varied and strong cultural influences of the nomadic East in Ukraine's past. According to Rudnytsky, the West that Ukraine dealt with was not the "real" West, but it was still "European" enough. But the East, which had exerted a formative influence on Ukraine, was not the archetypal Orient of nomads; it was an ancient, cultured, civilized, "historical," and thus European Byzantine Empire. No wonder that the result of the interaction of that "West" with this "East" was, for Rudnytsky, "the essentially Western (i.e. European) character of Ukraine."[404]

Ukrainian historical thought outside Soviet Ukraine went on to develop these theoretical propositions. For example, Ihor Ševčenko, utilizing the theoretical concept for the *Annales* School, argued that "in this case of Byzantium we should not speak of the influence exerted upon Ukraine by the East but by a part of Mediterranean civilization."[405] He also reintroduces the criterion already familiar from the discussion about the lack of native high culture in "non-historical" nations: In early modern times, such culture reached the Ukrainians through the Polish language. Thus, Poland once again emerges as the modern Ukrainian "West" but on a par with the new "East," which was actually located in the north — Muscovy.[406]

---

402 Ibid., 6.

403 Ibid.

404 Ibid., 3.

405 Ihor Ševčenko, "Ukraine between East and West," *Harvard Ukrainian Studies* 16, nos. 1–2 (June 1992): 174–83, here 174–75. Reprinted also in Ihor Ševčenko, *Ukraine between East and West: Essays on Cultural History to the Early Eighteenth Century* (Edmonton: Canadian Institute of Ukrainian Studies Press, 1996).

406 Ibid., 177–78.

Interestingly, Ševčenko's essay provoked a impassioned response from the Polish Ukrainianist Wladyslaw A. Serczyk. He was ready to admit that Ukraine was "part of Western Europe," which, for him, meant being part of Poland: "[When] most of the Ukrainian lands were included in the [Polish-Lithuanian] Commonwealth and the Ukrainian economic, political, and spiritual elites yielded to a visible and rapid Polonization, the civilizational development of Ukraine proceeded to an ever-increasing extent according to Western models."[407] Although ostensibly in agreement with the Ukrainian notion of accessing Europe through Poland, this statement also resembled the traditional Polish colonial narrative of "bringing civilization" to Ukraine. For that reason, it brought Serczyk into conflict with the "national paradigm" in Ukrainian historiography. For him, "Ukraine was to become East" the moment its lands were included in the Russian Empire or its predecessor, Muscovy. Consequently, the Khmelnytsky Uprising of 1648 "precipitated and then perpetuated the process of the expansion of the influences of the East."[408] At the same time, most Ukrainian historians would interpret the Khmelnytsky Uprising not simply as an act that detached the core Ukrainian lands from Poland and soon (in 1654) brought them to Russia. The uprising also gave birth to the Ukrainian independent and, later, autonomous Cossack state, and it remains a major state- and nation-building event in Ukrainian history.

Serczyk concludes his argument by juxtaposing twentieth-century Ukrainian strivings for independence, as based on "models of Western democracy," with the Soviet power, which "accepted without reservations the Oriental humility, submissiveness, and servility manifested towards the stronger party."[409] After the publication of Edward W. Said's *Orientalism*, the cogency of such assertions did not remain unquestioned. Still, the main problem with

---

407 Wladyslaw A. Serczyk, "Ukraine between East and West: Some Reflections on Professor Ševčenko's Essay," *Harvard Ukrainian Studies* 16, nos. 3–4 (December 1992): 433–40, here 434.

408 Ibid., 435.

409 Ibid., 436.

Serczyk's model is, rather, the fact that, in a typically colonialist move, it voids the agency of Ukraine itself. It was "Western" while a part of Poland, and "Eastern" while a part of Russia. But did the Ukrainian community have its own culture at all, even with all possible Eastern and Western influences on it?

Living in Imaginary Europe

In the early 1990s post-communist Ukrainian historiography accepted from the diaspora scholarship this leitmotif of "Westernness" in the national imagination. In 1995 a two-volume collection of Ivan L. Rudnytsky's essays was published in Kyiv. The first two reviews that appeared in Ukraine are of special interest here.. The journal *Polityka i Chas* (Politics and Time) published a review article by the noted historian Stanislav Kulchytsky under the revealing title, "Through the Keen Eye of the Talented Researcher: The Ukrainian Past from the Point of View of European History." Kulchytsky stresses that, "according to the two-volume work, the Ukrainian historical process developed over the centuries though with delay, in compliance with the Western European scenario."[410] It is worth noting that the reservation about "delay" is reminiscent of the similar positions of the delay or incompleteness observable in other Postcolonial national histories trying to construct their version of a "European" master-narrative.[411]

The influential journal *Suchasnist* (Contemporaneity) published a review by the prominent literary scholar Dmytro Nalyvaiko, which was even more symptomatic. He begins with the statement that Rudnytsky's essays "are timely and sometimes prophetic in the process of building the independent Ukrainian state."[412] The affirmation of the essentially European and Western character of Ukraine is, of course, "of principal importance."[413]

---

410 Stanislav Kulchytsky, "Hostrym zorom talanovytoho doslidnyka: Mynule Ukrainy z ohliadu na ievropeisku istoriiu," *Polityka i chas*, no. 1 (1996): 57–66, here 58.

411 Chakrabarty, "Postcoloniality and the Artifice of History."

412 Dmytro Nalyvaiko, "Pro 'Istorychni ese' Ivana Lysiaka-Rudnytskovo," *Suchasnist*, no. 1 (1996): 151–57, here 151.

413 Ibid., 152.

Nalyvaiko quotes at length from Rudnytsky's essay "The Role of Ukraine in Modern History," describing the ideology of the Ukrainian intelligentsia in the nineteenth and early twentieth centuries. The historian Mykola Kostomarov "contrasted the Kyivan tradition of liberty and individualism with the Muscovite tradition of authoritarianism and the subordination of the individual to the collective." Later Ukrainian thinkers "saw Ukraine, because of its deeply engrained libertarian attitude, as an organic part of the European community of nations, of which despotic Muscovy-Russia had never been a true and legitimate member."[414]

That a Ukrainian scholar of the post-Soviet period is citing the words of a late émigré colleague about their nineteenth-century predecessors makes this quotation especially interesting. It highlights the continuity of concerns about the location of the nation vis-à-vis "Europe" and the "East." They were present in the liberal national imagination of the nineteenth century, in the milieu of postwar émigré thinkers, and among the new national intellectual elites of post-communist Ukraine.[415]

Both reviews at least implicitly highlight those aspects of Rudnytsky's texts that were most important for the national self-image and formation of a post-communist narrative of Ukrainian history. In fact, Nalyvaiko openly claims that Rudnytsky's two-volume *Historical Essays* will serve "the formation of national self-consciousness in the Ukrainian people, their culture, and their state."[416] The rule of canonization, however, is to exclude or under-emphasize certain topics in a canonized text. For example, the real conclusion of Rudnytsky's essay "Ukraine between East and West" is as follows: "Ukraine, located between the worlds of Greek Byzantine and Western cultures, and a legitimate member of both, attempted, in

---

414 Ibid., 154; Rudnytsky, "Role of Ukraine in Modern History," 18.
415 On the "European" character of Ukraine as "imagined" in post-Soviet Ukraine during the early- to themid-1990s, see Andrew Wilson, *Ukrainian Nationalism in the 1990s: A Minority Faith* (Cambridge: Cambridge University Press, 1997), 173–77; Kataryna Wolczuk, "History, Europe, and the 'National Idea': The 'Official' Narrative of National Identity in Ukraine," *Nationalities Papers* 28, no. 4 (2000): 671–94.
416 Nalyvaiko, "Pro 'Istorychni ese' Ivana Lysiaka-Rudnytskoho," 157.

the course of its history, to unite the two traditions in a living syn-
thesis." He goes on to say that this "great task, which appears to be
the historical vocation of the Ukrainian people, remains unfulfilled,
and still lies in the future."[417] In other words, Ukraine's cultural
identity remains unsettled—a much more complex interpretation
than the eagerly quoted, out-of-context sentence on the Western, or
European, character of Ukraine. In fact, the following sentence after
the oft-quoted statement on "the essentially Western (i.e. European)
character of Ukraine" reads: "But this does not imply the denial of
powerful non-Western elements in the Ukrainian national type.
Common European characteristics have not been abolished or superseded but modified under the impact of forces emanating from
the East."[418] Of course, now that Rudnytsky's texts have been canonized in Ukraine, it is natural that some of his finer points will be
marginalized or avoided.

In Ukraine, like elsewhere, through canonization selected
texts are presumed to serve certain hegemonic functions with reference to the dominant values and structures of the society.[419] The
location of Ukraine between East and West, between Europe and
its elusive "Other," then, is clearly one of the principal concerns of
the modern Ukrainian national imagination.

Some other aspects of the "imaginary historical geography" of
Ukraine may be fruitfully explored from a postcolonial standpoint.
Just to outline a few of them, both of Ukraine's principal incarnations of "the East" and "the West," Russia and Poland, for most of
the modern period were themselves struggling to define their own
position vis-à-vis Europe. This point was made by the then chair of
Ukrainian History at Harvard, Roman Szporluk, in his 1996 article
in the Ukrainian journal *Suchasnist*, which had moved from New
York to Kyiv in 1992. This fact symbolized the joint efforts of

---

417 Rudnytsky, "Role of Ukraine in Modern History," 9.
418 Ibid., 3.
419 Dominick La Capra, "Canons, Texts, and Contexts," in Dominick La Capra, *Representing the Holocaust: History, Theory, Trauma* (Ithaca, N.Y.: Cornell University
Press, 1994), 20–25.

Ukrainian and diaspora thinkers to define the location of the nation.[420] Of course, the "older" nations and successors of the empires that had failed to come to terms with their imperial past are not exempt from concerns about their precise cultural-geographical positioning.[421] In an unorthodox theoretical essay, Alexander J. Motyl also showed that it is the conceptual binary opposition between Russia and "not-Russia" (referring to the non-Russian republics of the former Soviet Union lumped together) that "permits the West to stand above them both, as arbiter and savoir."[422]

Thus, the clear-cut binary opposition between East and West here is impossible by definition. Another rewarding direction of research might be the construction of "Ukraine" by Western historians, geographers, travelers, and writers. An excellent 2010 book by Larry Wolff covers Galicia under Habsburg rule, while the only work that has been published about other periods is an outdated compendium of selected translations without scholarly apparatus.[423] One might also suggest that in 1917–21 Western historians who served as advisers to the victorious allies in their construction

---

420 See Roman Shporluk [Szporluk], "Ukraina: Vid imperskoi peryferii do suverennoi derzhavy," *Suchasnist*, no. 11 (1996): 74–87, here 80–81.

421 On Poland, see Andrzej Walicki, *Poland between East and West: The Controversies over Self-Definition and Modernization in Partitioned Poland* (Cambridge, Mass.: Harvard Ukrainian Research Institute, 1994). On Russia's "personality problem," see Mark Bassin, "Russia between Europe and Asia: The Ideological Construction of Geographical Space," *Slavic Review* 50, no. 1 (Spring 1991): 1–17; Iver B. Neumann, *Russia and the Idea of Europe: A Study in Identity and International Relations* (New York: Routledge, 1996).

422 Alexander J. Motyl, "Negating the Negation: Russia, Not-Russia, and the West," *Nationalities Papers* 22, no. 1 (1994): 263–71, here 271.

423 Larry Wolff, *The Idea of Galicia: History and Fantasy in Habsburg Political Culture* (Stanford: Stanford University Press, 2010); Volodymyr Sichynsky, *Ukraine in Foreign Comments and Descriptions from the VIth to the XXth Centuries* (New York: Ukrainian Congress Committee of America, 1953). Although there is no systematic analysis of how Western travelers and politicians represented Ukraine, there are two helpful surveys of the portrayal of Ukraine in Russian and Polish historiographies. See Stephen Velychenko, *National History As Cultural Process: A Survey of the Interpretations of Ukraine's Past in Polish, Russian, and Ukrainian Historical Writing from the Earliest Times to 1914* (Edmonton: Canadian Institute of Ukrainian Studies Press, 1992); idem, *Shaping Identity in Eastern Europe and Russia: Soviet-Russian and Polish Accounts of Ukrainian History, 1914–1991* (New York: St. Martin's Press, 1993).

of the new Europe "imagined" Ukraine more "effectively" than the Ukrainians themselves. The best-known example is Sir Lewis Namier, who served at the time in the Political Intelligence Department of the British Foreign Office and exercized considerable influence on the British policy toward Poland and its national minorities (especially the Galician Ukrainians).[424] As during Napoleon's expedition to Egypt, discussed by Edward Said, the projects of studying the "Other" and shaping this identity were closely connected, if not united.

The Postcolonial Canon and Postmodern Iconoclasts

Further implications of the "national imagination" for Ukrainian history writing during the 1990s included the *type* of history required to be successful. Returning to the discussion of von Hagen's essay "Does Ukraine Have a History?", one of its main concerns about post-communist Ukrainian historiography was the establishment in Ukraine of "a new integral nationalist dogma, a primitive diaspora narrative that charts the prehistory of the independent Ukrainian state as the teleological triumph of an essentialist, primordial Ukrainian nation."[425] Von Hagen thought that this new — and dangerous — version of Ukrainian history had the potential to be as dogmatic and teleological as the Soviet grand narrative. He argued instead for another, "postmodern(ist)," model that would take into account the political and cultural discontinuities of Ukrainian history and the permeable cultural frontiers that "bound" Ukrainian identity.[426] (Indeed, many decades later the Revolution of Dignity (Euromaidan) established Ukrainian civic identity with political rather than cultural boundaries.)

---

424 See Taras Hunczak, "Sir Lewis Namier and the Struggle for Eastern Galicia, 1918–1920," *Harvard Ukrainian Studies* 1, no. 2 (June 1977): 198–210; Mark R. Baker, "A Tale of Two Historians: The Involvement of R.W. Seton-Watson and Lewis Namier in the Creation of New Nation-States in Eastern Europe at the End of the First World War." M.A. thesis, University of Alberta, 1993.

425 Mark von Hagen, "Does Ukraine Have a History?," 665.

426 Ibid., 669.

Some participants of the debate, however, advocated the "right" of independent Ukraine to have its own teleological national myth. And rightly so, since, as Serhii Plokhy showed in his reply to von Hagen, the role of a highly elaborate historical myth was crucial during the formation of the stateless Eastern European nations.[427] It was once again a non-historian, George G. Grabowicz, who brought a postcolonial view into the discussion of post-communist Ukrainian historiography. (In Ukrainian literary studies in the West, the relevance of postcolonial theory to the analysis of Ukrainian culture had by then been established by the Australian literary scholar Marko Pavlyshyn and his school. In Ukraine, Tamara Hundorova became an early proponent and influential promoter of Postcolonial Studies.)[428] Grabowicz stressed that Ukraine did have a colonial experience, albeit without the classical ingredient of race; a Ukrainian background was no impediment to upward mobility and high office in either the Russian Empire or the Soviet Union. Ukraine's colonial status could be detected in the economic sphere, but was most obvious in the realm of culture, though even there "the colonial model easily meld[ed] with the provincial one."[429] Grabowicz limited himself to a few constructive and insightful propositions for explaining the notion of national victimhood present in the national paradigm of Ukrainian history. His most important contribution is the notion of (postcolonial) collective trauma: "Polemic and defensiveness, and the lacrimogenesis that von Hagen and others see on the present east European scene

---

427 Serhii M. Plokhy, "The History of a 'Non-Historical' Nation: Notes on the Nature and Current Problems of Ukrainian Historiography," *Slavic Review* 54, no. 3 (Fall 1995): 709–16.

428 See Marko Pavlyshyn, "Postcolonial Features in Contemporary Ukrainian Culture," *Australian Slavonic and East European Studies* 6, no. 2 (1992): 41–55; and articles by Anna Berehulak, George G. Grabowicz, and Marko Pavlyshyn in Marko Pavlyshyn and J. E. M. Clarke, eds., *Ukraine in the 1990s* (Melbourne: Monash University, Slavic Section, 1992). Perhaps the best example of Tamara Hundorova's application of Postcolonial Studies to the analysis of Ukrainian culture is her book *Transytna kultura: Symptomy postkolonialnoi travmy* (Kyiv: Hrani-T, 2013).

429 George G. Grabowicz, "Ukrainian Studies: Framing the Contexts," *Slavic Review* 54, no. 3 (Fall 1995): 674–90, here 678.

are less the products of re-warmed nationalist dogmas (although they are that) than the consequence of deep and still unhealed collective traumas."[430] Contributions to Ukrainian Studies, argues Grabowicz, are still articulated in the mode of polemic, self-assertion, and national self-healing rather than self-analysis and revision. Although Grabowicz's interpretation is persuasive, the postcolonial anxieties and frustrations of Ukrainian historical scholarship needed not only to be justified, but also critically examined.

During the mid- to late-1990s, the first promising attempt at this kind of re-evaluation was made in Ukraine. In a paradigmatic postcolonial situation closely resembling the rebellion of the Subaltern Studies group against the grand narrative of the Indian imperial-educated nationalist elite, several Ukrainian historians raised their voices against the idealization of Mykhailo Hrushevsky (1866–1934). The legacy of this greatest representative of Ukrainian populist historiography, who served briefly in 1917–18 as speaker of the Ukrainian revolutionary parliament, was for decades besmirched or suppressed in Soviet Ukraine but revered in the diaspora. With the establishment of the independent Ukrainian state in 1991, the post-Soviet national elites quickly placed Hrushevsky into the new national canon. A book about his life was published in 1992 under the title *The Great Ukrainian* and with a foreword by President Leonid Kravchuk.[431] The rehabilitation of Hrushevsky's name was swift and almost acrobatic.[432] People who for decades had denounced him as a "bourgeois nationalist" and "German spy" suddenly began to quote his every word piously as the highest truth. The publication of a new edition of his monumental ten-volume

---

430   Ibid., 681.

431   See Leonid Kravchuk, "Slovo do chytacha," in *Velykyi Ukrainets: Materialy z zhyttia i dialnosti M. S. Hrushevskoho*, ed. A. P. Demydenko (Kyiv: Veselka, 1992), 5–6.

432   That is, in the aftermath of Ukrainian independence. On the struggle of the national-democratic opposition for Hrushevsky's "rehabilitation" in the late 1980s, see Bohdan W. Klid, "The Struggle over Mykhailo Hrushevsky: Recent Soviet Polemics," *Canadian Slavonic Papers* 33, no. 1 (March 1991): 32–45.

History of Ukraine-Rus' was a major national event. His portrait replaced Lenin's in the assembly hall at the Institute of Ukrainian History of the National Academy of Sciences.

The pompous official celebration of Hrushevsky's 130th anniversary in 1996, complete with ritualistic speeches about his "genius," elicited an interesting reaction from two historians known for their engagement with Western historical concepts. The leading authority on the early modern period and perhaps the most prominent female historian in post-Soviet Ukraine, Nataliia Yakovenko, published a newspaper article entitled "History Knowable and Unknowable."[433] Challenging the new dogmas of "national history," she writes that Ukrainian historians faithfully followed the official line in emulating Hrushevsky, with the result that "the Ukrainian historical scholarship of the 1990s [was] haunted by the *Zeitgeist* of the nineteenth century, which did not suspect that history [was] unknowable." Yakovenko emphasizes that history "as it really was" could not be written and that every historian reflected in his or her writings the ideas, morals, and culture of contemporary society. Thus, Yakovenko was effectively protesting against the enshrinement of the nineteenth-century national-populist approach represented by Hrushevsky in a new, dogmatic grand narrative, and questioning the validity of capital-H History *wie es eigentlich gewesen*,[434] which the former communist elites were turning into their legitimizing tool.

The second, even more politically conscious, intervention was made by the young scholar of nineteenth-century Ukraine, Yaroslav Hrytsak, in the same newspaper. He clearly identified the pompous jubilee and the appearance of the grey-bearded historian

---

433 Nataliia Iakovenko, "Istoria piznavana i nepiznavana," *Den*, 25 September 1996, 6.

434 "The way it really was." This expression belongs to the prominent German positivist historian Leopold von Ranke. Quoted after R. G. Collingwood, *The Idea of History*, rev. ed., ed. and with an introduction by Jan Van Der Dussen (Oxford: Clarendon Press, 1993), 130.

on the new 50-hryvnia bill as indications of "integrating Hrushevsky into the official ideology."[435] Hrushevsky's national-populist
and, subsequently, socialist-federalist views, as well as his adherence (except for a short period in 1918–20) to the federation with
Russia have made the historian a suitable forefather for a hastily-
constructed intellectual pedigree of a new Ukrainian elite that came
mainly from the old Soviet bureaucracy and Russophone industrial
managers. As for Hrushevsky's historical scheme, it "furnished the
scholarly base for the Ukrainian national myth."[436] Carried to its
logical conclusion, Hrytsak's argument would reveal that the new
Ukrainian elite adopted basically the same populist national myth
that was created by the nineteenth-century, liberal, middle-class
imagination.

Symptomatically, the Yakovenko-Hrytsak deconstructive effort elicited responses from two quarters. Speaking once again for
the academic establishment, Yaroslav Isaievych combined his defense of Hrushevsky with the assertion of the knowability of history
and an attack on "the postmodernist trend" in Western historiography that denied it. This trend had presumably influenced Yakovenko but, as Isaievych assured the reader, there had been "more
and more critics of postmodernism in the West," so practicing historians and the public did not have to worry and could continue, in
his words, "to seek the truth."[437] He also argued that the "voluntary
adoption" of Hrushevsky's ideas by the historical profession in
Ukraine could not be compared to the "forced, out of fear of police
and other repressions, imposition of ideological schemes" in the
former Soviet Union.[438]

The second rejoinder, by Les Herasymchuk, originated rather
from the milieu of patriotic Ukrainian writers. He celebrated the

---

435 Iaroslav Hrytsak, "Reabilitatsia Hrushevskoho i lehitymatsia nomenklatury,"
     Den, 29 October 1996, 6.
436 Ibid.
437 Iaroslav Isaevych, "Tverdzhennia pro nepiznavanist istorii styraie hran mizh
     falsyfikatsiieiu ta poshukom istyny," *Den*, 13 November 1996, 6.
438 Ibid.

Ukrainian "ethno-psychosphere," which has been formed "for hundreds and thousands of years." Hrushevsky should not be wronged because he is a part of the "great spiritual heritage" that belongs to the present and next generations of Ukrainians "by right of birth."[439] By revealing the positions among the intellectual elites, this polemic, typical of a postcolonial situation, provided interesting material for the global project of Postcolonial Studies aimed at documenting the links among ideologies, power, and knowledge as they developed in the post-imperial context.

* * *

The debates among diaspora historians in the 1970s, 1980s, and 1990s, as well as those with the participation of their colleagues from Ukraine, who joined this global conversation by the 1990s, look different from the vantage point of the 2020s. One can see in retrospect that the role of Ukrainian history in the decolonization of the field of "Russian and East European" history was really at the heart of those discussions. Yet, the dialogue between Ukrainian literary scholars, who had discovered by then the value of Postcolonial Studies for studying the Ukrainian culture under and after imperial rule, and Ukrainian historians both in Ukraine and in the diaspora, was not yet established. It took many decades, two revolutions, and the Russian invasion to establish decolonization as an important concept in Ukrainian politics and historical scholarship.

---

439 Les Herasymchuk, "Vyhnaty tradytsiiu z modernoho suspilstva oznachaie pozbutysia zemli pid nohamy," *Den*, 3 December 1996, 6.

10. National, European, or Multicultural?

Ukrainian History Textbooks Reimagine the Country's Past

Post-Soviet Hybridity

When the Soviet Union collapsed in 1991, Ukrainian school textbooks still celebrated the socialist "friendship of peoples." Mikhail Gorbachev's *glasnost* was late in arriving in the Ukrainian SSR, where the conservative party boss Volodymyr Shcherbytsky made few concessions to the democratic opposition before being forced into retirement in 1989. That year, academic historians started cautiously exploring the Western and pre-Soviet perspectives on Ukrainian history, but school textbooks followed this trend only after independence.[440]

Their starting point was the late-Soviet concept of Ukrainian history, which fused the elements of a Marxist class approach with a peculiar version of ethnic history resting on the notions of the Russo-Ukrainian brotherhood and Russian guidance. The "friendship of peoples" paradigm served as the obligatory model for discussing the relations between the Ukrainian and Russian nations and, in general, the peoples of the Soviet Union, although it applied to the portrayal of their coexistence in the Russian Empire as well. In fact, the "friendship of peoples" was one way of talking about imperial hierarchies without using the word "empire." Since Stalin's time, a nation's inclusion into the tsarist empire was decreed "progressive" mainly because it established a historical connection with the Russian people. In Ukraine, the alleged age-old striving to unite with "fraternal" Russia was enshrined during the 1940s and 1950s as the national idea of ethnic Ukrainians.[441]

---

440 Fedir Turchenko, *Ukraina – povernennia istorii: Heneza suchasnoho pidruchnyka* (Kyiv: Heneza, 2016), 11–13.

441 See Serhy Yekelchyk, *Stalin's Empire of Memory: Russian-Ukrainian Relations in the Soviet Historical Imagination* (Toronto: University of Toronto Press, 2004).

In its fully developed form during the late Soviet period, this concept of the Ukrainian past included several major components. Official historical narratives started with Kyivan Rus' as the "common cradle" of the Russian, Ukrainian, and Belarusian peoples, then proceeded to the "reunification" of Ukraine with Russia in 1654. The master narrative continued to emphasize the Russian leadership during the Revolution, when the evil "Ukrainian bourgeois nationalists" attempted to undermine the historical unity with Russia. However, according to Soviet textbooks, it was not they but the Bolsheviks who established a Ukrainian polity in the form of the Ukrainian SSR and subsequently, in the course of the Great Patriotic War, gathered within it practically all the Ukrainian lands, which had long been divided among different states. The war allegedly proved the Ukrainian people's commitment to their historical unity with Russia, as opposed to a capitalist nation-state that would be a puppet of foreign imperialists.

The undoing of this late-Soviet historical model did not become the drastic change that one would expect. First, the component of ethnic history was already present in the Soviet narrative, and only the national idea had to be changed from joining Russia to joining Europe. Second, the revision was neither wholesale nor immediate. The administrations of presidents Leonid Kuchma (1994–2005) and Viktor Yanukovych (2010–2014), which are often characterized as "pro-Russian," actually pursued a more ambiguous politics of memory. The historian Andrii Portnov has aptly called it hybrid or heterogeneous, because it allowed for the coexistence of seemingly incompatible interpretations in the context of diverse regional identities.[442] To put it simply, history textbooks combined the elements of the old Soviet approach with those of the Ukrainian national narrative that had been preserved in the diaspora and transferred from there back to Ukraine.[443] On the ground,

---

442 Andrei Portnov, *Uprazhneniia s istoriei po-ukrainski* (Moscow: OGI-Polit.ru-Memorial, 2010), 101–3.

443 This is true of the transformation in Ukrainian historiography in general. See Chapter 2 of this book.

teachers in Lviv could emphasize some aspects of these hybrid narratives and those in the Donbas, completely different ones. This am-
bivalence became gradually erased after the Orange Revolution
(2004–5) and more decisively, after the Revolution of Dignity (2013–
14) and the beginning of Russian aggression in 2014. This process
unfolded most visibly but not exclusively in connection with the
misleadingly called "decommunization" policies (starting in 2015)
and the activities of the Institute of National Memory aimed at undoing the legacy of Russian and Soviet rule.[444] The 2016 revisions to
the school curricula were similar in spirit, introducing for the first
time, for example, a notion already tested elsewhere in Eastern Europe—that of the "Soviet occupation" (initially, only in reference to
the outcome of the Ukrainian Revolution of 1917–21).[445]

Chronologically, the important signposts on the road to a
Ukrainian national narrative, no matter how hybrid, included the
introduction of the concept of the Ukrainian "national revival"
within the Habsburg and Romanov empires (in Vitaly Sarbei's textbook during the early 1990s) and Fedir Turchenko's rehabilitation
of the nationalist side both during the Revolution and World War
II in his popular textbooks that appeared in 1994 and 1996, respectively.[446] However, it was the interpretation proposed by Stanislav
Kulchytsky in the report of the working group of historians that he
headed between 1997 and 2004, as well as in his textbooks, which
came to prevail in the narratives of twentieth-century Ukrainian
history.[447] His interpretation allowed for the two presumably equal
trends in the Ukrainian resistance movement during the war: the
pro-Soviet and the nationalist.

---

444 See Oxana Shevel, "Decommunization in Post-Euromaidan Ukraine: Law and
Practice," *PONARS Eurasia*, January 2016, http://www.ponarseurasia.org/
memo/decommunization-post-euromaidan-ukraine-law-and-practice.

445 "Prohrama dlia zahalnoosvitnikh navchalnykh zakladiv. Istoriia Ukrainy. 10–
11 klasy. Riven standartu," 7, https://mon.gov.ua/ua/osvita/zagalna-
serednya-osvita/navchalni-programi/navchalni-programi-dlya-10-11-klasiv.

446 Turchenko, *Ukraina—povernennia istorii*, 47–58.

447 See Oksana Myshlovska, "Establishing the 'Irrefutable Facts' about the OUN
and UPA: The Role of the Working Group of Historians on OUN-UPA Activities in Mediating Memory-Based Conflict in Ukraine," *Ab Imperio*, no. 1 (2018):
223–54.

This type of hybridity (in the sense of combining the elements of Soviet or Russian interpretations with those taken from the Ukrainian national paradigm) continues to survive in present-day textbooks, but there is also a deeper kind of hybridity marking the persistence of the Soviet-style understanding of social change and subjects of history.[448]

Writing Ukraine into Europe

In considering the development of the new, "European" narrative of the Ukrainian past, one can see its complex interaction with the "national paradigm" and the Soviet legacy of history writing. The initial stage of this process involved a largely declarative Europe-anization of Ukrainian history, which was often accomplished by Soviet-style methods. The actual transformation of Ukrainian history textbooks according to European models is going to take a long time.

It is worth noting that the European idea acquired new meaning in Ukraine after the Orange Revolution and the Revolution of Dignity. Under President Kuchma the notion of Ukraine's European policy orientation coexisted with the view of Russia as also potentially European, even with the idea that the two countries could join Europe together.[449] In 2002, the historians of the two countries held a joint conference on "Russia and Ukraine in the European Cultural Space."[450] However, Russia's own "Eurasianist" choice under Putin, as well as the Russian's leader's condemnation of pro-Western Ukrainian revolutionaries, established in Ukraine the dichotomy between "Europe" and "Russia" as two opposing political choices. For many, this dualism rested on the long history of essentializing "Europe" and "Asia" as incompatible political and cultural entities—and assigning Russia to "Asia." Disentangling

---

448 On this, see Chapter 3 of this book.

449 Kataryna Wolczuk, "History, Europe, and the 'National Idea': The 'Official' Narrative of National Identity in Ukraine," *Nationalities Papers* 28, no. 4 (2000): 671–94, here 685.

450 Georgiy Kassianov [Kasianov], "Common Past, Different Visions: The Ukrainian-Russian Encounters over School History Textbooks, 1990s–2010s," *Bildung and Erziehung* 75, no. 2 (2022): 145–63, here 153.

the political choice and the historical stereotype will one day become a challenge for Ukrainian historians, but at present they are focusing on something else: the final purge of Soviet historical interpretations.

When looking at Ukrainian history textbooks, one notices immediately that the titles of chapters and sections often coincide, either word for word or in part. This is because it is the program, approved by the Ministry of Education, which determines the main issues to be covered in the History curriculum. The textbook authors then try to tailor the structure of their texts to coincide with the program as much as possible. What happens as a result is that, by determining the chapter and paragraph titles, the Ministry defines the overall narrative frame. For instance, if the section of the program and title of a chapter is about the "Ukrainian state," then clearly the authors have to take a statist approach in this chapter and focus on a Ukrainian state as their central theme. Or, if a chapter's title reads "Ukraine's Participation in European Economic and Cultural Processes," then clearly the textbooks' argument is going to be about Ukraine having been a part of Europe during that particular historical period. What will be implicit in this argument is, of course, that Ukraine was not — or not really — part of the "Asiatic" Russian Empire.

What are the salient points marking the post-2014 textbook narratives? One marks the transition from calling the medieval state of the Eastern Slavs Kyivan Rus' — a term invented by modern historians — to referring to it as Rus'-Ukraine. (The chronicles called this polity simply the land of Rus', thus leaving it to later historians to invent the name for the state.) The Ukrainian historian Mykhailo Hrushevsky (1866–1934) popularized the hyphenated name "Ukraine-Rus'" with the publication of his multivolume *History of Ukraine-Rus'* beginning in 1898. His original intention was to bridge the different terminology used by Ukrainian patriots in the Habsburg and Romanov empires, but the term also undermined the identification of medieval Rus' with Russia, while claiming it for

Ukrainian history.[451] Present-day textbooks are opaque about their very similar ideological agenda; one of them explains instead that historians have every right to use the term "Rus'-Ukraine" because most of this state's territory now belongs to Ukraine: "The territory of present-day Ukraine constituted the political, economic, and cultural center of this large medieval empire."[452]

Students find out from their textbooks that this medieval empire was both European and "multinational." But what exactly made the Kyivan state European—and thus implicitly different from that of Muscovy and the Russian Empire? A modern historian would look at the shared social and cultural processes. However, it would not make for a strong argument to claim, as one textbook does, that the similarity between primitive Paleolithic labor tools unearthed by Ukrainian archeologists and ones found in Germany, Poland, and Slovakia demonstrates that "from the very beginning of history the territory of Ukraine developed as part of Europe."[453]

Textbook authors also argue that the traditional periodization of the medieval period in Europe is fully applicable to Ukraine because the Kyivan state was "an organic component of medieval Europe."[454] Yet, there are serious problems in trying to fit Ukrainian history into the usual chronological borders of the Early, Classical, and Late Middle Ages, not to mention the absence of Latin as the universal language of learning. Soviet scholars had experienced difficulties with the application of the concept of feudalism to Kyivan Rus', but had to use it because it was important for Marxist theory.

---

451 See Serhii Plokhy, *Unmaking Imperial Russia: Mykhailo Hrushevsky and the Writing of Ukrainian History* (Toronto: University of Toronto Press, 2005), 167–71.

452 Iu. Iu. Svidersky, N. Iu. Romanyshyn, and T. V. Laduchenko, *Istoriia Ukrainy: Pidruchnyk dlia 7 klasu zahalnoosvitnikh navchalnykh zakladiv* (Kyiv: Hramota, 2015), 33–34. The same term, but without any explanation, is used alternately with the "Kyivan State" in N. M. Hupan, I. I. Smahin, and O. I. Pometun, *Istoriia Ukrainy: Pidruchnyk dlia 7 klasu zahalnoosvitnikh navchalnykh zakladiv* (Kyiv: Osvita, 2016).

453 Svidersky et al., *Istoriia Ukrainy*, 5.

454 V. A. Smolii and V. S. Stepankov, *Istoriia Ukrainy: Pidruchnyk dlia 7 klasu zahalnoosvitnikh navchalnykh zakladiv* (Kyiv: Heneza, 2007), 7.

Decades later, Ukrainian textbook authors kept it because it con-nected the Kyivan polity to Western Europe.[455] When everything else fails, there is also a circular geographic argument: "The period-ization of Ukrainian history coincides with the periodization of the Medieval period in other European countries. This is not incidental. Ukraine is located in East-Central Europe, and pan-European his-torical processes did not bypass it. Therefore, it is natural that the history of Ukraine is a component of European history."[456]

However, one region of Ukraine is excluded occasionally from this essentialist Medieval Europeanness—the Southeast, where pro-Russian political parties predominated in recent decades, ena-bling the Russian annexation of the Crimea and parts of the Donbas. In ancient times, the Southeast "constituted the western section of the Great Steppe." The attacks of the nomads arriving through this corridor "undermined the economic and military might of our an-cestors, and distracted them from the amelioration of their land."[457] It is difficult not to notice here an implicit reference to present-day events, as well as the unproblematic "othering" of this crucial re-gion.

Textbook authors experience similar difficulties with the no-tion of Ukraine as a multiethnic land. One textbook even defines the Kyivan state as an "empire" populated by over twenty peoples, while another calls it "an early Feudal multinational empire similar to Charlemagne's empire."[458] The term "empire" is probably in-tended to underscore Ukraine's past greatness, and it is used here in a positive sense; later, the same textbook speaks of Rus'-Ukraine as a "multiethnic state."[459] In contrast, it has an unequivocally neg-ative connotation in textbooks dealing with the Modern period. Much more common in textbooks covering the Ukrainian history before the twentieth century is the positive affirmation of Ukraine

455 Svidersky et al., *Istoriia Ukrainy*, 82.
456 Ibid., 11.
457 Ibid.
458 Smolii and Stepankov, *Istoriia Ukrainy*, 80.
459 Svidersky et al., *Istoriia Ukrainy*, 179.

as the motherland of all its nationalities – usually without any discussion of historical relations among them. One conceptual slippage in particular makes this omission possible: the failure to define the "Ukrainian people."

Thus, students are told that "the Ukrainian land became the Motherland not only of Ukrainians, but also Belarusians, Russians, Crimean Tatars, Jews, Greeks, Karaims, Hungarians, Romanians, Moldovans, Gagauz, Poles, and Armenians – of everyone who, by the will of fate, connected their lives with Ukraine. The history of Ukraine is the common history of the entire Ukrainian people."[460] In this quote, the "Ukrainian people" clearly stands for the multiethnic population of the land that is now Ukraine.

However, the task of constructing a friendly, multinational Ukraine soon begins to interfere with the equally important ideological agenda of separating the Ukrainians from the Russians as early as possible. For that purpose, textbook authors need a different ethnic concept of the Ukrainian people. Thus, it is already during the Great Migration (fourth to seventh centuries) that the "foundations were laid for the formation of the three different East Slavic peoples: Belarusians, Russians, and Ukrainians."[461] This statement also undermines the Soviet notion of the Old Rus' nationality as the common cradle of the three East Slavic nations. But when exactly did Ukrainians become a separate ethnic group? The authors claim that it was the adoption of Christianity in the late tenth century that helped establish the political and cultural unity of the East Slavic tribes: "The Ukrainian ethnos was formed as a result."[462]

However, the multicultural aspect is not really discussed. The authors state that there were other ethnic groups living in this polity, but they never really engage the question of the relations between them and the East Slavic majority or whether one can telescope back the modern notion of multiculturalism, which is linked to the equally modern concept of citizenship.

---

460 Ibid., 9.
461 Ibid., 18.
462 Ibid., 61.

Defining the Nation

The next salient point is that the concept of nation operates in many textbooks on two different levels. On the one hand, there is a notion, universally accepted in Ukraine, of the national revival that took place from the late eighteenth to the early twentieth century, and which is understood as a "recovery" of national consciousness or "revival" of historical memory.[463] This notion is based on the sound research of Western scholars on the social composition and ideological evolution of the Ukrainian national movement, but interpreted through the lens of Romantic nationalism, which in this case is supposed to be the object of study, but becomes instead a methodology. The concept of the Ukrainian nation thus introduced is an anthropomorphic one, typical of the primordialist school: A nation is like a fully-formed person, who is asleep but needs to be awakened by patriots. Once this happens, the nation proceeds naturally to fighting for its own state: "What results from the revival is the emergence and growth of the movement for restoring a native nation-state."[464] Ernest Gellner famously defined this type of patriotic beliefs as "sleeping-beauty" nationalism.[465]

Intriguingly, though, such a concept of the nation does not conform to the actual definition of nation that one finds in the same textbook: "A nation is a historical community of people that is formed based on the common territory they inhabit, [their] language, cultural features, character, [and] economic connections."[466] This is the well-known definition that Stalin offered in his 1913 work on *Marxism and the National Question*, except that the textbook does not mention the author and, in any case, the authors probably did not take it directly from Stalin's work but from a long tradition of Soviet textbooks and dictionaries that defined a nation precisely

---

463 O. Reient and O. Malii, *Istoriia Ukrainy: Pidruchnyk dlia 9 klasu zahalnoosvvitnikh navchalnykh zakladiv*, 2nd ed. (Kyiv: Heneza, 2011), 14–15.

464 Ibid., 14.

465 See Ernest Gellner, *Nations and Nationalism* (Ithaca, N.Y.: Cornell University Press, 1983), 48.

466 Reient and Malii, *Istoriia Ukrainy*, 8.

this way. This is a good example of a holdover from the Soviet dogmatic version of Marxism, and there are more similar instances in
other textbooks.

But such dualism creates a problem for understanding the
concept of nation. If a nation only wakes up at the time of the national revival, than who were the Ukrainians before that point?
Some textbooks solve this difficulty by distinguishing between an
ethnos and a nation — the latter is defined as an ethnos that "entered
the sphere of political life and determines independently its political aim, tasks, and ways of achieving them."[467] It may seem that the
textbook author is stressing here the work of modern national imagination and perhaps even national mobilization, albeit through
continued reliance on an anthropomorphic depiction of both nation
and ethnos as united organisms. In reality, such a definition admits
the possibility of bringing back primordialism though the back-
door: "The Ukrainian people remained in the condition of an ethnos
for over a thousand years."[468] Furthermore, nineteenth-century ra-
cial-anthropology notions of the Ukrainian national character can
be introduced as fully valid, in particular the supposedly eternal
democratic inclinations of freedom-loving Ukrainians, as well as
their dreamy disposition, romantic emotionality, and fatalism.[469]

Yet, in the end, this textbook's actual description of Ukrainian
nation building during the nineteenth century is also based on Stalin's "objective" criteria. In addition to a common territory and historical past, these include economic ties, although the latter link
back to ethnic features: "Fairs united the Ukrainian economy into a
single Ukrainian national market" and, more generally, trade "as-
sisted the formation of features common to the majority of the
Ukrainian people."[470] Here one starts to wonder how to reconcile
this nation-building role of capitalist trade with the predominance

---

467 O. K. Strukevych, *Istoriia Ukrainy: Pidruchnyk dlia 9 klasu zahalnoosvitnikh navchalnykh zakladiv* (Kyiv: Hramota, 2009), 13.

468 Ibid.

469 Ibid., 20.

470 Ibid., 91.

of Jews in trade and among the urban population in some regions, which this author also notes.[471]

Prominent in Ukrainian history textbooks is the term "national liberation movement" (*natsionalno-vyzvolnyi rukh*). It is applied across the board, starting with the Bohdan Khmelnytsky rebellion of the mid-sixteenth century. At least one textbook also insists that Khmelnytsky had a clear plan—even a "program" of Ukrainian statebuilding. The notion of "national liberation" is also applied to the discussion of the nineteenth century, even to its early decades, when patriotic intellectuals had only begun formulating the cultural foundations of their people's identity.[472] If one is to believe that the Cyril and Methodius Brotherhood (1845–47) marked the emergence of an "all-national Ukrainian ideology shared by the Ukrainian aristocracy and peasantry alike,"[473] then, indeed, the only task of Ukrainian activists would appear to be liberating their land from Russian imperial control. In reality, before 1917 their main task was reaching out to the peasantry, which had to be recruited for membership in a modern nation and, during 1917 and 1918, transitioning from the notion of a socialist federation to that of independent Ukraine.

The Nation-State and Its Elites

The concept of a national liberation movement is especially common in the discussion of the Ukrainian Revolution of 1917–20 and the activities of the Ukrainian nationalist guerrillas during and immediately after World War II. This term is also used for the dissident movement in the postwar Soviet Union and the mass political mobilization in the years before the Soviet collapse. For example, the Ukrainian dissidents of the 1960s and 1970s "became a living

---

471   Ibid., 30 and 210.
472   Reient and Malii, *Istoriia Ukrainy*, 5.
473   Ibid., 89.

representation of the indestructible nature of the Ukrainian national liberation movement, Ukraine's striving for a better life and the creation of a sovereign independent state."[474]

The authors conveniently ignore the fact that the majority of Ukrainian dissidents used the works of Lenin to criticize the late Soviet state, and few pushed for outright independence. In other words, the struggle for "national liberation" appears to be present constantly in Ukrainian history. This teleology of national liberation would look familiar to previous generations of Ukrainians, who studied from Soviet textbooks. The historical experience of the Ukrainian nation should be narrated as reflecting its principal aim, be it the reunification with Russia or the acquisition of a Ukrainian nation-state. If it is the latter, it introduces perfect logic into the attempts to establish the continuity of the state tradition, because it would make sense that the primordial nation was constantly attempting to establish its statehood.

It is easy to see that this statist understanding needs to be reconciled with the relatively more complex concept of a nation requiring a national revival in order to develop fully. This task is achieved through an emphasis on the national elites. Of course, scholars who have sought to explain the peculiarities of nation building in Eastern Europe have also relied on the concept of non-existent national elites (because the nobility had assimilated) and the development during the nineteenth century of a new type of national elite comprised of intellectuals, who then start reaching out to the masses. But these followers of Miroslav Hroch proceed from the notion of a modern nation—as an imagined community and a horizontal brotherhood—only really coming into existence with the mobilization of the masses.[475] On the contrary, the textbooks imply that the "people" were always Ukrainian, but the state existed only during periods when the elites were "true" to their nation.

---

474 F. H. Turchenko, P. P. Panchenko, and S. M. Tymchenko, *Novitnia istoriia Ukrainy (1939–pochatok XXI st.): Pidruchnyk dlia 11 klasa zahalnoosvitnikh navchalnykh zakladiv*, 5th ed. (Kyiv: Heneza, 2006), 166.

475 See, e.g., Alexander Maxwell, "Twenty-Five Years of A-B-C: Miroslav Hroch's Impact on Nationalism Studies," *Nationalities Papers* 36, no. 6 (November 2010): 773–76.

Thus, one commonly encounters in textbooks the definition of Kyivan Rus' as the "first Ukrainian princely state" and the Principality of Galicia-Volhynia as the "second Ukrainian princely state."[476] After that, the Ukrainian lands belonged to other states, until the next attempt to resume the national state tradition, the Khmelnytsky Rebellion.

Another important narrative thread is the participation of the Ukrainian lands in "European cultural processes" and multiculturalism, which comes back at various points and often in interesting ways. One recent textbook, for example, makes an outlandish claim about the Ukrainian history and the history of the Crimean Tatars, namely, that the Ukrainians and the Crimean Tatars shared a "similar historical fate" and that they were "united by a single motherland." Such an interpretive turn goes contrary to the main tenets of national history as the history of the nation, and can only be explained by the Russian annexation of the Crimea in 2014 and the subsequent emphasis in Ukraine on the Crimean Tatars as the peninsula's true owners. The claim that Ukraine and the Crimea constituted a "single motherland" long before the Soviet Union came into existence is paradoxical. The Ukrainian national narrative continues to glorify the Zaporozhian Cossacks as the defenders of their country against the raids of those very same Crimean (and Nogay) Tatars. As we can see, the concept of Motherland becomes very plastic here, which is generally a good thing because it defies any ethnic exclusivity.

The Nation-State and Its Others

At least, this is how things look in theory. It is instructive to examine the representations of another ethnic group, whose presence in the Ukrainian lands has been significant throughout history – the Jews. The Jews first appear (without any explanations of where they came from), together with the Greeks, Bulgarians, and Arme-

---

476 Svidersky et al., *Istoriia Ukrainy*, 179.

nians, as traders at Kyiv's public markets during the tenth and eleventh centuries.[477] After that they disappear again for a long period. Students are told that by the late eighteenth century, Jews constituted 3.5 percent of the population in Right-Bank Ukraine and 10 percent in Galicia, which made them the second-largest national minority after the Poles.[478]

Yet there is nothing about the relations between the Jewish and Ukrainian communities or major changes in Jewish cultural life, such as the Haskalah. Moreover, on the rare occasions when the Jews are mentioned, the authors include them on the list of aliens, who took certain social sectors away from the indigenous population. Thus, in the early nineteenth century in the Ukrainian lands of the Russian Empire, "Traders were predominantly Russians, Jews, and merchants of foreign origins (especially in the South), while tradesmen were Ukrainians."[479] Students do not discover what place the Jews occupied in the division of labor in the Habsburg Empire, and why, but are told merely that some small towns in Galicia were "almost completely Jewish" and that Jews constituted approximately a third of the population in larger urban centers, including Lviv: "Traditionally their life was based on the precepts of the Talmud."[480]

In this framework, it is only natural that Ukrainians are going to reclaim their social and economic place. Indeed, this is what the authors see happening in Galicia as modern market relations develop and peasants start "squeezing out the intermediaries of other national backgrounds, primarily Jews."[481] Fortunately, this process did not involve "bloody excesses," because the Ukrainian Catholic Church "did not foment xenophobia and hatred of the Jews, who were of a different creed, but, on the contrary, called for religious

477 Svidersky et al., *Istoriia Ukrainy*, 94.
478 Reient and Malii, *Istoriia Ukrainy*, 22.
479 Ibid., 24.
480 Ibid., 29.
481 Ibid., 156.

tolerance and reconciliation."[482] This is, of course, an attempt to explain away the pogroms of 1881 in the Russian Empire, which are not mentioned in the textbook, even though many of them took place in what is now Ukraine. The authors imply that interethnic tensions resulted from economic competition, but the Ukrainian "national" church mitigated them, unlike the (implicitly xenophobic) Russian Orthodox Church.

The Holocaust is mentioned in Ukrainian textbooks, but exclusively as a Nazi crime committed in Ukraine. They shy away from any discussion of the role the largely Ukrainian auxiliary police played in the Holocaust or the Jewish question in the ideology of the Organization of Ukrainian Nationalists.[483] Similarly, textbooks discuss only in an evasive way the ethnic cleansing of Polish civilians in Volhynia in 1943.[484] This event is framed as the result of the Ukrainian nationalist insurgents' failed attempt to "establish an understanding with the Polish national forces."[485] In addition to sharing (implicitly) the blame for the ethnic cleansing with the Polish underground, such an interpretation also bypasses the larger historical context. The Volhynian tragedy needs to be contextualized as part of complex Ukrainian-Polish relations, which involved an escalation of violence during the war years. At the same time, coordinated mass attacks on Polish civilians initiated in a single night throughout Volhynia were without precedent. Nationalist ideology and the wartime experience of mass murder must be part of the explanation.[486]

---

482 Ibid., 157.

483 This observation fits in with the findings of Johan Dietsch, "Textbooks and the Holocaust in Independent Ukraine: An Uneasy Past," *European Education*, 44, no. 3 (October 2012): 67–94.

484 Other textbooks do not mention the Volhynian events at all. See, e.g., O. I. Pometun and N. M. Hupan, *Istoriia Ukrainy: Pidruchnyk dlia 11 klasu zahalnoosvitnikh navchalnykh zakladiv* (Kharkiv: Sytsyia, 2012).

485 Turchenko et al., *Novitnia istoriia Ukrainy*, 45.

486 See Timothy Snyder, "The Causes of the Polish-Ukrainian Ethnic Cleansing, 1943," *Past & Present*, no. 179 (May 2003): 197–234; Andrii Portnov, *Poland and Ukraine: Entangled Histories, Asymmetric Memories*, Forum Transregionale Studien Essays, no. 7 (Berlin: Forum Transregionale Studien, 2020).

The methodology of constructing a history textbook in present-day Ukraine is also worth considering. An approach that is becoming increasingly popular in the upper grades is introducing longer excerpts from primary sources, seemingly a device for developing pupils' ability to interpret historical evidence. But both the selection and the exact positioning of these texts in the textbook can be more telling than direct interpretive commentary by its authors.

For example, a textbook supplement for Grade 10 — actually, several chapters printed in 2015 as a thin paperback to bring the textbook's chronological coverage with the changed curriculum — opens with a very long quote from a book that an émigré Ukrainian author published shortly after the Revolution of 1917–20. The quote is so long that one does not see immediately where it ends, because it continues for over two pages. It can be mistaken easily for a text written by the authors, and for all intents and purposes it does serve as an introduction to the book. It is this quote, rather than the authorial analysis, which introduces such important notions as the "inhumane rule of the Bolsheviks" and the "general terror against Ukrainians," which they implemented.[487] This information is introduced through the voice of an émigré Ukrainian politician, but in such a way that it can be mistaken for the voice of the textbook authors. Such a method of presenting major conceptual points is similar to the Soviet convention of quoting Marx or Lenin at length instead of formulating and substantiating their own conceptual vision. When one finds in the same publication small inserts of authorial voice, they simply continue the line that the Soviet power in Ukraine was a rule by "occupiers."[488]

Searching for Ukrainian Capitalism, War, and Revolution

In general, recent textbooks structure their narrative of World War II around the thesis of "two currents" in the resistance movement in Ukraine, the nationalist guerrillas and the Soviet partisans.[489]

---

487 Vitalii Vlasov and Stanislav Kulchytsky, *Istoriia Ukrainy 1921–1938: Navchalnyi posibnyk dlia zahalnoosvitnikh navchalnykh zakladiv* (Kyiv: Litera, 2015), 4.

488 Ibid., 21.

489 Turchenko at al., *Novitnia istoriia Ukrainy*, 23.

Such a take on the war diminishes the contribution of the millions of Ukrainians who fought in the ranks of the Red Army — numerically the largest group by far of ethnic Ukrainians (and Soviet Ukrainian residents of other ethnic backgrounds), who fought on the Allied side in the war. Conveniently enough, framing the Ukrainian war experience as a story of two, implicitly equal resistance movements also diminishes and, in many textbooks, erases completely the existence of the volunteer SS Galicia Division. Just like the experience of Ukrainians in the Red Army, the case of those who volunteered for the SS Galicia Division calls for careful historical contextualization — something that is difficult to achieve in a school textbook. Still, omitting such a discussion or cutting it short is not a productive solution. It is telling that such an approach to the war is not the result of the Russian attack on Ukraine in 2014. It can be found in textbooks published during President Yanukovych's term of office.

Another salient point is the one-sided discussion of the Revolution of 1917–20, with its social component given short shrift. Curiously enough, one can identify in textbooks a number of holdovers from the Soviet social sciences, but not necessarily any assessments of key events. The agrarian revolt of 1917–18 and the upending of urban social relations are usually missing because the overall story is framed as part of Ukrainian state building, its principal milestones being the creation of the Ukrainian People's Republic and the Hetman State. For textbook authors, the concept of a Ukrainian state is the central point of their narrative, whereas the notion of a social revolution is suspect; the latter is seen either as part of the Bolshevik plot to take over Ukraine or an unfortunate social phenomenon that contributed to the Bolshevik victory over the Ukrainian national governments. Hence, the focus on the Ukrainian "state-building process" in 1917–20.[490]

The combination of Soviet holdovers in methodology with the aim of privileging nation and state building produces paradoxical

---

490 Kulchytsky and Lebedieva, *Istoriia Ukrainy,* 175 and 285.

224 NATIONAL, EUROPEAN, OR MULTICULTURAL?

results. Two textbooks in this sample featured a discussion of monopolistic capitalism as the late stage of capitalism — an explanation
of why the revolution was historically predetermined that is taken
from Lenin via old Soviet textbooks. This concept leads nowhere
because the Ukrainian Revolution in the new textbooks is not a social revolt, but a national one. The textbook by Reient and Malii develops this contradiction to the fullest. On the one hand, it uses recognizable Marxist language in discussing the development of the
"rural bourgeoisie" and "rural proletariat" in the Ukrainian countryside following the reform of 1861. The authors also reproduce
Lenin's definition of "monopolistic capitalism," although they call
it a "new" rather than "last" stage of capitalism.[491] At the same time,
they refrain from discussing the development of a revolutionary
movement. Throughout the textbook, they emphasize the essential
goodness of native Ukrainian capitalists, who allegedly cared well
for their workers. The textbook authors finally attempt to suppress
Marxist language in favor of a clerical nativism in a chapter with
the bewildering title "Church and Religious Life in the Second Half
of the Nineteenth Century. Ukrainian Entrepreneurs-Benefac-
tors."[492] There, students learn that, because the Russian Orthodox
Church was in crisis, many seminary students "joined the ranks of
the godless revolutionaries." Since these revolutionaries could become "even more dangerous enemies of everything Ukrainian than
their Orthodox predecessors," it was even more important that
Ukrainian capitalists step in to support "Ukrainian spirituality and
culture."[493]

Conclusion

To sum up, the representative selection of textbooks analyzed in
this chapter demonstrates a rather slow transition to Western models. The European narrative remains largely declarative, because no
Western-style historical methods are introduced. Social history, the

---

491 Reient and Malii, *Istoriia Ukrainy*, 145–46 and 154; see also Kulchytsky and Le-
    bedieva, *Istoriia Ukrainy*, 23 and 67.
492 Reient and Malii, *Istoriia Ukrainy*, 217.
493 Ibid., 218.

history of everyday life, womens' history, and the history of various minorities remain on the margins of Ukrainian textbooks, whereas in the West they have long been seen as fundamental. The national paradigm and political history continue predominating in Ukrainian school textbooks.

However, the reality on the ground, at least before the start of the all-out Russian invasion in 2022, has been different, because teachers had their own political or regionalist sympathies. The regional nature of Ukrainian politics created pockets of post-Soviet nostalgia and pro-Russian sentiment in many eastern and southeastern regions. For example, in 2016 a group of Ukrainian teachers in Zaporizhia, which included a school principal, was investigated by the Ukrainian security service for their membership in pro-Russian social networks and the anti-Ukrainian statements they made there.[494] The new language about "Soviet occupation" has also caused unease among some teachers.[495] An independent association of Ukrainian schoolteachers of history and social science, *Nova doba* (New Age), has been working for two decades to assist teachers in the transition to new programs, but its visibility remains relatively low.[496]

Given that national history and Ukraine's European choice have emerged as an important ideological battleground in Russia's war on Ukraine, it is crucial that Ukrainian historical narratives transition from a declarative Europeanness to writing the history of Ukraine in a modern European way. Teaching students to deconstruct colonial narrative frameworks and understand Ukraine as a multiethnic political community based on democratic choice would give Ukraine an advantage over the rigid and confrontational kind of imperialistic history taught in Putin's Russia.

---

494 *KP v Ukraini*, 16 August 2016, 5.

495 *Vesti*, 12 August 2016, 4.

496 See its web site: Vseukrainska asotsiatsiia vykladachiv istorii ta sotsialnykh nauk "Nova doba": https://www.novadoba.org.ua/.

Conclusion

Russia's all-out invasion of Ukraine has highlighted aspects of modern Ukrainian history writing that were obscured by traditional categories of analysis. It was too easy to dismiss the significance of the transformations in Ukrainian historical scholarship by focusing on the persistence of Soviet-style conceptualization, adhering to the new orthodoxy of the "national paradigm," and borrowing interpretations from the diaspora. Even the perennial concern of representing Ukrainian history as part of European history could appear naïve and parochial — overcompensation for the never-completed transition from the Soviet school of history that linked Ukraine to Russia.

Yet, by decisively rejecting Putin's historical mythologies, Ukrainians have demonstrated the vitality of their new historical narratives, thus forcing the West to look closely at what reading of the past animated their valiant struggle. It became clear that, in the Ukrainian case, the national paradigm played a progressive role as a tool for deconstructing the imperial version of their history. It then began evolving into a constellation of more open-ended narratives informed by modern Western approaches: regional history, microhistory, women's history, oral history, new cultural history, transnational history, and many others.

It turned out that the Ukrainian diaspora had acted as more than a custodian of the historical models from the 1920s and 1930s. By the 1990s, when diaspora historians re-established contact with Ukraine, they were no longer stereotypical émigrés publishing in Ukrainian but highly educated Western professionals not united by any ideology. Rather than dispensing nationalistic dogma, diaspora historians introduced their Ukrainian colleagues to sophisticated Western approaches, particularly the study of the development of the modern Ukrainian nation.

Before long it became clear that certain Western approaches were eminently transferable. Regional history and Borderland Studies, to name a few, actually have a long tradition in Ukraine going back to the 1920s, a foundation on which spatial history could

227

also be developed. New cultural history was indispensable for the study of imperial identities and cultural hierarchies. Oral history took off in the study of the Holodomor and World War II, but soon expanded beyond these fields. Women's history provided modern instruments for conducting research on this once neglected but now burgeoning discipline.

The quest for joining European historical narratives turned out to be a decolonization strategy that outgrew the constraints of geopolitics to reveal its potential for transnational and comparative history informed by Postcolonial Studies. Indeed, the notion that Ukrainian history belonged to the joint European past acquired new meaning with the emergence of a new Ukrainian identity. The two Ukrainian revolutions in the twenty-first century and success-ful resistance to Russian aggression demonstrated the power of the modern Ukrainian idea representing the democratic choice of a multiethnic political community. This civic Ukrainian nation also required modern historical narratives, its values anchored in Ukraine's past.

Public history played a major role in this transition. With the decommunization policies having evolved into decolonization by 2019, historians as civic activists mobilized to speak on behalf of the new Ukraine. One can see in retrospect that many previous histor-ical debates in Ukraine and the diaspora were really about decolo-nization and subversion of imperial narratives. But now that the Ukrainian state and the historical profession have articulated this, it is time for historians to follow Ukrainian literary scholars in dis-covering the significance of Postcolonial Studies. This discipline will contribute greatly to analyzing Ukraine's imperial past and the vestiges of Sovietness in culture and everyday life.

Finally, writing Ukrainian history has become a global enter-prise. No clear divide now exists between historians based in Ukraine and abroad because international mobility and joint pro-jects have made them part of a transnational collective working on a shared set of research objectives. The Ukrainian historical profes-sion, no longer stuck in the limbo of "post-Soviet transition," is making a welcome and long-overdue contribution to European and global historical scholarship. Ukraine matters and with it, its his-tory.

Bibliography

Amato, Anthony J. *The Carpathians, the Hutsuls, and Ukraine: An Environmental History.* Lanham, Md.: Lexington Books, 2020.

Anderson, Benedict. *Imagined Communities: Reflections on the Origin and Spread of Nationalism.* Rev. ed. London: Verso, 1991.

Antonovych, Dmytro, ed. *Ukrainska kultura.* Kyiv: Lybid, 1993.

Arel, Dominique. "The Scholar, Historian, and Public Advocate: The Contributions of Paul Robert Magocsi to Our Understanding of Ukraine and Central Europe." *Nationalities Papers* 39, no. 1 (January 2011): 125-27.

Aristov, Vadim. *Aleksei Shakhmatov i rannee letopisanie.* Kyiv: Laurus, 2018.

Badora, N. "Filosofsko-kulturolohichni idei u tvorchosti I. Lysiaka-Rudnytskoho." *Visnyk Kyivskoho natsionalnoho universytetu im. Tarasa Shevchenka, Ukrainoznavstvo,* no. 4 (2000): 45-49.

Bækken, Håvard, and Johannes Due Enstad. "Identity under Siege: Selective Securitization of History in Putin's Russia." *Slavonic and East European Review* 98, no. 2 (2020): 321-44.

Baker, Mark R. "A Tale of Two Historians: The Involvement of R.W. Seton-Watson and Lewis Namier in the Creation of New Nation-States in Eastern Europe at the End of the First World War." M.A. thesis. University of Alberta, 1993.

Balynsky, Ihor, Iaroslav Hrytsak, and Tarik Siril Amar, eds. *Strasti za Banderoiu.* Kyiv: Hrani-T, 2010.

Baran, V. D. *Davni sloviany.* Ukraina kriz viky 3. Kyiv: Alternatyvy, 1998.

Baran, V. K. and V. M. Danylenko. *Ukraina v umovakh systemnoi kryzy (1946–1980-ti rr.).* Ukraina kriz viky 13. Kyiv: Alternatyvy, 1999.

Bassin, Mark. "Russia between Europe and Asia: The Ideological Construction of Geographical Space." *Slavic Review* 50, no. 1 (Spring 1991): 1-17.

Berezhnaya, Liliya, and John-Paul Himka, eds. *The World to Come: Ukrainian Images of the Last Judgment.* Cambridge, Mass.: Ukrainian Research Institute, Harvard University, 2014.

Betlii, Olena. "Istoryk na pozovakh iz prostorom, abo Chy mozhlyva sinkhronizovana istoriia." *Ukrainskyi humanitarnyi ohliad,* nos. 16–17 (2012): 132-51.

Bilenky, Serhiy, ed. *Fashioning Modern Ukraine: The Writings of Mykola Kostomarov, Volodymyr Antonovych and Mykhailo Drahomanov.* Edmonton and Toronto: CIUS Press, 2013.

_____. *Imperial Urbanism in the Borderlands: Kyiv, 1800–1905.* Toronto: University of Toronto Press, 2018.

_____. *Romantic Nationalism in Eastern Europe: Russian, Polish, and Ukrainian Political Imaginations.* Stanford: Stanford University Press, 2012.

"Bilshist ukraintsiv pohodzhuiutsia, shcho Holodomor 1932–33 rokiv buv henotsydom ukrainskoho narodu." *Hromadskyi Prostir,* 17 November 2014. https://www.prostir.ua/?news=bilshist-ukrajintsiv-pohodzh uyutsya-scho-holodomor-1932-33-rokiv-buv-henotsydom-ukraj-inskoho-narodu.

Bociurkiw, Bohdan. *The Ukrainian Greek Catholic Church and the Soviet State (1939–1950).* Edmonton and Toronto: Canadian Institute of Ukrainian Studies Press, 1996.

Bokan, Volodymyr, and Leontii Polovyi. *Istoriia kultury Ukrainy.* 2nd ed. Kyiv: MAUP, 2001.

Bondar, S. V. "I. Lysiak-Rudnytskyi: Osoblyvosti formuvannia narodu ta natsii." *Visnyk Kyivskoho natsionalnoho universytetu im. Tarasa Shevchenka: Filosofiia, Politolohiia,* nos. 49–51 (2003): 9–14.

Brandenberger, David. *National Bolshevism: Stalinist Mass Culture and the Formation of Modern Russian National Identity.* Cambridge, Mass.: Harvard University Press, 2002.

Brandenberger, David, and Mikhail Zelenov. "Editors' Introduction." In *Stalin's Master Narrative: A Critical Edition of the History of the Communist Party of the Soviet Union (Bolsheviks), Short Course,* edited by David Brandenberger and Mikhail Zelenov, 1–85. New Haven: Yale University Press, 2019.

Buniatian, K. P., V. Iu. Murzin, and O. V. Symonenko. *Na svitanku istorii. Ukraina kriz viky 1.* Kyiv: Alternatyvy, 1998.

Chakrabarty, Dipesh. "Postcoloniality and the Artifice of History: Who Speaks for 'Indian' Pasts?" *Representations* 37 (Winter 1992): 1–26.

Chatterjee, Partha. *Nationalist Thought and the Colonial World – A Derivative Discourse.* London: Zed Books, 1986.

_____. *The Nation and Its Fragments: Colonial and Postcolonial Histories.* Princeton: Princeton University Press, 1993.

Cherepanova, S. O., ed. *Ukrainska kultura: Istoriia i suchasnist.* Lviv: Svit, 1994.

Chyzhevsky, D. I. *Istoriia ukrainskoi literatury.* Kyiv: Akademiia, 2003.

Coleman, Heather J. *Russian Baptists and Spiritual Revolution.* Bloomington: Indiana University Press, 2005.

Coleman, Heather J., and Mark Steinberg, eds. *Sacred Stories: Religion and Spirituality in Modern Russia.* Bloomington: Indiana University Press, 2007.

Collingwood, R. G. *The Idea of History*. Edited by Jan Van Der Dussen. Rev. ed. Oxford: Clarendon Press, 1993.

Dabrowski, Patrice M. *The Carpathians: Discovering the Highlands of Poland and Ukraine*. Ithaca, N.Y.: Cornell University Press, 2021.

Danylenko, V. M., ed. *Povoienna Ukraina: Narysy sotsialnoi istorii (druha polovyna 40-kh–seredyna 50-kh rr.)*. 2 vols. Kyiv: Instytut istorii Ukrainy NANU, 2010.

Das, Veena. "Subaltern as Perspective." In *Subaltern Studies VI: Writings in South Asian History and Society*, edited by Ranajit Guha, 311–24. Delhi: Oxford University Press, 1989.

Datsenko, V. S. "Pryntsypy liberalizmu i problema natsiietvorennia u politychnii filosofii I. P. Lysiaka-Rudnytskoho." *Filosofiia i politolohiia v konteksti suchasnoi kultury*, no. 8 (2014): 184–88.

Departament obrazovaniia Iaroslavskoi oblasti. "Press-konferentsiia Edinoi Rossii i Minprosveshcheniia Rossii ob ekspertize ukrainskikh uchebnikov." 31 March 2022. https://www.youtube.com/watch?v=g5GnejdJiL0.

Dietsch, Johan. "Textbooks and the Holocaust in Independent Ukraine: An Uneasy Past." *European Education* 44, no. 3 (October 2012): 67–94.

Diggins, John P. "Arthur O. Lovejoy and the Challenge of Intellectual History." *Journal of the History of Ideas* 67, no. 1 (2006): 181–208.

Domańska, Maria. "The Myth of the Great Patriotic War As a Tool of the Kremlin's Great Power Policy." *OSW Commentary*, 31 December 2019. https://www.osw.waw.pl/en/publikacje/osw-commentary/2019-12-31/myth-great-patriotic-war-a-tool-kremlins-great-power-policy#_ftn8.

Doroschenko, Dmytro. *Die Ukraine und Deutschland: Neun Jahrhunderte Deutsch-Ukrainischer Beziehungen*. Munich: Ukrainische Freie Universitat, 1994.

Doroshenko, Dmytro. *A Survey of Ukrainian History*. Edited, updated (1914–75), and an Introduction by Oleh W. Gerus. Winnipeg: Humeniuk Publication Foundation, 1975.

_____. *History of the Ukraine*. Edited by G. W. Simpson. Translated by Hanna Chykalenko-Keller. Edmonton: Institute Press, 1939.

_____. *Moi spomyny pro davnie-mynule (1901–1914)*. Winnipeg: Tryzub, 1949.

_____. *Narys istorii Ukrainy*. 2 vols. Warsaw: Ukrainskyi naukovyi instytut, 1932–33.

"Doslidzhennia." Tsentr miskoi istorii Tsentralno-Skhidnoi Ievropy. https://www.lvivcenter.org/academic/research/.

Drahomanov, Mykhailo. "Avstro-ruski spomyny." In his *Literaturno-publitsystychni pratsi*, 263–74. Vol. 2. Kyiv: Naukova dumka, 1970.

Dysa, Kateryna. *Istoriia z vidmamy: Sudy pro chary v ukrainskykh voievodstvakh Rechi Pospolytoi XVII–XVIII stolit*. Kyiv: Krytyka, 2008.

Dziuba, Ivan. "Chy usvidomliuiemo natsionalnu kulturu iak tsilisnist?" *Ukraina: Nauka i kultura* 22 (1988): 309–25.

Editorial Board. "Peredmova do piatytomnyka." In *Istoriia ukrainskoi kultury u piaty tomakh*, edited by B. Ie. Paton, 7–32. Vol. 1. Kyiv: Naukova dumka, 2001.

Editorial Board. "Predislovie." In *Istoriia Ukrainskoi SSR*. Edited by Iu. Iu. Kondufor, 5–16. Vol. 1. Kyiv: Naukova dumka, 1981.

Ekelchik, Sergei. [Serhy Yekelchyk]. *Istoriia Ukrainy: Stanovlenie sovremennoi natsii*. Translated by N. Klimchuk [M. Klymchuk] and E. Leenson. Kyiv: K. I. S., 2010.

Eley, Geoff, and Keith Nield. "Farewell to the Working Class?" *International Labor and Working-Class History*, no. 57 (Spring 2000): 1–30.

Filipchuk, Oleksandr. *Zabutyi sviatyi: Kniaz Volodymyr Velykyi mizh Skhodom i Zakhodom*. Kyiv: Laurus, 2020.

Franko, Ivan, and Volodymyr Hnatiuk. "I my v Ievropi: Protest halytskykh rusyniv proty madiarskoho tysiacholittia." In Franko, Ivan. *Zibrannia tvoriv*. 55 vols.. Vol. 46, bk. 2, 339–50. Kyiv: Naukova dumka, 1986.

Gellner, Ernest. *Nations and Nationalism*. Oxford: Blackwell, 1983.

Gerasimov, Ilya. "The Belarusian Postcolonial Revolution: Field Reports." *Ab Imperio*, no. 3 (2020): 259–72.

_____. "Ukraine 2014: The First Postcolonial Revolution: Introduction to the Forum." *Ab Imperio*, no. 3 (2014): 22–44.

Gerasimov, Ilya, and Marina Mogilner. "Deconstructing Integration: Ukraine's Postcolonial Subjectivity." *Slavic Review* 74, no. 4 (Winter 2015): 715–22.

Gerus, Oleh W. "The Reverend Semen Sawchuk and the Ukrainian Orthodox Church in Canada." *Journal of Ukrainian Studies* 16, no. 1 (Summer 1991): 61–88.

Gladkii, Iurii. *Gumanitarnaia geografiia kak nauchnoe znanie*. Moscow: Direktmediia, 2016.

Grabowicz, George G. "Some Further Observations on 'Non-historical' Nations and 'Incomplete' Literatures: A Reply to Ivan L. Rudnytsky." *Harvard Ukrainian Studies* 5, no. 3 (September 1981): 369–80.

_____. ""The Magocsi Problem" (*Problema Magochoho*): A Preliminary Deconstruction and Contextualization." *Nationalities Papers* 39, no. 1 (January 2011): 111–16.

_____. "Ukrainian Studies: Framing the Contexts." *Slavic Review* 54, no. 3 (Fall 1995): 674–90.

Guha, Ranajit. *Elementary Aspects of Peasant Insurgency in Colonial India.* Delhi: Oxford University Press, 1983.

_____. "The Prose of Counter-insurgency." In *Subaltern Studies II: Writings on South Asian History and Society.* edited by Ranajit Guha. 1–42. Delhi: Oxford University Press, 1983.

Halushka, A., I. Hyrych, et al., *U kihtiakh dvohlavykh orliv: Tvorennia modernoi natsii: Ukraina pid skipetramy Romanovykh i Habsburhiv.* Kharkiv: KSD, 2016.

Halushko, Kyrylo. "Na porozi novoi Ukrainy: Iak kryza staroho svitu porodyla ukrainsku natsiiu." *Dilova Stolytsia,* 10 March 2017. https://www.dsnews.ua/nasha_revolyutsiya_1917/na-poroge-novoy-ukrainy-kak-krizis-starogo-mira-rodil-ukrainskuyu-10032017220000.

Hann, Chris. "Intellectuals, Ethnic Groups and Nations: Two late Twentieth-Century Cases." In *Notions of Nationalism,* edited by Sukumar Periwal, 106–28. Budapest: Central European University Press, 1995.

Hann, Chris, and Paul Robert Magocsi, eds. *Galicia: A Multicultured Land.* Toronto: University of Toronto Press, 2005.

Harvard Ukrainian Research Institute. "The MAPA Digital Atlas of Ukraine Program Aims to Advance Ukrainian Studies Using GIS." https://gis.huri.harvard.edu/about.

Hegel, Georg Wilhelm Friedrich. *The Philosophy of History.* New York: Dover, 1956.

Herasymchuk, Les. "Vyhnaty tradytsiiu z modernoho suspilstva oznachaie pozbutysia zemli pid nohamy." *Den,* 3 December 1996.

Himka, John-Paul. *Galician Villagers and the Ukrainian National Movement in the Nineteenth Century.* Edmonton: Canadian Institute of Ukrainian Studies, 1988.

_____. *Last Judgment Iconography in the Carpathians.* Toronto: University of Toronto Press, 2009.

_____. *Religion and Nationality in Western Ukraine: The Greek Catholic Church and the Ruthenian National Movement in Galicia, 1870–1900.* Montreal and Kingston: McGill-Queen's University Press, 2000.

_____. *Socialism in Galicia: The Emergence of Polish Social Democracy and Ukrainian Radicalism.* Cambridge, Mass.: Harvard Ukrainian Research Institute, 1983.

_____. "The Construction of Nationality in Galician Rus': Icarian Flights in Almost All Directions." In *Intellectuals and the Articulation of the Nation*, edited by Ronald G. Suny and Michael D. Kennedy, 109–64. Ann Arbor: University of Michigan Press, 1999.

_____. "Young Radicals and Independent Statehood: The Idea of Independent Ukraine, 1890–1895." *Slavic Review* 41, no. 2 (Summer 1982): 219–35.

_____. *Ukrainian Nationalists and the Holocaust: OUN and UPA's Participation in the Destruction of Ukrainian Jewry, 1941–1944*. Stuttgart: Ibidem, 2021.

Himka, John-Paul, and Andriy Zayarnyuk, eds. *Letters from Heaven: Popular Religion in Russia and Ukraine*. Toronto: University of Toronto Press, 2006.

Himka, John-Paul, and Hans-Joachim Torke, eds. *German-Ukrainian Relations in Historical Perspective*. Edmonton: Canadian Institute of Ukrainian Studies Press, 1994.

Hobsbawm, Eric J., and Terence Ranger, eds. *The Invention of Tradition*. New York: Cambridge University Press, 1983.

Holovko, B. A. "Spetsyfika vykladannia filosofskykh dystsyplin u natsionalnomu ahrarnomu universyteti." In *Humanitarna osvita: Dosvid i problemy*, edited by M. I. Bletskan, 95–100. Uzhhorod: Grazhda, 1999.

Holubets, Mykola. "Mystetstvo." In *Istoriia ukrainskoi kultury*, edited by Ivan Krypiakevych. 4th ed. Kyiv: Lybid, 2002.

Honcharenko, M. V. "Kultura i natsiia." In *Kultura ukrainskoho narodu: Navchalnyi posibnyk*, edited by V. M. Rusanivsky. 5–21. Kyiv: Lybid, 1994.

Horobets, Viktor. "Naskilky novoiu ie 'nova sotsialna istoriia' v ukrainskomu prochytanni? (Vid redaktsiinoi kolehii)." *Sotsium: Almanakh sotsialnoi istorii* 5 (2005): 7–9.

Hrabovych, Hryhorii [George Grabowicz]. *Do istorii ukrainskoi literatury: Doslidzhennia, ese, polemika*. Kyiv: Osnovy, 1997.

Hrechenko, V., I. Chornyi, V. Kushneruk, and V. Rezhko. *Istoriia svitovoi ta ukrainskoi kultury*. Kyiv: Litera, 2005.

Hrinchenko, Halyna, and Valentyna Kudriashova. "Pedahohichna diialnist Ivana Ohiienka." In *Ivan Ohiienko i utverdzhennia humanitarnoi nauky ta osvity v Ukraini*, edited by M. V. Levkivsky. 5–16. Zhytomyr: Zhurfond, 1997.

Hrinchenko, Helinada, ed. *Slukhaty, chuty, rozumity: Usna istoriia Ukrainy XX–XXI stolit*. Kyiv: Ukrainska asotsiatsiia usnoi istorii, 2021.

Hroch, Miroslav. *A Comparative Analysis of the Social Composition of Patriotic Groups among the Smaller European Nations*. Translated by Ben Fowkes. New York: Cambridge University Press, 1985.

_____. *Die Vorkämpfer der nationalen Bewegung bei den kleinen Völkern Europas: Eine vergleichende Analyse zur gesellschaftlichen Schichtung der patriotischen Gruppen*. Prague: Universita Karlova, 1968.

_____. *Social Preconditions of National Revival in Europe: A Comparative Analysis of the Social Composition of Patriotic Groups among the Smaller European Nations*. Translated by Ben Fowkes. Cambridge: Cambridge University Press, 1985.

Hrushevsky, Michael. *A History of Ukraine*. Edited by O. J. Frederiksen. Preface by George Vernadsky. New Haven: Yale University Press for the Ukrainian National Association, 1941.

Hrushevsky, Mykhailo. "'Malorosiiskiia pesni' Maksymovycha i stolittia ukrainskoi naukovoi pratsi." *Ukraina*, no. 6 (1927): 1–13.

_____. "Step i more v istorii Ukrainy: Kilka sliv shchodo plianu i perspektyv tsoho doslidu." *Ukrainskyi istoryk*, nos. 3–4 (1991–1992): 54–68.

Hryniuk, Stella. *Peasants with Promise: Ukrainians in Southeastern Galicia, 1880–1900*. Edmonton: Canadian Institute of Ukrainian Studies Press, 1991.

Hrytsak, Iaroslav [Yaroslav]. "Iakykh-to kniaziv buly stolytsi u Kyievi? Do konstruiuvannia istorychnoi pam'iati halytskykh ukraintsiv u 1830–1930-ti roky." *Ukraina Moderna*, no. 6 (2001): 77–95.

_____. "Ivan Lysiak-Rudnytsky: Narys intelektualnoi biohrafii." *Suchasnist*, no. 11 (1994): 73–96.

_____. *Narys istorii Ukrainy: Formuvannia modernoi ukrainskoi natsii XIX–XX st.* Kyiv: Heneza, 1996.

_____. "Paradoksy ukrainskoi modernizatsii." In *Strasti za natsionalizmom: Istorychni ese*, edited by Iaroslav Hrytsak, 37–45. Kyiv: Krytyka, 2004.

_____. "Porady na zle i na dobre." *Gazeta.ua*, August 7, 2011. http://gazeta.ua/articles/grycak-jaroslav/_poradi-na-zle-i-na-dobre/393431.

_____. *Prorok u svoii vitchyzni: Franko ta ioho spilnota (1856–1886)*. Kyiv: Krytyka, 2006.

_____. "Reabilitatsia Hrushevskoho i lehitymatsia nomenklatury." *Den*, 29 October 1996.

_____. "Ukrainska istoriohrafiia 1991–2001: Desiatylittia zmin." *Ukraina Moderna*, no. 9 (2005): 43–68.

_____. *Podolaty mynule: Hlobalna istoriia Ukrainy*. Kyiv: Portal, 2022.

Hrytsak, Ia., and I.-P. Khymka [John-Paul Himka]. "Lystuvannia Ivana Lysiaka-Rudnytskoho i Romana Rozdolskoho." *Ukraina Moderna*, nos. 2–3 (1999): 376–413.

Hrytsak, Yaroslav. *Franko and His Community*. Translated by Marta Daria Olynyk. Brighton, Mass.: Academic Studies Press, 2018.

———. "'Icarian Flights in Almost All Directions' Reconsidered." In "Confronting the Past: Ukraine and Its History: A Festschrift in Honour of John-Paul Himka," edited by Andrew Gow, Roman Senkus, and Serhy Yekelchyk. Special issue, *Journal of Ukrainian Studies* 35–36 (2010–11): 81–89.

———. "Ivan L. Rudnytsky and His Visit to the Soviet Union (1970)." In *Cossacks in Jamaica, Ukraine at the Antipodes: Essays in Honor of Marko Pavlyshyn*, edited by Alessandro Achilli, Serhy Yekelchyk, and Dmytro Yesypenko, 543–53. Boston: Academic Studies Press, 2020.

Hrytsenko, Oleksandr, ed. *Narysy ukrainskoi populiarnoi kultury*. Kyiv: Ukrainskyi tsentr kulturnykh doslidzhen, 1998.

Hunczak, Taras. "Sir Lewis Namier and the Struggle for Eastern Galicia, 1918–1920." *Harvard Ukrainian Studies* 1, no. 2 (June 1977): 198–210.

Hundorova, Tamara. *Transytna kultura: Symptomy postkolonialnoi travmy*. Kyiv: Hrani-T, 2013.

Hupan, N. M., I. I. Smahin, and O. I. Pometun. *Istoriia Ukrainy: Pidruchnyk dlia 7 klasu zahalnoosvitnikh navchalnykh zakladiv*. Kyiv: Osvita, 2016.

Hurzhii, O. I., and T. V. Chukhlib, *Hetmanska Ukraina*. Ukraina kriz viky 8. Kyiv: Alternatyvy, 1999.

Iakovenko, N. [Nataliia] M. *Narys istorii Ukrainy z naidavnishykh chasiv do kintsia XVIII stolittia*. Kyiv: Heneza, 1997.

Iakovenko, Nataliia. "Istoria piznavana i nepiznavana." *Den*, 25 September 1996.

———. *Paralelnyi svit: Doslidzhennia z istorii uiavlen ta idei v Ukraini XVI–XVII st*. Kyiv: Krytyka, 2002.

———. "'Pohreb tilu moiemu vybyraiu s predky moiemy': Mistsia pokhovannia volynskykh kniaziv u XV–seredyni XVII stolit." *Ukraina: Kulturna spadshchyna, natsionalna svidomist, derzhavnist*, no. 20 (2011): 784–808.

———. "U kolorakh proletarskoi revoliutsii." *Ukrainskyi humanitarnyi ohliad*, no. 3 (2000): 58–78.

———. *Vstup do istorii*. Kyiv: Krytyka, 2007.

Iaremchuk, Vitalii. *Mynule Ukrainy v istorychnii nautsi URSR pisliastalinskoi doby*. Ostroh: Vydavnytstvo Natsionalnoho universytetu "Ostrozka akademiia," 2009.

Iartys, A., and V. Melnyk, eds. *Lektsii z istorii svitovoi ta vitchyznianoi kultury.* 2nd ed. Lviv: Svit, 2005.

Iefimenko, Hennadii, Iana Prymachenko, and Oksana Iurkova. *Ukraina radianska: Iliuzii ta katastrofy komunistychnoho "raiu": 1917–1938.* Kharkiv: KSD, 2017.

Iekelchyk, S. [Serhii] "Zustrich z kanadskym istorykom Dzh.-P. Hymkoiu." *Ukrainskyi istorychnyi zhurnal*, no. 12 (1991): 152.

Iekelchyk, Serhii [Serhy Yekelchyk]. "Iakshcho kolonialnyi, znachyt my ne buly vidpovidalni za mynule." *Korydor.* October 19, 2016. http://www.korydor.in.ua/ua/stories/sergij-yekelchyk-pamjatre-prezentacija- kultura.html.

Ievseev, Ie. T., S. A. Kanavenko, V. I. Kovalov, and V. V. Hrebeniuk. *Istoriia kultury Ukrainy.* Kharkiv: Kharkivskyi natsionalnyi avto-dorozhnyi instytut, 2001.

Isaievych, Iaroslav. "Tverdzhennia pro nepiznavanist istorii styraie hran mizh falsyfikatsiieiu ta poshukom istyny." *Den*, 13 November 1996.

_____. "Ukrainian Studies — Exceptional or Merely Exemplary?" *Slavic Review* 54, no. 3 (Fall 1995): 702–8.

Istoriia Vsesoiuznoi kommunisticheskoi partii (bolshevikov): Kratkii kurs. Moscow: OGIZ, 1946.

Kappeler, Andreas. "From an Ethnonational to a Multiethnic to a Transnational Ukrainian History." In *A Laboratory of Transnational History: Ukraine and Recent Ukrainian Historiography*, edited by Georgiy Kasianov and Philipp Ther, 51–81. Budapest: Central European University Press, 2009.

_____. *Kleine Geschichte der Ukraine.* Munich: C. H. Beck, 1994.

_____. *Mala istoriia Ukrainy.* Translated by O. Blashchuk. Kyiv: K. I. S., 2007.

Karlovskyi, Denys. "Okupanty na zakhoplenykh terytoriiakh boriutsia z pidruchnykamy istorii, Stusom i Banderoiu." *Ukrainska Pravda.* March 24, 2022. https://www.pravda.com.ua/news/2022/03/24/7334252/.

Kasianov, Georgiy. "'Nationalized' History: Past Continuous, Present Perfect, Future ...." In *A Laboratory of Transnational History: Ukraine and Recent Ukrainian Historiography*, edited by Georgiy Kasianov and Philipp Ther, 7–24. Budapest: Central European University Press, 2009.

Kasianov, Georgiy, and Oleksii Tolochko. "National Histories and Contemporary Historiography: The Challenges and Risks of Writing a New History of Ukraine." *Harvard Ukrainian Studies* 34, nos. 1–4 (2015-2016): 79–106.

Kasianov, Georgiy, and Philipp Ther, eds. *A Laboratory of Transnational History: Ukraine and Recent Ukrainian Historiography*. Budapest: Central European University Press, 2009.

Kasianov, Georgiy, and Philipp Ther. Introductionto *A Laboratory of Transnational History: Ukraine and Recent Ukrainian Historiography*, edited by Georgiy Kasianov and Philipp Ther, 1–4. Budapest: Central European University Press, 2009.

Kasianov, Heorhii [Georgiy]. *Danse macabre: Holod 1932–1933 rokiv u politytsi, masovii svidomosti ta istoriohrafii (1980-ti–pochatok 2000-kh)*. Kyiv: Nash chas, 2010.

_____. *Past Continuous: Istorychna polityka 1980-kh–2000-kh: Ukraina ta susidy*. Kyiv: Laurus and Antropos-Logos-Film, 2018.

Kassianov [Kasianov], Georgiy. "Common Past, Different Visions: The Ukrainian-Russian Encounters over School History Textbooks, 1990s–2010s." *Bildung and Erziehung* 75, no. 2 (2022): 145–63.

Khymka, Dzhon-Pol [John-Paul Himka]. *Zarodzhennia polskoi sotsial-demokratii ta ukrainskoho radykalizmu v Halychyni (1860–1890)*. Translated by S. Levchenko. Kyiv: Osnovni tsinnosti, 2002.

Khymka, Ivan [John-Paul Himka]. "Istoriia Ukrainy ta ukraintsiv u Kanadi u Viddili istorii ta klasyky Albertskoho universytetu." In *Zakhidnokanadskyi zbirnyk*. Vol. 3, edited by Yar Slavutych, 99–119. Edmonton: NTSh, 1998.

Khymka, Ivan Pavlo [John-Paul Himka]. "Nash istoryk, nasha epokha: Ivan Lysiak-Rudnytsky." *Krytyka* XVIII, nos. 1–2 (195–96) (November 2014): 4–8.

Kis, Oksana, ed. *Ukrainski zhinky u hornyli modernizatsii*. Kharkiv: KSD, 2017.

Klapchuk, S. M., and V. F. Ostafiichuk, eds. *Istoriia ukrainskoi kultury: Zbirnyk materialiv i dokumentiv*. Kyiv: Vyshcha shkola, 2000.

_____. *Istoriia ukrainskoi ta zarubizhnoi kultury*. 4th ed. Kyiv: Znannia-Pres, 2002.

Klid, Bohdan W. "The Struggle over Mykhailo Hrushevsky: Recent Soviet Polemics." *Canadian Slavonic Papers* 33, no. 1 (March 1991): 32–45.

Kohut, Zenon E. *Making Ukraine: Studies on Political Culture, Historical Narrative, and Identity*. Edmonton: Canadian Institute of Ukrainian Studies Press, 2011.

Kondufor, Iu. Iu. and A. H. Shevelev, eds. *Istoriia Ukrainskoi RSR*. 8 vols. Kyiv: Naukova dumka, 1977–79.

Kondufor, Iu. Iu., ed. *Druzhba i bratstvo russkogo i ukrainskogo narodov*. 2 vols. Kyiv: Naukova dumka, 1982.

_____. ed. *Istoriia Ukrainskoi SSR*. 10 vols. Kyiv: Naukova dumka, 1980–85.

Koposov, Nikolai. *Memory Laws, Memory Wars: The Politics of the Past in Europe and Russia.* New York: Cambridge University Press, 2017.

Kordan, Bohdan S. *Canada and the Ukrainian Question, 1939–1945.* Montreal: McGill-Queen's University Press, 2001.

Kotenko, Anton. "Povernennia prostoru." *Ukrainskyi humanitarnyi ohliad,* no. 15 (2010): 45–60.

_____. "Space Oddity." *Ukrainskyi humanitarnyi ohliad,* no. 18 (2013): 172–76.

_____. "The Ukrainian Project in Search of National Space, 1861–1914." PhD diss. Budapest: Central European University, 2013.

Kotkin, Stephen. "Class, the Working Class, and the Politburo." *International Labor and Working-Class History,* no. 57 (Spring 2000): 48–52.

Kotliar, M. F. *Halytsko-Volynska Rus.* Ukraina kriz viky 5. Kyiv: Alternatyvy, 1998.

Koval, M. V. *Ukraina v Druhii svitovii i Velykii Vitchyznianii viinakh (1939–1945 rr.).* Ukraina kriz viky 12. Kyiv: Alternatyvy, 1999.

Kozachenko, Antin. *Ukrainska kultura: Ii mynuvshyna i suchasnist.* Kharkiv: Proletar, 1931.

Kozak, M. P. "Rytmy kultury i arytmiia epokhy." In *Kultura ukrainskoho narodu: Navchalnyi posibnyk,* edited by V. M. Rusanivsky. 213–65. Kyiv: Lybid, 1994.

KP v Ukraini. 16 August 2016.

Kravchenko, Bohdan. *Sotsialni zminy i natsionalna svidomist v Ukraini XX st.* Translated by V. Ivashko and V. Korniienko. Kyiv: Osnovy, 1997.

_____. "Zminy v strukturi robitnychoi kliasy na Ukraini (1897–1970 rr.)." *Suchasnist,* no. 2 (1980): 7–25.

Kravchenko, Volodymyr. *Kharkov/Kharkiv: Stolitsa pogranichia.* Vilnius: European Humanities University Press, 2010.

_____. "Lystuvannia Romana Shporliuka z Ivanom Lysiakom-Rudnytskym i Iuriiem Shevelovym (1962–1982 rr.)." *Skhid-zakhid: Istorykokulturolohichnyi zbirnyk,* nos. 9–10 (2008): 208–94.

_____. *Narysy z ukrainskoi istoriohrafii epokhy natsionalnoho vidrodzhennia (druha polovyna XVIII–seredyna XIX st.).* Kharkiv: Osnova, 1996.

_____. *Ukraina, imperiia, Rosiia: Vybrani statti z modernoi istorii ta istoriohrafii.* Kyiv: Krytyka, 2011.

Kravchuk, Leonid. "Slovo do chytacha." In *Velykyi Ukrainets: Materialy z zhyttia i dialnosti M. S. Hrushevskoho,* edited by A. P. Demydenko, 5–6. Kyiv: Veselka, 1992.

Krawchenko, Bohdan. *Social Change and National Consciousness in Twentieth-Century Ukraine.* London: Macmillan, 1985.

Krawchenko [Kravchenko], Bohdan, and Roman Serbyn, eds. *Famine in Ukraine (1932–1933)*. Edmonton: Canadian Institute of Ukrainian Studies, 1986.

Krechetova, Diana. "Okupanty vyluchaiut z bibliotek ukrainski knyzhky, shchob znyshchyty ikh." *Ukrainska Pravda*. May 25, 2022. https://life.pravda.com.ua/culture/2022/05/25/248802/.

Kruzhytskyi, S.D., V. M. Zubar, and A. S. Rusiaeva. *Antychni derzhavy Pivnichnoho Prychornomoria*. Ukraina kriz viky 2. Kyiv: Alternatyvy, 1998.

Krypiakevych, Ivan. "Pobut." In *Istoriia ukrainskoi kultury*, edited by Ivan Krypiakevych. 4th ed. Kyiv: Lybid, 2002.

Krypiakevych, Ivan, and Mykola Holubets, eds. *Velyka istoriia Ukrainy*. Supplemented by Dmytro Doroshenko and Iaroslav Pasternak. Winnipeg: Ivan Tyktor, 1948.

Kulchitskii [Kulchytskyi, Kulchytsky], S. V. *Pochemu on nas unichtozhal? Stalin i ukrainskii Golodomor*. Kyiv: Ukrainska pres-hrupa, 2007.

Kulchytsky, Stanislav. *The Ukrainian Famine of 1932–1933: An Anatomy of the Holodomor*. Translated by Ali Kinsella. Edmonton and Toronto: Canadian Institute of Ukrainian Studies Press, 2018.

Kulchytskyi, S. [Stanislav] V. *Holodomor 1932–33 rokiv iak henotsyd: trudnoshchi usvidomlennia*. Kyiv: Nash chas, 2007.

_____. "Hostrym zorom talanovytoho doslidnyka: Mynule Ukrainy z ohliadu na ievropeisku istoriiu." *Polityka i chas*, no. 1 (1996): 57–66.

_____. *Ukraina mizh dvoma viinamy (1921–1939 rr.)*. Ukraina kriz viky 11. Kyiv: Alternatyvy, 1999.

Kulchytskyi, S.V. ed. *Narysy povsiakdennoho zhyttia Radianskoi Ukrainy v dobu NEPu (1921–1928 rr.)*. 2 vols. Kyiv: Instytut istorii Ukrainy NANU, 2010.

Kulikov, Volodymyr, and Iryna Sklokina, eds. *Pratsia, vysnazhennia ta uspikh: Promyslovi monomista Donbasu*. Lviv: FOP Shumylovych, 2018.

Kuzio, Taras. "A Multi-Vectored Scholar for a Multi-Vectored Era: Paul Robert Magocsi." *Nationalities Papers* 39, no. 1 (January 2011): 95–104.

Kuznetsova, L.V. "Problemy vykladannia teorii ta istorii natsionalnoi kultury v osvitnikh zakladakh Ukrainy." In *Ukrainska kultura: Zmist i metodyka vykladannia*, edited by A. K. Bychko, 97–104. Kyiv: Navchalno-metodychnyi kabinet vyshchoi osvity Ministerstva osvity, 1993.

La Capra, Dominick, ed. "Canons, Texts, and Contexts." In *Representing the Holocaust: History, Theory, Trauma*, 20–25. Ithaca, N.Y.: Cornell University Press, 1994.

Lefebvre, Henri. *The Production of Space*. Oxford: Blackwell, 1991.

Lenin, V. I. "Pamiati Gertsena." In *Polnoe sobranie sochinenii*. 55 vols. 255–62. Vol. 21. Moscow: Politizdat, 1958–1966.

Lewin, Moshe. *Russian Peasants and Soviet Power: A Study of Collectivization*. Translated by John Biggart and Irene Nove. Preface by Alec Nove. London: Allen and Unwin, 1968.

Lisovyi, Vasyl. "I. Lysiak-Rudnytskyi—istoryk ukrainskoi politychnoi dumky." *Politolohichni chytannia*, no. 4 (1993): 207–26.

Luckyj, George S. N. *Between Gogol' and Ševčenko: Polarity in the Literary Ukraine, 1798–1847*. Munich: W. Fink, 1971.

_____. *Literary Politics in the Soviet Ukraine, 1917–1934*. New York: Columbia University Press, 1956.

_____. *Literary Politics in the Soviet Ukraine, 1917–1934*. Rev. and updated ed. Durham, N.C.: Duke University Press, 1990.

_____. *Young Ukraine: The Brotherhood of Saints Cyril and Methodius, 1845–1847*. Ottawa: University of Ottawa Press, 1991.

Luckyj, George S. N., and R. Lindheim, eds. *Towards an Intellectual History of Ukraine: An Anthology of Ukrainian Thought from 1710 to 1995*. Toronto: University of Toronto Press, 1996.

Lupul, Manoly R. "The Establishment of the Canadian Institute of Ukrainian Studies at the University of Alberta: A Personal Memoir." *Journal of Ukrainian Studies* 18, nos. 1–2 (Summer-Winter 1993): 1–32.

_____. *The Politics of Multiculturalism: A Ukrainian-Canadian Memoir*. Edmonton and Toronto: Canadian Institute of Ukrainian Studies, 2007.

Lysiak-Rudnytskyi, Ivan. "Dyskusiini vystupy na mizhnarodnomu istorychnomu kongresi." In *Istorychni ese*, edited by Frank Sysyn and Iaroslav Hrytsak. Translated by Marta Badik, et al., 409–18. Vol 2. Kyiv: Osnovy, 1994.

_____. *Istorychni ese*. 2 vols. Edited by Frank Sysyn and Iaroslav Hrytsak. Translated by Marta Badik et al. Kyiv: Osnovy, 1994.

_____. "Iz Drahomanivskykh studii." In *Istorychni ese*, edited by Frank Sysyn and Iaroslav Hrytsak. Translated by Marta Badik, et al., 289–98. Vol. 1. Kyiv: Osnovy, 1994.

_____. *Mizh istoriieiu ta politykoiu: Statti do istorii i krytyky ukrainskoi suspilno-politychnoi dumky*. Munich: Suchasnist, 1973.

_____. "Natsionalizm." In *Istorychni ese*, edited by Frank Sysyn and Iaroslav Hrytsak. Translated by Marta Badik, et al., 247–59. Vol. 2. Kyiv: Osnovy, 1994.

_____. "Natsionalizm i totalitaryzm (vidpovid M. Prokopovi)." In *Istorychni ese*, edited by Frank Sysyn and Iaroslav Hrytsak. Translated by Marta Badik, et al., 489–96. Vol. 2. Kyiv: Osnovy, 1994.

_____. "Navkolo mizhnarodnoho istorychnoho kongresu u Vidni." In *Istorychni ese*, edited by Frank Sysyn and Iaroslav Hrytsak. Translated by Marta Badik, et al., 419–35. Vol. 2. Kyiv: Osnovy, 1994.

_____. "Rusyfikatsiia chy malorosiianizatsiia?" In *Istorychni ese*, edited by Frank Sysyn and Iaroslav Hrytsak. Translated by Marta Badik, et al., 471–76. Vol. 2. Kyiv: Osnovy, 1994.

_____. "Struktura ukrainskoi istorii v XIX stolitti." In *Istorychni ese*, edited by Frank Sysyn and Iaroslav Hrytsak. Translated by Marta Badik, et al., 193–202. Vol. 1. Kyiv: Osnovy, 1994

_____. "Viacheslav Lypynsky." In *Istorychni ese*, edited by Frank Sysyn and Iaroslav Hrytsak. Translated by Marta Badik, et al., 131–48. Vol. 2. Kyiv: Osnovy, 1994.

_____. "V oboroni intelektu." In *Istorychni ese*, edited by Frank Sysyn and Iaroslav Hrytsak. Translated by Marta Badik, et al., 381–407. Vol. 2. Kyiv: Osnovy, 1994.

Lytvyn, V. M. *Ukraina na mezhi tysiacholit (1991–2000 rr.)*. Ukraina kriz viky 14. Kyiv: Alternatyvy, 2000.

Lytvyn, V. M. ed. *Ekonomichna istoriia Ukrainy*. Vol. 1. Kyiv: Nika-Tsentr, 2011.

Mace, James E. *Communism and the Dilemmas of National Liberation: National Communism in Soviet Ukraine, 1918–1933*. Cambridge, Mass.: Harvard Ukrainian Research Institute, 1983.

Magocsi, Paul R. *The Shaping of a National Identity: Subcarpathian Rus', 1848– 1948*. Cambridge, Mass.: Harvard University Press, 1978.

Magocsi, Paul Robert. *A History of Ukraine: The Land and Its Peoples*. 2 eds. Toronto: University of Toronto Press, 1987, 2010, rev. 2013.

_____. "Concluding Observations on the Symposium." *Nationalities Papers* 39, no. 1 (January 2011): 129–34.

_____. *The Roots of Ukrainian Nationalism: Galicia As Ukraine's Piedmont*. Toronto: University of Toronto Press, 2002.

_____. *Ukraine: An Illustrated History*. Toronto: University of Toronto Press, 2007.

Maksimovich, Mikhail [Mykhailo Maksymovych], ed. "Predislovie." In *Malorossiiskiia pesni*. Moscow: Avgust Semen, 1827. i–xxxviii.

Mälksoo, Maria. "'Memory Must Be Defended': Beyond the Politics of Mnemonical Security," *Security Dialogue* 46, no. 3 (2015): 221–37.

_____. *The Politics of Becoming European: A Study of Polish and Baltic Post-Cold War Security Imaginaries*. London: Routledge, 2010.

_____. "The Postcolonial Moment in Russia's War against Ukraine." *Journal of Genocide Research.* Published online. 11 May 2022. https://www.tandfonline.com/doi/full/10.1080/14623528.2022.20 74947.

Malyshko, L. M. "Pro deiaki aspekty vykladannia ukrainskoi natsionalnoi kultury v tekhnichnomu vuzi." In *Ukrainska kultura: Zmist i metodyka vykladannia,* edited by A. K. Bychko, 117–24. Kyiv: Navchalno-metodychnyi kabinet vyshchoi osvity Ministerstva osvity, 1993.

Marchenko, M. I. *Istoriia ukrainskoi kultury: Z naidavnishykh chasiv do seredyny XVII st.* Kyiv: Radianska shkola, 1961.

Marples, David R. *Chernobyl and Nuclear Power in the USSR.* New York: St. Martin's Press and Edmonton: Canadian Institute of Ukrainian Studies, 1986.

_____. *Heroes and Villains: Creating National History in Contemporary Ukraine.* Budapest: Central European University Press, 2007.

_____. *Holodomor: Causes of the 1932–1933 Famine in Ukraine.* Saskatoon: Heritage Press, 2011.

_____. *Stalinism in Ukraine in the 1940s.* New York: St. Martin's Press, 1992.

_____. *Ukraine in Conflict: An Analytical Chronicle.* Bristol, UK: E-International Relations, 2017/ www.e-ir.info/wp-content/uploads/2017/05/Ukraine-in-Conflict-E-IR.pdf.

_____. *Ukraine under Perestroika: Ecology, Economics and the Workers' Revolt.* New York: St. Martin's Press, 1991.

Marples, David R., and Frederick V. Mills, eds. *Ukraine's Euromaidan: Analyses of a Civil Revolution.* Stuttgart: Ibidem, 2015.

Martin, Terry. *The Affirmative Action Empire: Nations and Nationalism in the Soviet Union, 1923–1939.* Ithaca, N.Y.: Cornell University Press, 2001.

Masliichuk, Volodymyr. "Marksystski skhemy ukrainskoi istorii: Matvii Iavorskyi, Volodymyr Sukhyno-Khomenko, Mykola Horban." *Ukraina Moderna,* no. 3 (2009): 63–77.

_____. "Orest Subtelny." *Historians.ua,* August 1, 2016. https://www.historians.in.ua/index.php/en/institutsiji-istorichnoji-nauki-v-ukrajini/1955-volodymyr-masliychuk-orest-subtelnyi.

_____. *Provintsiia na perekhresti kultur: Doslidzhennia z istorii Slobidskoi Ukrainy XVII–XIX st.* Kharkiv: Kharkivskyi pryvatnyi muzei miskoi sadyby, 2007.

"Materialy k press-konferentsii 'Ukrainskie uchebniki kak instrument propagandy nenavisti.'" *Edinaia Rossiia.* March 30, 2022. https://er.ru/pages/analiz.

Maxwell, Alexander. "Twenty-Five Years of A-B-C: Miroslav Hroch's Impact on Nationalism Studies." *Nationalities Papers* 36, no. 6 (November 2010): 773–76.

Ministerstvo nauky i osvity Ukrainy. "Prohrama dlia zahalnoosvitnikh navchalnykh zakladiv. Istoriia Ukrainy. 10–11 klasy. Riven standartu." https://mon.gov.ua/ua/osvita/zagalna-serednya-osvi ta/navchalni-programi/navchalni-programi-dlya-10-11-klasiv.

Mishchenko, Kateryna, ed. *The Book of Kyiv/Kyivska knyzhka*. Kyiv: Medusa, 2015.

Misto: Istoriia, kultura, suspilstvo: E-zhurnal urbanistychnykh studii. http://mics.org.ua/?p=41.

Motyl, Alexander J. "Negating the Negation: Russia, Not-Russia, and the West." *Nationalities Papers* 22, no. 1 (1994): 263–71.

_____. "The Paradoxes of Paul Robert Magocsi: The Case for Rusyns and the Logical Necessity of Ukrainians." *Nationalities Papers* 39, no. 1 (January 2011): 105–9.

Motyl, Oleksandr [Alexander]. "Orhanizatsiia ukrainskykh natsionalistiv i robitnytstvo (kilka zavvah)." *Suchasnist*, no. 2 (1980): 51–63.

Myshlovska, Oksana. "Establishing the 'Irrefutable Facts' about the OUN and UPA: The Role of the Working Group of Historians on OUN-UPA Activities in Mediating Memory-Based Conflict in Ukraine." *Ab Imperio*, no. 1 (2018): 223–54.

Nalyvaiko, Dmytro. "Pro 'Istorichni ese' Ivana Lysiaka-Rudnytskoho." *Suchasnist*, no. 1 (1996): 151–57.

Naumenko, Volodymyr. *Iak ne treba vykladaty istoriiu ukrainskoi kultury.* Kyiv: Petro Barskyi, 1918.

Neumann, Iver B. *Russia and the Idea of Europe: A Study in Identity and International Relations.* New York: Routledge, 1996.

"Newly Mapped Data Leads to New Insights." Harvard Ukrainian Research Institute, 11 June 2018. https://huri.harvard.edu/news/ newly-mapped-data-leads-new-insights.

Ohiienko, Ivan. *Ukrainska kultura.* Kyiv: Nasha kultura i nauka, 2002.

_____. *Ukrainska kultura: Korotka istoriia kulturnoho zhyttia ukrainskoho naroda.* Kyiv: Ie. Cherepovskyi, 1918.

Oleinikov, M. Ia. *Saur-Mogila: Putevoditel.* Donetsk: Donbass, 1976.

O'Loughlin, John, Gerard Toal, and Vladimir Kolosov, "Who Identifies with the 'Russian World'? Geopolitical Attitudes in Southeastern Ukraine, Crimea, Abkhazia, South Ossetia, and Transnistria," *Eurasian Geography and Economics* 57, no. 6 (2016): 745–78.

Onyschenko, Natalia, and Iryna Kohut, eds. "Transformatsii miskoho prostoru." Special issue, *Spilne*, no. 2 (2010). https://commons.
com.ua/uk/zhurnal-spilne-2-transformatsiyi.

Orlova, Violetta. "Rosiiany pochaly borotbu z ukrainskymy knyzhkamy na
okupovanykh terytoriiakh." *UNIAN*. March 24, 2022.
https://www.unian.ua/war/viyna-v-ukrajini-rosiyani-na- okupo-
vanih-teritoriyah-nishchat-ukrajinski-knizhki-novini-vtorgnennya-
rosiji-v-ukrajinu- 11758072.html

Otrishchenko, Natalia, ed. *Sykhiv: Prostory, pam'iati, praktyky.* Lviv: FOP
Shumylovych, 2018.

Ovsiiuk, Oksana. *Zhyttia pislia okupatsii: Pobut kyian, 1943–1945 rr.* Kyiv:
Duliby, 2017.

Parnikoza, I. Iu. "Kyivski ostrovy ta pryberezhni urochyshcha na Dnipri —
pohliad kriz viky." *Myslenne drevo*. http://www.myslenedrevo.
com.ua/uk/Sci/Kyiv/Islands.html.

Pavko, A. I. "Chy potribno vyvchaty politychnu istoriiu Ukrainy u vyshchii shkoli?" *Ukrainskyi istorychnyi zhurnal*, no. 2 (2005): 204–7.

Pavlyshyn, Marko. "Post-Colonial Features in Contemporary Ukrainian
Culture." *Australian Slavonic and East European Studies* 6, no. 2 (1992):
41–55.

_____. "Ruslana, Serduchka, Jamala: National Self-Imaging in Ukraine's
Eurovision Entries." In *Eurovisions: Identity and the International Politics of the Eurovision Song Contest since 1956*, edited by Julie Kalman,
Ben Wellings, and Keshia Jacotine, 129–50. London: Palgrave Macmillan, 2019.

Pavlyshyn, Marko, ed. "Ukrainska kultura z pohliadu postmodernizmu."
In *Kanon ta iconostas*, 213–22. Kyiv: Chas, 1997.

Pavlyshyn, Marko, and J. E. M. Clarke, eds. *Ukraine in the 1990s.* Melbourne:
Monash University, Slavic Section, 1992.

Pipes, Richard. *The Formation of the Soviet Union: Communism and Nationalism, 1917–1923.* Cambridge, Mass.: Harvard University Press, 1954.

Plokhii [Plokhy], Serhii. *Brama Ievropy: Istoriia Ukrainy vid skifskykh voien do
nezalezhnosti.* Translated by R. Klochko (Kharkiv: KSD, 2016).

Plokhy, Serhii. "Between History and Nation: Paul Robert Magocsi and the
Rewriting of Ukrainian History." *Nationalities Papers* 39, no. 1 (January 2011): 117–24.

_____. *The Gates of Europe: A History of Ukraine* (New York: Basic Books,
2015).

_____. *Ukraine and Russia: Representations of the Past.* Toronto: University
of Toronto Press, 2008.

_____. *Unmaking Imperial Russia: Mykhailo Hrushevsky and the Writing of Ukrainian History*. Toronto: University of Toronto Press, 2005.

Plokhy, Serhii, ed. *The Future of the Past: New Perspectives on Ukrainian History*. Cambridge, Mass.: Harvard Ukrainian Research Institute, 2017.

Plokhy, Serhii M. "The History of a 'Non-Historical' Nation: Notes on the Nature and Current Problems of Ukrainian Historiography." *Slavic Review* 54, no. 3 (Fall 1995): 709–16.

Plokhy, Serhii, and Frank E. Sysyn. *Religion and Nation in Modern Ukraine*. Edmonton and Toronto: Canadian Institute of Ukrainian Studies Press, 2003.

Polishchuk, E. P. "Pro mistse kursu istorii kultury v systemi humanitarnoi osvity." In *Humanitarna osvita: Dosvid i problemy*, edited by M. I. Bletskan, 485–92. Uzhhorod: Grazhda, 1999.

Pometun, O. I., and N. M. Hupan. *Istoriia Ukrainy: Pidruchnyk dlia 11 klasu zahalnoosvitnikh navchalnykh zakladiv*. Kharkiv: Sytsyia, 2012.

Popovych, Myroslav. *Narys istorii kultury Ukrainy*. 2nd ed. Kyiv: ArtEk, 2001.

Portnikov, Vitalii. "Nash Hrushevskyi: Pamiati Oresta Subtelnoho." *Espreso TV*, 26 July 2016. http://espreso.tv/article/2016/07/26/nash_grushevskyy_pamyati_oresta_subtelnogo.

Portnov, Andrei [Andrii]. "O grazhdanskoi vovlechennosti, intellektualnoi nepredvziatosti i izuchenii pamiati." *Ab Imperio*, no. 1 (2011): 12–20.

_____. *Uprazhneniia s istoriei po-ukrainski*. Moscow: OGI-Polit.ru-Memorial, 2010.

Portnov, Andrii. *Poland and Ukraine: Entangled Histories, Asymmetric Memories*, Forum Transregionale Studien Essays, 7. Berlin: Forum Transregionale Studien, 2020.

Potichnyj, Peter J., and Howard Aster, eds. *Ukrainian-Jewish Relations in Historical Perspective*. 3 eds. Edmonton: Canadian Institute of Ukrainian Studies, 1988, 1990, 2010.

Potichnyj, Peter J., ed. *Poland and Ukraine: Past and Present*. Edmonton and Toronto: Canadian Institute of Ukrainian Studies, 1980.

Potichnyj, Peter J. et al., eds. *Ukraine and Russia in Their Historical Encounter*. Edmonton: Canadian Institute of Ukrainian Studies Press, 1992.

Prakash, Gyan, ed. *After Colonialism: Imperial Histories and Postcolonial Displacements*. Princeton: Princeton University Press, 1995.

_____. "Postcolonial Criticism and Indian Historiography." *Social Text* 31/32 (1992): 8–19.

_____. "Subaltern Studies as Postcolonial Criticism." *American Historical Review* 99, no. 5 (December 1994): 1475–90.

Pritsak, Omeljan, Taras Hunczak, Ivan L. Rudnytsky, et al. "Problems of Terminology and Periodization in the Teaching of Ukrainian History: Round-table Discussion." In *Rethinking Ukrainian History*, edited by Ivan L. Rudnytsky and John-Paul Himka, 233–68. Edmonton: Canadian Institute of Ukrainian Studies, 1981.

Problema OUN-UPA: Zvit robochoi hrupy istorykiv pry Uriadovii komisii z vyvchennia diialnosti OUN i UPA. Kyiv: Instytut istorii Ukrainy NANU, 2004.

Prymak, Thomas M. "Dmytro Doroshenko: A Ukrainian Émigré Historian of the Interwar Period." *Harvard Ukrainian Studies* 25, nos. 1–2 (Spring 2001): 31–56.

_____. "Dmytro Doroshenko and Canada." *Journal of Ukrainian Studies* 30, no. 2 (Winter 2005): 1–25.

_____. *Gathering a Heritage: Ukrainian, Slavonic, and Ethnic Canada and the USA*. Toronto: University of Toronto Press, 2014.

_____. *Maple Leaf and Trident: The Ukrainian Canadians during the Second World War*. Toronto: Multicultural History Society of Ontario, 1988.

_____. *Mykhailo Hrushevsky: The Politics of National Culture*. Toronto: University of Toronto Press, 1987.

_____. *Mykola Kostomarov: A Biography*. Toronto: University of Toronto Press, 1996.

Putin, Vladimir. "Ob istoricheskom edinstve russkikh i ukraintsev," President Rossii, 12 July 2021. http://www.kremlin.ru/events/president/news/66181.

Radzykevych, Volodymyr. "Pysmenstvo." In *Istoriia ukrainskoi kultury*, edited by Ivan Krypiakevych. 4th ed. Kyiv: Lybid, 2002.

Reient, O., and O. Malii. *Istoriia Ukrainy: Pidruchnyk dlia 9 klasu zahalnoosvitnikh navchalnykh zakladiv*. 2nd ed. Kyiv: Heneza, 2011.

Remy, Johannes. *Brothers or Enemies: The Ukrainian National Movement and Russia from the 1840s to the 1870s*. Toronto: University of Toronto Press, 2016.

Riabchuk, Anastasiia. "'Formuvannia' i 'zanepad' robitnychoho klasu (Sproba ohliadu)." *Ukraina Moderna*, no. 3 (2009): 126–42.

Rublov, O. S., and Iu. A. Cherchenko. *Stalinshchyna i dolia zakhidnoukrainskoi intelihentsii: 20–50-ti roky XX st.*.Kyiv: Naukova dumka, 1994.

Rublov, O. S., and O. P. Reient, *Ukrainski vyzvolni zmahannia 1917–1921 rr.* Ukraina kriz viky 10. Kyiv: Alternatyvy, 1999.

Rudnytsky, Ivan L. "Carpatho-Ukraine: A People in Search of Their Identity." In his *Essays in Modern Ukrainian History*, edited by Peter L. Rudnytsky, 353–74. Edmonton: Canadian Institute of Ukrainian Studies, University of Alberta, 1987.

_____. "Drahomanov as Political Theorist." In his *Essays in Modern Ukrainian History*, edited by Peter L. Rudnytsky, 203–54. Edmonton: Canadian Institute of Ukrainian Studies, University of Alberta, 1987.

_____. *Essays in Modern Ukrainian History*. Edited by Peter L. Rudnytsky. Edmonton: Canadian Institute of Ukrainian Studies, University of Alberta, 1987.

_____. "Franciszek Duchiński and His Impact on Ukrainian Political Thought." In his *Essays in Modern Ukrainian History*, edited by Peter L. Rudnytsky, 187–202. Edmonton: Canadian Institute of Ukrainian Studies, University of Alberta, 1987.

_____. "Hipolit Vladimir Terlecki." In his *Essays in Modern Ukrainian History*, edited by Peter L. Rudnytsky, 143–72. Edmonton: Canadian Institute of Ukrainian Studies, University of Alberta, 1987.

_____. "Michał Czajkowski's Cossack Project during the Crimean War: An Analysis of Ideas." In his *Essays in Modern Ukrainian History*, edited by Peter L. Rudnytsky, 173–86. Edmonton: Canadian Institute of Ukrainian Studies, University of Alberta, 1987.

_____. "Observations on the Problem of 'Historical' and 'Non-Historical' Nations." *Harvard Ukrainian Studies* 5, no. 3 (September 1981): 358–68.

_____. "Observations on the Problem of 'Historical' and 'Non-historical' Nations." In his *Essays in Modern Ukrainian History*, edited by Peter L. Rudnytsky, 37–48. Edmonton: Canadian Institute of Ukrainian Studies, University of Alberta, 1987.

_____. "Soviet Ukraine in Historical Perspective." In his *Essays in Modern Ukrainian History*, edited by Peter L. Rudnytsky, 463–76. Edmonton: Canadian Institute of Ukrainian Studies, University of Alberta, 1987.

_____. "The First Ukrainian Political Program: Mykhailo Drahomanov's 'Introduction' to *Hromada*." In his *Essays in Modern Ukrainian History*, edited by Peter L. Rudnytsky, 255–82. Edmonton: Canadian Institute of Ukrainian Studies, University of Alberta, 1987.

_____. "The Fourth Universal and Its Ideological Antecedents." In his *Essays in Modern Ukrainian History*, edited by Peter L. Rudnytsky, 389–416. Edmonton: Canadian Institute of Ukrainian Studies, University of Alberta, 1987.

_____. "The Intellectual Origins of Modern Ukraine." In his *Essays in Modern Ukrainian History*, edited by Peter L. Rudnytsky, 123–42. Edmonton: Canadian Institute of Ukrainian Studies, University of Alberta, 1987.

_____. "The Role of the Ukraine in Modern History." *Slavic Review* 22, no. 2 (June 1963): 199–216.

_____. "The Role of Ukraine in Modern History." In his *Essays in Modern Ukrainian History*, edited by Peter L. Rudnytsky, 11–36. Edmonton: Canadian Institute of Ukrainian Studies, University of Alberta, 1987.

_____. "The Ukrainian National Movement on the Eve of the First World War." In his *Essays in Modern Ukrainian History*, edited by Peter L. Rudnytsky, 375–88. Edmonton: Canadian Institute of Ukrainian Studies, University of Alberta, 1987.

_____. "Trends in Ukrainian Political Thought." In his *Essays in Modern Ukrainian History*, edited by Peter L. Rudnytsky, 91–122. Edmonton: Canadian Institute of Ukrainian Studies, University of Alberta, 1987.

_____. "Ukraine between East and West." In his *Essays in Modern Ukrainian History*, edited by Peter L. Rudnytsky, 1–10. Edmonton: Canadian Institute of Ukrainian Studies, 1987.

_____. "Volodymyr Vynnychenko's Ideas in the Light of His Political Writings." In his *Essays in Modern Ukrainian History*, edited by Peter L. Rudnytsky, 417–36. Edmonton: Canadian Institute of Ukrainian Studies, University of Alberta, 1987.

Rudnytsky, Ivan L., and John-Paul Himka, eds. *Rethinking Ukrainian History*. Edmonton: Canadian Institute of Ukrainian Studies, University of Alberta, 1981.

Rusyna, O.V. *Ukraina pid tataramy i Lytvoiu*. Ukraina kriz viky 6. Kyiv: Alternatyvy, 1998.

Sarbei, V. H. *Do vyroblennia kontseptsii bahatotomnoi "Istorii ukrainskoho narodu" (rozdumy i propozytsii)*. Kyiv: Instytut istorii Ukrainy NANU, 1994.

_____. *Natsionalne vidrodzhennia Ukrainy*. Ukraina kriz viky 9. Kyiv: Alternatyvy, 1999.

Savaryn, Petro. "Spohady uchasnyka: Polityka, bahatokulturnist, Kanadskyi instytut ukrainoznavstva, abetkova Entsyklopediia Ukrainy-2." In *Zakhidnokanadskyi zbirnyk*. Vol. 3, edited by Yar Slavutych, 317–82. Edmonton: 1998.

"Savur-Mohyla Left without Obelisk Because of Shelling: Photo." *Tsenzor.net*, 21 August 2014. https://censor.net/en/p299092.

Schlögel, Karl. *Im Raume lesen wir die Zeit: Über Zivilisationsgeschichte und Geopolitik*. Munich: Carl Hanser, 2003.

Semchyshyn, Myroslav. *Tysiacha rokiv ukrainskoi kultury*. 2nd ed. Kyiv: Druha ruka-Feniks, 1993.

Serczyk, Wladyslaw A. "Ukraine between East and West: Some Reflections on Professor Ševčenko's Essay." *Harvard Ukrainian Studies* 16, nos. 3–4 (December 1992): 433–40.

Sereda, Ostap. "From Church-Based to Cultural Nationalism: Early Ukrainophiles, Ritual-Purification Movement and Emerging Cult of Taras Shevchenko in Austrian Eastern Galicia in the 1860s." *Canadian-American Slavic Studies* 40, no. 1 (2006): 21–47.

Ševčenko, Ihor. "Ukraine between East and West." *Harvard Ukrainian Studies* 16, nos. 1–2 (June 1992): 174–83.

_____. *Ukraine between East and West: Essays on Cultural History to the Early Eighteenth Century*. Edmonton: Canadian Institute of Ukrainian Studies Press, 1996.

Shamrai, Serhii. *Kyivska kozachchyna 1855 r. (Do istorii selianskykh rukhiv na Kyivshchyni)*. Kyiv: Vseukrainska Akademiia nauk, 1928.

Shevel, Oxana. "Decommunization in Post-Euromaidan Ukraine: Law and Practice." *PONARS Eurasia*, January 2016. http://www.ponars eurasia.org/memo/decommunization-post-euromaidan-ukraine-law-and-practice.

_____. "The Battle for Historical Memory in Postrevolutionary Ukraine." *Current History* 115, no. 783 (2016): 258–63.

Shevelov, Iurii. "Postskryptum redaktora." *Suchasnist*, no. 2 (1980): 157–59.

Shkandij, Myroslav. *Modernists, Marxists, and the Nation: The Ukrainian Literary Discussion of the 1920s*. Edmonton: Canadian Institute of Ukrainian Studies Press, 1992.

Shporliuk [Szporluk], Roman. "Zamist obitsianoi statti." *Suchasnist*, no. 2 (1980): 26–33.

_____. "Ukraina: Vid imperskoi peryferii do suverennoi derzhavy." *Suchanist*, no. 11 (1996): 74–87.

Shtohryn, Iryna, ed. *AD 242: Istoriia muzhnosti, braterstva ta samopozhertvy*. Kharkiv: KSD, 2016.

Shvaiba, Nadiia. "Komisiia Poludnevoi Ukrainy VUAN (1926–1930 rr.)." *Naukovi zapysky Instytutu ukrainskoi arkheohrafii ta dzherelo-znavstva im. M. S. Hrushevskoho NANU* 12 (2006): 328–38.

Shynkaruk, V., and Ie. Bystrytskyi, eds. *Fenomen ukrainskoi kultury: Metodolohichni zasady osmyslennia*. Kyiv: Feniks, 1996.

Sichynsky, Volodymyr. *Ukraine in Foreign Comments and Descriptions from the VIth to the XXth Centuries*. New York: Ukrainian Congress Committee of America, 1953.

Simpson, G. W. Introduction to *History of the Ukraine*, by Dmytro Doroshenko, 3–15. Translated and abridged by Hannah Chykalenko-Keller. Edmonton: The Institute Press, 1939.

Skaba, A. D., ed. *Vinok druzhby*. Vol. 3, *Dukhovnyi rozkvit ukrainskoho narodu*. Kyiv: Politvydav, 1972.

Sliusarenko, A. H., V. I. Husev, and V. M. Lytvyn, eds. *Novitnia istoriia Ukrainy, 1900–2000: Pidruchnyk dlia studentiv istorychnykh spetsialnostei vyshchykh navchalnykh zakladiv*. Kyiv: Vyshcha shkola, 2002.

Smolii, V. [Valerii] A., and V. S. Stepankov, *Istoriia Ukrainy: Pidruchnyk dlia 7 klasu zahalnoosvitnikh navchalnykh zakladiv*. Kyiv: Heneza, 2007.

_____. *Ukrainska natsionalna revoliutsiia (1648–1676 rr.)*. Ukraina kriz viky 7. Kyiv: Alternatyvy, 1999.

Smolii, V. A., ed. *Entsyklopediia istorii Ukrainy*. 10 vols. Kyiv: Naukova dumka, 2003–2013.

_____. *"Istoriia Ukrainy": Materialy do rozrobky kontseptsii natsionalnoho hrand-naratyvu; Zaproshennia do dyskusii*. Kyiv: Instytut istorii Ukrainy NANU, 2011.

_____. *U leshchatakh totalitaryzmu: Pershe dvadtsiatyrichchia Instytutu istorii NAN Ukrainy (1936–1956 rr.)*. Vol. 1. Kyiv: Instytut istorii Ukrainy, 1996.

Smolii, Valerii, ed. *Istoriia Ukrainy: Navchalnyi posibnyk*. 3rd ed. Kyiv: Alternatyvy, 2002

_____. "Peredmova." In *Istoriia Ukrainy: Navchalnyi posibnyk*. 3rd ed., edited by Valerii Smolii, 3–8. Kyiv: Alternatyvy, 2002.

Snyder, Timothy. "The Causes of the Polish-Ukrainian Ethnic Cleansing, 1943." *Past & Present*, no. 179 (May 2003): 197–234.

_____. "The War in Ukraine Is a Colonial War." *The New Yorker*. 28 April 2022. https://www.newyorker.com/news/essay/the-war-in-ukraine-is-a-colonial-war-colonial-war.

Soja, Edward W. *Postmodern Geographies: The Reassertion of Space in Critical Social Theory*. London: Verso, 1989.

Spivak, Gayatri Chakravorty. "Can the Subaltern Speak?" In *Marxism and the Interpretation of Culture*, edited by Cary Nelson and Lawrence Grossberg, 271–313. Urbana: University of Illinois Press, 1988.

_____. "Subaltern Studies: Deconstructing Historiography." In *Subaltern Studies IV: Writings in South Asian History and Society*, edited by Ranajit Guha, 338–63, Delhi: Oxford University Press, 1985.

_____. "The Rani of Sirmur: An Essay in the Reading of the Archives." *History and Theory* 24, no. 3 (1985): 247–72.

Starchenko, Nataliia. *Ukrainski svity Rechi Pospolytoi: Istorii pro istoriiu*. Kyiv: Laurus, 2021.

Stiazhkina, Olena. *Smak radianskoho: Izha i idtsi v mystetstvi zhyttia i mystetstvi kino (seredyna 1960-kh–seredyna 1980-kh)*. Kyiv: Dukh i litera, 2021.

Strukevych, O. K. *Istoriia Ukrainy: Pidruchnyk dlia 9 klasu zahalnoosvitnikh navchalnykh zakladiv*. Kyiv: Hramota, 2009.

Stryjek, Tomasz. *Jakiej przeszłości potrzebuje przyszłość?: Interpretacje dziejów narodowych w historiografii i debacie publicznej na Ukrainie 1991–2004.* Warsaw: Instytut Studiów Politycznych PAN/Oficyna Wydawnicza RYTM, 2007.

Subtelny, Orest. "The Current State of Ukrainian Historiography." *Journal of Ukrainian Studies* 18, nos. 1–2 (Summer–Winter 1993): 33–54.

Subtelny, Orest. *Ukraine: A History.* 4 eds. Toronto: University of Toronto Press, 1988, 1994, 2000, 2009.

Subtelnyi [Subtelny], Orest. *Istoriia Ukrainy.* Translated by Iurii Shevchuk. Kyiv: Lybid, 1991.

Svarnyk, Halyna. "Kilka shtrykhiv do ideinoi biohrafii Dmytra Dontsova." *Ukraina Moderna*, no. 1 (1996): 150–56.

Svidersky, Iu. Iu., N. Iu. Romanyshyn, and T. V. Laduchenko. *Istoriia Ukrainy: Pidruchnyk dlia 7 klasu zahalnoosvitnikh navchalnykh zakladiv.* Kyiv: Hramota, 2015.

Symonenko, R. H. *Do kontseptsii bahatotomnoi "Istorii ukrainskoho narodu" (mizhnatsionalni i mizhnarodni aspekty).* Kyiv: Instytut istorii Ukrainy NANU, 1993.

Sysyn, Frank E. "Introduction to Mykhailo Hrushevsky's *History of Ukraine-Rus'.*" In *Historiography of Imperial Russia: The Profession and Writing History in a Multinational State,* edited by Thomas Sanders, 344–72. Armonk, N.Y.: M. E. Sharpe, 1999.

_____. "Introduction to the *History of Ukraine-Rus'.*" In Mykhailo Hrushevsky. *History of Ukraine-Rus'.* Vol. 1, *From Prehistory to the Eleventh Century,* , edited by Andrzej Poppe and Frank E. Sysyn, translated by Marta Skorupsky, xxii–xlii. Edmonton: Canadian Institute of Ukrainian Studies Press, 1997.

Sysyn, Frank E, and Iaroslav Hrytsak, eds. "Komentari." In *Istorychni ese,* translated by Marta Badik et al., 497–540. Vol. 2. Kyiv: Osnovy, 1994.

Szporluk, Roman. *Ukraine: A Brief History.* 2nd ed. Detroit: Ukrainian Festival Committee, 1982.

TASS. "Putin: Sovremennaia Ukraina tselikom i polnostiu byla sozdana kommunisticheskoi Rossiei." 21 February 2021. https://tass.ru/politika/13791307.

Ther, Philipp. "The Transnational Paradigm of Historiography and Its Potential for Ukrainian History." In *A Laboratory of Transnational History: Ukraine and Recent Ukrainian Historiography,* edited by Georgiy Kasianov and Philipp Ther, 81–114. Budapest: Central European University Press, 2009.

Tolochko, Aleksei [Oleksii]. *Ocherki nachalnoi Rusi.* Kyiv: Laurus, 2015.

Tolochko, O. P., and P. P. Tolochko. *Kyivska Rus*. Ukraina kriz viky 4. Kyiv: Alternatyvy, 1998.

Tomashivskyi, Stepan. *Kyivska kozachchyna 1855 r.* Lviv: NTSh, 1902.

Törnquist-Plewa, Barbara, and Yuliya Yurchuk. "Memory Politics in Contemporary Ukraine: Reflections from the Postcolonial Perspective." *Memory Studies* 12, no. 6 (December 2019): 699–720.

Troshchynskyi, V. P., and A. A. Shevchenko. *Ukraintsi v sviti*. Ukraina kriz viky 15. Kyiv: Alternatyvy, 1999.

Turchenko, Fedir. *Ukraina – povernennia istorii: Heneza suchasnoho pidruchnyka*. Kyiv: Heneza, 2016.

Turchenko, F. H., P. P. Panchenko, and S. M. Tymchenko. *Novitnia istoriia Ukrainy (1939–pochatok XXI st.): Pidruchnyk dlia 11 klasu zahalnoosvitnikh navchalnykh zakladiv*. 5th ed. Kyiv: Heneza, 2006.

Tymoshyk, M. [Mykola] S. *Holhofa Ivana Ohiienka: Ukrainoznavchi problemy v derzhavotvorchii, naukovii, redaktorskii ta vydavnychii diialnosti*. Kyiv: Zapovit, 1997.

Tymoshyk, Mykola. *"Lyshus naviky z chuzhynoiu…" Mytropolyt Ilarion (Ivan Ohiienko) i ukrainske vidrodzhennia*. Kyiv: Nasha kultura i nauka, 2000.

"U Kirovohradi ozvuchyly rezultaty opytuvannia pro pereimenuvannia mista." *Ukrainska Pravda*, 26 October 2015. https://www.pravda. com.ua/news/2015/10/26/7086321/

Ukrainskyi instytut natsionalnoi pam'iati. "UINP ta MKIP rozpochaly seriiu kruhlykh stoliv 'Derusyfikatsiia, dekomunizatsiia ta dekolonizatsiia u publichnomu prostori." 13 May 2022. https://uinp.gov.ua/pres-centr/novyny/uinp-ta-mkip-roz pochaly-seriyu-kruglyh-stoliv-derusyfikaciya-dekomuniza ciya-ta-dekolonizaciya-u-publichnomu-prostori1.

_____."Zavershennia dekomunizatsii – pochatok dekolonizatsii." 9 April 2019. https://uinp.gov.ua/pres-centr/novyny/zavershennya-deko munizaciyi-pochatok-dekolonizaciyi.

Velychenko, Stephen. *National History as Cultural Process: A Survey of the Interpretations of Ukraine's Past in Polish, Russian, and Ukrainian Historical Writing from the Earliest Times to 1914*. Edmonton: Canadian Institute of Ukrainian Studies Press, 1992.

_____. *Painting Imperialism and Nationalism Red: The Ukrainian Marxist Critique of Russian Communist Rule in Ukraine, 1918–1925*. Toronto: University of Toronto Press, 2015.

_____. "Post-Colonialism and Ukrainian History." *Ab Imperio*, no. 1 (2004): 391–404.

_____. *Shaping Identity in Eastern Europe and Russia: Soviet and Polish Accounts of Ukrainian History, 1914–1991.* New York: St. Martin's Press, 1993.

_____. *State Building in Revolutionary Ukraine: A Comparative Study of Governments and Bureaucrats, 1917–1922.* Toronto: University of Toronto Press, 2011.

"Verkhovna Rada pereimenuvala Kirovohrad u Kropyvnytskyi." *Den*, 14 July 2016. https://day.kyiv.ua/uk/news/140716-verhovna-rada-pereymenuvala-kirovograd-u-kropyvnyckyy.

Vermenych, Iaroslava. "Prostorove modeliuvannia istorii: Zmina paradyhm." In *Skhid i Pivden Ukrainy: Chas, prostir, sotsium*, edited by Iaroslava Vermenych, 16–53. Vol. 1. Kyiv: Instytut istorii Ukrainy NANU, 2014–16.

Vermenych, Iaroslava, ed. *Skhid i Pivden Ukrainy: Chas, prostir, sotsium.* 2 vols. Kyiv: Instytut istorii Ukrainy NANU, 2014–16.

Vesti. 12 August 2016.

"Vidpovid ukrainskykh istorykiv na stattiu V. Putina 'Pro istorychnu iednist rosiian ta ukraintsiv.'" Likbez: Istorychnyi Front, 4 September 2021. https://likbez.org.ua/ua/ukrayinska-vidguk-ukrayinskih-istorikiv-na-stattyu-v-putina-pro-istorichnu-yednist-rosiyan-ta-ukrayintsiv.html.

Vlasov, Vitalii, and Stanislav Kulchytskyi. *Istoriia Ukrainy 1921–1938: Navchalnyi posibnyk dlia zahalnoosvitnikh navchalnykh zakladiv.* Kyiv: Litera, 2015.

von Hagen, Mark. "Does Ukraine Have a History?" *Slavic Review* 54, no. 3 (Fall 1995): 658–673.

_____. "Revisiting the Histories of Ukraine." In *Laboratory of Transnational History: Ukraine and Recent Ukrainian Historiography*, edited by Georgiy Kasianov and Philipp Ther, 25–50. Budapest: Central European University Press, 2009.

Vorobev, A.M., and G. A. Lisovik, et al. *Ukrainskaia i zarubezhnaia kultura: Uchebnoe posobie.* Kyiv: Natsionalnyi aviatsionnyi universitet, 2002.

Vseukrainska asotsiatsiia vykladachiv istorii ta sotsialnykh nauk "Nova doba." https://www.novadoba.org.ua/.

Vushko, Iryna. "Historians at War: History, Politics, and Memory in Ukraine." *Contemporary European History* 27, no. 1 (2018): 112–24.

Walicki, Andrzei. *Poland Between East and West: The Controversies over Self-Definition and Modernization in Partitioned Poland.* Cambridge, Mass.: Harvard Ukrainian Research Institute, 1994.

White, Hayden. *Metahistory: The Historical Imagination in Nineteenth-Century Europe.* Baltimore: Johns Hopkins University Press, 1973.

Wilson, Andrew. *The Ukrainians: Unexpected Nation*. New Haven: Yale University Press, 2000.

_____. *Ukrainian Nationalism in the 1990s: A Minority Faith*. Cambridge: Cambridge University Press, 1997.

Wolczuk, Kataryna. "History, Europe, and the 'National Idea': The 'Official' Narrative of National Identity in Ukraine." *Nationalities Papers* 28, no. 4 (2000): 671–94.

Wolff, Larry. *The Idea of Galicia: History and Fantasy in Habsburg Political Culture*. Stanford: Stanford University Press, 2010.

Yekelchyk, Serhy. *Stalin's Citizens: Everyday Politics in the Wake of Total War*. New York: Oxford University Press, 2014.

_____. *Stalin's Empire of Memory: Russian-Ukrainian Relations in the Soviet Historical Imagination*. Toronto: University of Toronto Press, 2004.

_____. "The Body and National Myth: Motifs from the Ukrainian National Revival in the Nineteenth Century." *Australian Slavonic and East European Studies* 7, no. 2 (1993): 31–59.

_____. *The Conflict in Ukraine*. New York: Oxford University Press, 2015.

_____. "The Nation's Clothes: Constructing a Ukrainian High Culture in the Russian Empire, 1860–1900." *Jahrbücher für Geschichte Osteuropas* 49, no. 2 (2001): 230–39.

_____. *Ukraine: Birth of A Modern Nation*. New York: Oxford University Press. 2007.

_____. *Ukraine: What Everyone Needs to Know*, 2nd ed. New York: Oxford University Press, 2020.

Young, Robert. *White Mythologies: Writing History and the West*. London: Routledge, 1990.

Yurchuk, Yuliya. "Historians as Activists: History Writing in Times of War: The Case of Ukraine in 2014–2018." *Nationalities Papers* 49, no. 4 (2021): 691–709.

Yuzyk, Vera. "Biography—Senator Paul Yuzyk." Official Website of Honourable Senator Paul Yuzyk. https://yuzyk.com/biography/#Moving-Multiculturalism-from-Idea-to-Official-Recognition.

Zablotskaia, K. V., ed. *Istoriia mirovoi i ukrainskoi kultury: Uchebnoe posobie*. Donetsk: Ukrainskii kulturologicheskii tsentr, 1999.

Zabuzhko, Oksana. *Dvi kultury*. Kyiv: Znannia, 1990.

Zaiarniuk, Andrii [Zayarnyuk, Andriy]. *Idiomy emansypatsii: "Vyzvolni proiekty" i halytske selo v seredyni XIX stolittia*. Kyiv: Krytyka, 2007.

Zakovych, M. M., ed. *Ukrainska ta zarubizhna kultura: Navchalnyi posibnyk*. 3rd ed. Kyiv: Znannia, 2002.

Zayarnyuk, Andriy. *Framing the Ukrainian Peasantry in Habsburg Galicia, 1846–1914.* Edmonton and Toronto: Canadian Institute of Ukrainian Studies Press, 2013.

_____. *Lviv's Uncertain Destination: A City and Its Train Terminal from Franz Joseph I to Brezhnev.* Toronto: University of Toronto Press, 2020.

Ziac, Martin Fedor. "Professors and Politics: The Role of Paul Robert Magocsi in the Modern Carpatho-Rusyn Revival." *East European Quarterly* 35, no. 2 (June 2001): 213–32.

Zhezherun, V. T., and V. H. Rybalka, eds. *Ukrainska ta zarubizhna kultura.* Kharkiv: Slobozhanshchyna, 2003.

Zhurzhenko, Tatiana. *Borderlands into Bordered Lands: Geopolitics of Identity in Post-Soviet Ukraine.* Stuttgart: *ibidem*-Verlag, 2010.

UKRAINIAN VOICES

Collected by Andreas Umland